Amazing Sweden

Marie Dahlberg Lena Koller Maria Ravegård

SNOWFLING MEDIA

SNOWFLING media

© Marie Dahlberg, Lena Koller, Maria Ravegård, Gunnar Genell 2008

Repro and print: Fälth & Hässler, Värnamo Sweden 2008

Translation: Craig Andrew Pratt

Editor: Maria Wessberger

ISBN 978-91-85851-00-3

www.amazingsweden.com
www.snowflingmedia.com

Contents

Foreword

Amazing Sweden is a unique *smörgåsbord* of a book; an unabashed ode to the land up north that will hopefully guide the reader on an informative and pleasant journey through Swedish business, culture, history, design, innovation, cuisine and landscapes. We have insisted on creating an independent work free of corporate and government sponsorship. As a result no one has been able to buy a place in the book or influence the content in any way.

The *smörgåsbord* (literally sandwich table) is actually a traditional Swedish buffet that evolved out of the so called aquavit table that was popular until the smorgasbord made its breakthrough in the mid nineteenth century. The word smorgasbord is one of the few modern Swedish words that have found their way into both English and German. Strangely enough, visitors to Sweden are unlikely to find a smorgasbord mentioned on any restaurant menu.

So how can you summarize a country? The answer of course is you can't. How do you decide what is not worth mentioning and what qualifies as amazing? There is often a fine line between the two categories and no matter how you look at it there is no escaping the fact that the choices made by the book's creative team are entirely subjective.

Rest assured there have been many heated discussions. One of our yardsticks has been the question "Is this unique to Sweden?" a simple enough question it would seem, but difficult nonetheless as *The Definitive Guide to the World* has yet to be written (our next project perhaps?). Swedish traditions were an obvious starter as were the seasonal transitions and landscapes which are unique to this part of the world. The fact that a sparsely populated country of just over 9 million people has spawned so many innovations that have given rise to global companies is indeed remarkable, as is the sheer number of ingenious Swedish inventions and patents. Understandably we have chosen to highlight this phenomenon. Given that there are so many contenders, which criteria did we apply to companies and businesses before deciding to include them in the book?

The first requirement was the existence of a physical innovation; however the size of the company was also given consideration. Most important of all was the human story behind the success. Was it interesting enough? In some cases the story wasn't all that exciting but the sheer global muscle of the company concerned has been enough to earn them the epithet *amazing*. However, innumerable inventions have never reached the world market but this doesn't necessarily mean that they are less meaningful or ingenious.

An entrepreneurial spirit has also been a decisive factor.
So, what does it mean to be Swedish? Swedes politely remove their shoes when they visit. They will duly inform you when they intend to use the amenities and exactly what they intend to do there. This however is an example of a more general type of idiosyncrasy which is given scant attention in this book.

Multiculturalism is a sociological term with a variety of connotations. For example it is used to refer both to a government's ability to deal with a society whose members are of a variety of ethnic backgrounds as well as the inter-racial tolerance within a society. The term was first used in 1957 to describe the situation in Switzerland, but gained widespread popularity during the 1960's, particularly in the USA and Western Europe. The term *multicultural* is often used to describe a society that has been influenced by or includes a number of different cultures. This is often due to immigration and enriches all facets of the community from its art, music and literature through to its cuisine and fashion sensibilities.

Multiculturally is an adverb often used to describe how a government should treat different ethnic groups within the same nation. Most European states consist of a numerically dominant ethnic group – whose name is often reflected in the name of the country – and a greater or lesser number of ethnic minorities. This is also the case in Sweden but it is by no means a uniquely Swedish phenomenon.

This book is largely based on interviews with experts in various fields. For example when putting the chapter on architecture together we consulted a group of young Swedish architects. Similarly we were given invaluable assistance on the art chapter by two famous Swedish artists who kindly drew up a list for us. Strictly speaking all creative endeavors such as music, design, architecture and glass are unique, so once again our choices cannot be anything other than subjective. It's not easy drawing the line but it has to be done otherwise there would be no book.

Everyone has their own opinion of what is uniquely Swedish and what should have been included in the book. We are aware of this and know that we will be deluged with questions as to why certain things were excluded. We can offer no better answer than this: our personal response to the simple question "Amazing/not amazing?"

SWEDISH PRONUNCIATION

In this book we have chosen to spell Swedish place names in the Swedish manner.

There are several reasons for this: firstly in most cases there is no English alternative. Secondly, either the English names are extremely close to the Swedish versions (eg. Malmö/ Malmoe), or are archaic Latin names such as Dalecarlia and Scania for Dalarna and Skåne. Try asking a young Swede the way to Dalecarlia and see how far it gets you! Asking the way to Scania on the other hand will almost certainly find you on your way to the local truck factory. Finally, we do not want to underestimate our readers; we are sure that they are more than capable of getting their tongues around a little Swedish, and having done so, when they visit Sweden they will be much less likely to encounter blank looks or inadvertently wind up in automobile plants when asking for directions.

However, there are a few things you should know. To start with, there a few extra vowels in Swedish – that's right, the ones with the dots and rings:

Å is pronounced like the *or* in *store*

Ä is pronounced like the *ai* in *air*

Ö is pronounced like the *ur* in *burn*

Y is also a vowel, halfway between *ee* and *oo* (similar to the German *ü*).

K is often, although not always, pronounced sh especially in place names. Eg Linköping is pronounced *lin-shur-ping*. Kiruna on the other hand starts with a hard *k*.

Confusing? Well, why do you think most Swedes have learnt to speak such good English.

Whatever happened to the Swedish Viking?

The legend of the wild man of the North

The most famous Swedish icon is without doubt the Viking; no Nordic figure past or present is ever likely to attain their status. Even though a thousand years have passed, civilised Europe is still to fully recover from the shock of the wild men of the North – children of harsher climes – suddenly crashing ashore on the continental and British coasts. The Vikings spread death and destruction wherever they turned.

The modern world is full of Viking toys, most of them adorned with horns. Strangely enough, archaeologists have never found a single Viking helmet with such appendages.

The Viking is a central figure in Swedish cultural heritage – a character that evokes enormous interest not only in Sweden but around the world. For most people the very mention of the word *Viking* conjures up images of a cold blooded raider, someone who plundered and pillaged in all directions as the mood took him. However, the Viking was also a colonist who eventually came to govern large parts of Europe. The Viking Age is often portrayed as a golden period in Swedish history, and even though he is mostly remembered for his bloody raids, the Viking has been assigned the role of the archetypal Swede. The spoils of war were not the only reason the Vikings ventured into foreign waters. Commerce was also high on their list of priorities and led them to establish flourishing trade routes in many parts of the world.

Historians place the Viking Age at between 800 and 1050 AD, a period when Scandinavia was booming. At this time Lake Mälaren and its inlets were the seat of the Swedish Vikings. The island of Björkö in particular was a flourishing centre and today is a significant archaeological site that has proved to be a treasure trove of rune stones and Viking artefacts.

The Vikings were nothing if not pragmatists – if they couldn't conquer an area they traded with it. Skilled shipbuilders and navigators, they always managed to prosper in some way no matter where they wound up. However, despite their more positive attributes it seems that theirs is a name that is destined to live in infamy.

The first recorded instance of a Viking raid occurred in 793 AD at the Priory of Lindisfarne in North West England. Chronicler Simeon of Durham left this account: "And they came to the church of Lindisfarne, laid everything waste with grievous plundering, trampled the holy places with polluted steps, dug up the altars and seized all the treasures of the holy church. They killed some of the brothers, took some away with them in fetters, many they drove out, naked and loaded with insults, some they drowned in the sea …"

Norwegian and Danish Vikings set sail to the south and west, whereas the Swedes headed east into the mighty rivers that traverse Eastern Europe. During the Viking Age, Norse chieftains held sway in large tracts of Europe and the British Isles. In the west, Iceland and Greenland were colonised and in the east, trade routes were opened up from Scandinavia to the Orient.

One summer's day around the year 1000 AD, Leif Eriksson and his crew set sail from Greenland. They were in search of a land to the west that had been sighted by Bjarne Herjulfsson. Eriksson first made landfall in a place he christened Hellunda (Flat stone land – modern Baffin Island) before sailing on to Markland (Woodland – modern Labrador). From here they followed the coast to the site of modern day Boston where they settled. But here the trail mysteriously ends. One theory is that the milk drinking Vikings offered the *skraelings* (their word for Indians) some dairy products. The natives became violently ill and, suspecting treachery, slaughtered every last one of the visitors. We'll have to leave it up to the archaeologists to determine whether or not this yarn is actually true.

For a small country, Sweden has given the world a disproportionate number of icons; however it is the image of the Vikings that persists. No other Nordic figure is ever likely to approach their status. Over one thousand years later, Europe still shudders at the thought of long boats appearing ominously from beyond the horizon. The wild men of the North struck fear into the hearts of men, crashing ashore, taking everything they could get their hands on and destroying what they could not.

Even today, in those moments when a Swede feels particularly brave or powerful, he or she can be seen to beat their chest and say, "After all, I am a Viking".

The Viking Age is often portrayed as a golden period in Swedish history, and the Viking is perceived as the archetypal Swede. However, the image portrayed in films and cartoons differs somewhat from reality. The Viking name lives in infamy on account of their bloody raids but they were also successful merchants who returned to Sweden with ideas and artefacts from their travels.

▼ Viking Age sword in silver and copper from Halla on the island of Gotland.

Stockholm

Part of the "archipelago stew"

Nobody knows when the name *Stockholm* first came into use. Legend has it that pirates razed the town of Sigtuna in 1187 and the residents fled for their lives transporting their possessions in hollowed out logs. They decided that the place the logs floated ashore would be the site of a new town. The Swedish word for log is *stock* and the word *holm* means islet. Thus *Stock-holm*. Exactly where the logs landed is not clear; Stockholm consists of many islands and water is a constant presence. Stockholm is renowned as the world's cleanest city – a place where you can take a dip downtown or catch a salmon outside the Royal Palace.

A German theory claims the city got its name from visitors who erroneously believed it to be built on poles in the Venetian manner. Even though the area had been inhabited for many years, Stockholm's official date of birth is generally regarded as 19th August 1252. On this day, Birger Jarl, the unofficial ruler of the country during the reign of *Erik the Lisp and Lame*, sent a letter to the peasants in the region *Attundaland*, modern day *Uppland* north of Stockholm, kindly informing them that henceforth they were liable to pay tax to the cathedral.

Yet despite this, neither Birger Jarl nor his son Magnus Ladulås considered Stockholm to be the capital as the monarchs of this time were more or less nomads. Magnus did however support the town and built Klara monastery in the northern precinct where Klara Church stands today. By the end of the 13th century, Stockholm was slowly emerging as the capital city as the other major towns of Helgö, Birka and Sigtuna began to decline.

At the beginning of the 15th century, 5000 people lived in Stockholm, all of them in *Gamla Stan* – the Old Town. Conditions were appalling. Livestock roamed freely and a sewerage system was conspicuous by its absence. All kinds of waste was tossed out into the streets where it was trampled into the mud before eventually seeping into the water. Special wooden soles were worn on top of leather shoes to protect them from this fetid mess. Examples of these can be seen at the Museum of Medieval Stockholm.

If we fast forward to the 17th century we come to Gustavus Adolphus' ascension to the throne and an era that saw Sweden rise to superpower status in Europe. At this time Finland and large tracts around the Baltic were Swedish territory, including parts of northern Germany. This meant that Sweden exerted almost total control over the Baltic Sea. As the capital of the empire, Stockholm soon expanded beyond the Old Town. Streets were laid out according to a geometric civic plan with the Royal Palace and Parliament buildings at the centre. Stockholm became a mercantile centre and the King commissioned the building of imposing warships, the most impressive being the ill-fated Vasa which embarrassingly sank in sight of Stockholm on its maiden voyage. Her wreck was discovered in the 1960s whereupon she was salvaged and put on display at the magnificent Vasa Museum on Djurgården.

Gustavus Adolphus was succeeded by his daughter Kristina. Kristina had to all intents

Apart from its natural beauty, modern Stockholm is often lauded for its dynamic, creative urban scene. No matter what your passion may be, Stockholm has more than enough to offer in the way of shopping, cuisine, nightlife and the arts to satisfy even the most discerning of visitors.

Broadly speaking Stockholm can be divided into two main districts. The first, consisting of the vibrant city centre, the entertainment hub of Stureplan and exclusive Östermalm, is where you will find an outlet for any type of high-end consumption that takes your fancy. This is also where you will find most of the museums and galleries. The other main area consists of the island of Södermalm, which has a more bohemian and relaxed feel than its flashier counterpart to the north. Södermalm is famous for its diverse blend of fashion and design shops, restaurants, cosy cafeés and thriving markets. Modern Stockholm truly has something for everybody.

and purposes been raised as a man and was crowned in 1650 amid great pomp and circumstance. A patron of the arts and sciences, her four-year reign saw Stockholm flourish intellectually and creatively. However, she could never come to terms with her role as Head of State and in 1654, to everyone's astonishment, she abdicated, moved to Rome and converted to Catholicism. Ironic when one considers that her father had died fighting against the Papists.

During the 18th century Stockholm's population swelled to 75 000. It was at this time that the last great plague swept across Europe; a period when Stockholm had one of the highest concentrations of restaurants in Europe as well as the dubious honour of being one of her filthiest cities. The stench was said to be unbearable, particularly during the summer months. Gustav III who had now taken the throne supported the arts and sciences and formed the Swedish Academy and the Royal Academy of Science, the institutions that today award the Nobel Prizes for Literature, Physics and Chemistry. Gustav was murdered in 1792 during a masquerade ball at the Opera House, the victim of a plot amongst the nobility.

At the beginning of the 19th century Stockholm was an impoverished city. To make matters worse, cholera broke out in 1834 killing thousands of people particularly in the densely populated area of Kungsholmen. At the same time palatial apartments were being built in Östermalm. The city's first gasworks opened in the middle of the century, a significant event that enabled the illumination of the city at night.

Eldkvarn – the Fire Mill – was an enormous steam driven mill that stood on the site of the present day City Hall. The mill attracted a lot of attention as it constantly showered its surroundings with sparks. In 1878 the mill burnt to the ground in a conflagration that could be seen from all over the city. The blaze was witnessed by a twelve-year-old boy called Ragnar Österberg, who would grow up to be the architect responsible for the design of City Hall. Österberg was an ardent national romanticist and City Hall is a brilliant example of this architectural style. However, the building took so long to erect that new design trends emerged before it was completed and in 1919 the tower was crowned with a neo-classicist flourish. The interior is a wonderful pot-pourri of Vasa renaissance, neoclassicism and chinoiserie. City Hall has become an icon for Stockholm and is probably the world's most famous party venue. The annual Nobel Banquet is held here. As the name suggests, this is also the seat of the Stockholm City administration.

A new civic plan was drawn up in the 19th century with the intent of transforming Stockholm into a miniature Paris with broad, tree-lined avenues and traffic hubs such as Karlaplan. The Old Town however was spared, along with a few timber houses in the higher parts of Södermalm.

By the end of the 1870s Stockholm had one of the highest concentrations of telephones per capita in all of Europe and electricity illuminated the finer residences at just the push of a button. The wheels of industry turned day and night, and water and sewerage pipes were being laid across the city. But the 1800s were not simply a cavalcade of technical innovations. Industrialisation was accompanied by increased alcohol consumption and it is estimated that by the end of the century each Swede drank 46 litres of spirits per year. As a result the temperance movement took on an important role in society.

In the 20th century the Stockholm Municipal Council purchased large tracts of land outside the city. As part of the ambitious Project Own Home, these were divided into building blocks and rented out cheaply to those interested in building.

Eventually a new town emerged in Stockholm. An urban renewal plan had been formed in the 1930s but was put on hold due to the interceding world war, economically unfavourable conditions and political bureaucracy. A wave of demolition was finally unleashed upon the district of lower Norrmalm in the 1960s and 70s – planned destruction on a scale never before witnessed in a European city. This episode has come to be seen as a shameful chapter in Swedish urban history and many authors and journalists have expressed their disgust at the widespread carnage. As many as 450 buildings were torn down in the Klara District alone, with another couple of hundred in the rest of the inner city. They were replaced by offices and shops which meant that the downtown area simply died at night. In later years attempts have been made to redress the situation by converting disused parking buildings into apartment blocks and even building row houses on top of office buildings.

In February 1986, Prime Minister Olof Palme was shot and killed in the street on his way home to the Old Town after a night out at the cinema. He was walking without a bodyguard, arm in arm with his wife. The case remains unsolved and its handling has been the source of constant discussion in the media. Palme's murder changed the way Swedish politicians looked at personal security and these days you will seldom, if ever, see the Prime Minister on a tram or taking an evening stroll on the streets of Stockholm. On that fateful night in 1986, Stockholm made the painful transition from small town to big city.

The expression *Beauty on Water* is often used to describe Stockholm and justifiably so. The city is made up of 12 islands (15 if you count a few extra islets) and is woven together by 57 bridges. If you expand the city limits a bit the number swells to 30 000 islands, all of which can be reached by boat, some of them all year round. The massive fleet of boats plying these waters includes more than 20 that are over 100 years old, many of them powered by steam.

The Stockholm
Archipelago

"A landscape chopped up and stewed"

Hjalmar Söderberg

Björnö (Bear Island) Nature
Reserve at the furthest tip of the
Island of Ingarö is characteristic of the archipelago with its
cliffs, forests and small scale
horticulture squeezed into
narrow valleys. Accessible even
for those without a boat, it is a
popular destination for visitors
looking for a spot of sun and
swimming. Particularly popular
is the sandy beach at Torpesand
which looks out over the waters
of Nämdöfjärden.

The Royal Swedish Yacht Club has always played an important role at Sandhamn. Formed in 1830, it is one of the world's oldest and largest sailing organisations. Its annual Gotland Runt race attracts yachtsmen from around the world and gives the island an excuse to really dress up in style. While other islands in the archipelago live off fishing and agriculture, Sandhamn has become a sailing metropolis.

A large proportion of the more than one million leisure boats in Sweden are sail boats. The level of boat ownership in Sweden is amongst the highest in the world, which is hardly surprising given that the country has been blessed with over 60000 islands and 95000 navigable lakes. Needless to say, boating – with or without a motor – is amongst the Swedes' favourite past times.

The Baltic Sea is unique. An ancient fissure landscape, it is the largest body of brackish water in the world and supports a unique flora and fauna. Each one of its thousands of islands and skerries has its own character and beauty. Once upon a time a mountain cracked and formed a myriad of small islands. The Stockholm archipelago consists of around 30000 islands and new skerries are constantly appearing. A mighty mountain chain once dominated this area. What had been a desert area was eventually coated by a layer of ice two kilometres thick which chiselled and polished the landscape into the magnificent archipelago we see today. An archipelago beyond compare where vegetation decreases the further from the mainland one strays.

The first sea charts of this treacherous cluster of islands date from 1626 and mark the location of the island (Gunnil's öra) as 130 degrees southwest of the Svenska Högarna – the furthest outpost of the archipelago. Those who attempted to anchor here would inevitably run into difficulties because the island didn't exist. It was a mirage reflecting the Estonian islands of Ösel and Dagö. Navigating the archipelago should never be taken lightly even with modern navigational equipment and maps.

Unlike most other artists and writers, Swedish author Hjalmar Söderberg was said to be less than impressed by this part of the Baltic. He coined the phrase "a landscape chopped up and stewed" which is actually a fairly accurate description; sailing here is like navigating a huge beef stew. Many of the biggest names in Swedish art and literature have been inspired by the Stockholm archipelago, and since the middle of the 1800s they have been heading out to the old pilots' harbour at Sandhamn (Sand Harbour). This village with its maze of narrow streets was the place where August Strindberg drank his snaps with the local pilot, where Carl Larsson immortalised the inn keeper and Anders Zorn captured the sea on his canvas. It also inspired author Albert Engström's term *a floating smörgåsbord*. He took a buoyant wooden tray with food, beer and snaps and placed it in the water while he bobbed around in an inflatable ring together with other esteemed members of Sweden's cultural elite.

"Beautiful Sandhamn. Surrounded by water on three sides and sea on the other." August Strindberg penned these words in 1873 and the same is true today. The sea and the horizon give Sandhamn, or Sandö (Sand Island) as it is actually called, its special character. The island consists of sand, sand and more sand, interspersed with the occasional ancient granite outcrop. Sandhamn is famous for its bathing and as a place overrun by international sailors, but is also home to culturally significant sites and breathtaking landscapes.

Visiting Stockholm and not taking a boat trip out into the archipelago is like visiting Paris and not seeing the Eiffel Tower. It is a unique experience simply not to be missed.

The Monarchy

A French King and German Queen

The Swedish Royal Family:
(left to right) Princess
Madeleine, King Carl XVI Gustaf,
Queen Silvia. Prince Carl Philip
and Crown Princess Victoria.

The Swedish Royal Family consists of King Carl XVI Gustaf, Queen Silvia, Crown Princess Victoria, Prince Carl Philip and Princess Madeleine.

The Swedish monarchy is one of the oldest in the world and can trace its origins back more than a thousand years. No one really knows who the first Swedish kings were, although they were most likely powerful chieftains from high-status families. It wasn't until the Middle Ages that a centralized power structure emerged in the form of a King and his counsel.

The rules of succession were laid out during the reign of Gustav Vasa when it was decided that the right to inherit the Swedish crown would be ratified through so called succession agreements.

When French Marshal Jean Baptiste Bernadotte was elected as successor to the Swedish throne by the Swedish parliament in Örebro in 1810, a new order of succession was incorporated into Swedish law. From this point on the crown would go to the eldest prince. This was amended in 1980 and nowadays the throne passes to the eldest offspring regardless of gender. Sweden is a constitutional monarchy where the monarch's ambit is governed by law. As Head of State his function is primarily symbolic and his duties are restricted to ceremonial tasks. As King he is not permitted to express his personal political views which means that he must constantly watch his tongue. Walking this tightrope requires enormous discipline. The Monarchy is extremely popular in Sweden, even the Social Democrats who have governed the country for nearly seventy years seem to have forgotten that they are supposed to be republicans at heart. To suddenly start pushing for a republic would be no less than political suicide.

How did Sweden wind up with a French Marshal on the throne? Jean Baptiste Bernadotte rose to prominence as Governor of the Hansa Towns in Germany where he demonstrates excellent administrative abilities. At this time he comes into contact with Swedish officers that have been taken prisoner. In 1809 he participates in Napoleon's Austrian campaign but falls into disfavour and returns to Paris with his tail between his legs and without a commission. Suddenly the successor to the Swedish throne dies, allegedly from eating a poisoned pastry. Jean Baptiste Bernadotte is adopted by Karl XIII and given the Swedish name Karl Johan. In 1818 he ascends to the throne as King Karl XIV Johan. The current King of Sweden is the seventh consecutive Bernadotte and his motto is: *For Sweden – with the times.*

Silvia Sommerlath was working as an official hostess at the Olympic Games in 1972 when she met the King. Apparently things between them just clicked. A few years later church bells ring for the couple, Sweden has a beautiful new queen and the line of succession is secured.

When Crown Princess Victoria arrived in 1977 the Royal Family decided to leave the asphalt of the Old Town and the Royal Palace and move out to Drottningholm, Sweden's best preseveled example of 17th century royal architecture. Queen Hedvig Eleonora commissioned architect Nicodemus Tessin the Elder to build Drottningholm which is a perfect example of contemporary European architecture. Succeeding generations of royalty have left their mark on the buildings, which is why you will see influences from various periods.

Drottningholm has been designated a World Heritage Site by UNESCO. It is open to visitors all year round with the exception of the Royal Family's private residence which is not open to the public. The exotic Chinese Pavilion, Drottningholm Palace Theatre and spectacular parks all contribute to creating a unique environment.

The crown, the scepter, the orb and the key are the principal regal symbols for the country and represent the traditions of the monarchy. The regalia, each with their own particular symbolism, are brought forth at important royal ceremonies such as coronations, christening, weddings and funerals.

Among the main royal symbols you will also find the large and small coats of arms of the Kingdom. These were originally the King's personal coats of arms and not the Kingdom's.

▶ The changing of the guard and parade of guards are popular attractions. During the summer months the Royal Guard and band march or ride through the streets of Stockholm to the outer courtyard of the Royal Palace. The Royal Guard has protected the Royal Palace since 1523 at which time they consisted of 100–200 soldiers. These days military units from all over Sweden take turns standing guard, forming an important part of the Royal Family's security apparatus and the defence system of Stockholm.

The balance of power

A palette of red, blue, green and yellow

Sweden can be considered to be an ancient democracy where written rules have existed for the governing of the country since the middle of the 14th century. Sweden is a parliamentary democracy where *Riksdagen* (parliament) represents the population and determines how long a government may sit in power. Rules for this are laid out in the constitution. The first laws began to be passed in the 1600s and have been successively revised ever since. Parliament acquired more power during the prolonged period of peace in the 1700s when practically all authority became vested in the four estates and the party system began to emerge. Many of the traditions observed in parliament originate from this period.

In the year 1772 Gustav III's bloodless coup results in more power reverting to the King. In 1809 a new constitution based on Montesquieu's principles is ratified clarifying the distribution of power between the King and parliament. The judiciary and government authorities are granted more independence and the office of Judiciary Ombudsman, to whom citizens can turn with complaints about authorities, is created. This is the first position of this type anywhere in the world. The form of government in operation in 1809 remains practically unchanged until 1974 when the current model is introduced. The most significant change made at this time is that the King is divested of any political power and becomes a ceremonial Head of State. This is quite a leap from the constitution of 1809 which decrees that "… the Kingdom of Sweden shall be governed by a King".

Ministerial rule is forbidden in Sweden where it is seen as a form of corruption. A minister is forbidden from influencing a government body or agency to act in a particular way in regard to a particular matter. In many countries, ministers are held accountable for all decisions of their department and are permitted and expected to intervene. This is not the way it works in Sweden where it is actually an offence.

In 1971 Sweden abandons the two-house system and adopts a single house consisting of 350 members. The system soon proves vulnerable when the 1973 election finishes in a dead heat with the Socialist and Conservative blocks each winning 175 seats. This leads to a so-called *lottery* parliament where important decisions are made with the assistance of a lottery. These days the House consists of 349 members and Sweden goes to the polls once every four years.

The Swedish constitution consists of four articles which take precedence over all other laws and lay the foundations for modern Swedish society. The first law guaranteeing freedom of the press was passed as early as 1766 and assured every member of society the right to express and disseminate their views without fear of censorship. In the same spirit, Sweden's most recent constitutional article assures freedom of speech and, while similar to the law governing freedom of the press, it is primarily concerned with broadcast media.

The constitution also lays down the rules of succession which were amended as recently as 1980 to allow female succession. Previously a woman could only be the monarch if there were no males among her siblings. Princess Victoria is therefore the first ever Crown Princess. The right to form or join an association is a fundamental principle of democracy. It is often said that the growth of the temperance, trade union and Free Church movements in Sweden at the end of 19th century benefited the development of democracy. By engaging in these popular movements, the men and women on the street learned the rules governing public meetings, how to keep protocols, debate and interact with government bodies. In other words, they learned the rules of the democratic game.

In 1921 all men and women are given the right to vote. Only now can we say that parliament is truly democratic. Suddenly women could even be elected to parliament. Compared to other countries the modern Swedish parliament has a large proportion of women — currently around fifty percent.

Rosenbad, the site of various government offices, is where the cabinet meets every Thursday. The Prime Minister's office is located on the seventh floor and commands impressive views of Stockholm's waterways.

The name *Rosenbad* comes from a popular bath house that existed here in the 1680's. The current building was designed by the architect Ferdinand Boberg (1860–1946) – a pioneer of the Jugend style of architecture in Sweden – who intended it to be a symbol of modern Nordic society.

Götaplatsen and Carl Milles' statue of *Poseidon*.

26

Göteborg

City of Swedish cars and seafood

With a population of approximately 600 000 Göteborg is Sweden's second largest city – a miniature Nordic San Francisco which, just like its Californian counterpart, is characterised by water, bridges, hills, trams and excellent seafood restaurants. Its residents steadfastly insist upon calling it *"the face of Sweden"*, something that the people of Stockholm naturally take issue with.

It is actually possible to travel across Sweden by boat via the Göta Canal which traverses the land and connects the Baltic and North Seas. The construction of this remarkable feat of engineering commenced in 1810 and is generally regarded as the beginning of the industrialisation of Sweden. The painstaking task of digging the canal was assigned to soldiers who dug for 20 years in order to spare ships the long journey around the coast.

Göteborg was founded in 1621 by King Gustav II Adolf of Sweden, although much of the civic planning was carried out by Dutch and German drainage engineers – a necessity given that the city stood on extensive marshlands. The site however had been inhabited for several thousand years – a fact mentioned in the Icelandic Sagas and corroborated by the finding of the 10th century Viking vessel, the Askekärr ship – the only one in Sweden and the best preserved example in Scandinavia.

The activities of British merchants and industrial magnates in the 18th century helped Göteborg develop into a hub for international commerce, and during the East India Company's heyday the city became the main European centre for the trade of products from the Far East.

In 1745 the East Indiaman Götheborg was returning home after her third journey to China – a journey that had lasted nearly three years. Fully laden with tea, china, silk and spices, this jewel of the Swedish merchant fleet ran aground and sank within sight of New Elfsborgs Castle, a 17th century fort built to protect Göteborg from the Danes and which later became a prison for lifers and finally a museum. Divers who visited the wreck in the 1980s confirmed that

▲ The *Göteborgsoperan* which looks out over the Göta River has both a unique interior and exterior and is well worth a visit. This beautiful architectural creation was designed by Jan Izikowitz.

there is little left of the original ship; however the surrounding area proved to be a treasure trove of exciting finds. A marine archaeological expedition was mounted and, once a layer of mud had been excavated, opened a door to a bygone century that offered adventures on the high seas and trade with exotic cultures. A dream was soon born – to recreate the ship.

And now the dream has become a reality. The East

Indiaman Götheborg is once again sailing the seven seas in full compliance with modern safety regulations for ocean going vessels. The project is a successful combination of modern research and 18th century maritime craftsmanship.

Media coverage both in Sweden and abroad has been extensive and has helped arouse people's-interest in the new East Indiaman. To date, over a million people, many of them eminent guests and delegates, have visited the Terra Nova Shipyard in Göteborg and witnessed the reconstruction of one of the largest ships of the 18th century.

The Götheborg has naturally received a lot of attention in China. Minister for Foreign Affairs, Mr Li Zhaoxing, and Vice Premier, Madame Wu Yi, visited Terra Nova and extended an invitation for the ship to visit their country. Both spoke of the East Indiaman's significance as a symbol for trade and cultural relations between the two countries. Initial sailing trials were held in 2005 and soon after the ship was christened by H.M. Queen Silvia and the hawsers finally thrown off.

Lobster fishing is as natural on the west coast as elk hunting is in other parts of the country. Lobster season opens at the end of September each year when the entire west coast breaks out in a giant seafood party. On the first day of the season the sea is packed with boats jostling for the best positions. Several places in Bohus County offer Lobster Safaris followed by a sumptuous lobster dinner.

When the Götheborg is in full sail it is impossible to distinguish her from the original ship. Indeed, above the water line she certainly appears to be the genuine article as most of her modern equipment is hidden deep within the hull. A vision which many believed to be impossible has been realised and this imposing historic vessel is asail once more, even venturing as far as China where she plied the waters in the 1700s. She has been performing an inestimable public relations service for Sweden ever since.

To date, more than 300 000 people from five continents have had the unique experience of walking her decks.

NAKED ISLES OF GRANITE. WHO NEEDS SWAYING PALM TREES AND SAND?

Imagine an archipelago of 3000 smoothly polished granite islands where your kayak can silently glide ashore. Where you can pitch a tent and watch the sun sink slowly into the sea without someone telling you to move on. This, Ladies and Gentlemen, is unique. This is Sweden and Bohus County.

The first tourists found their way to Bohus County in the 1800s when sea bathing and kelp enticed well-heeled city folk to the picturesque fishing villages along the coast. Well-known doctors embraced the trend espousing the beneficial effects of bathing on both the body and soul.

A dip a day keeps the doctor away it was said. Carl Curman, a balneologist from Lysekil wrote: "Cold sea bathing is an excellent curative, provided it is suitable for the patient, but is a double-edged sword that can cause more damage than good if used irresponsibly … the weaker and less acclimatised one is and the colder the air and water, the less time one can spend bathing".

Special baths were built in Marstrand, Lysekil, Gustavsberg and Strömstad, as well as in several other locations. Those that remain are as popular today as they were in their heyday and serve as beautiful reminders of a bygone era. Swedish bathing enthusiasts bathe all year round – even the bitter Swedish winter doesn't deter them! When the ice lies thick at the base of the ladders, they simply call upon an ingenious device called *the ice master* to clear it away and pro-vide access to the exhilaratingly chilly water below.

Bohus County is kelp and cliffs, sea bathing and shellfish, all wonderfully framed in a spec-tacular landscape.

◀ The chalk white minarets and pagoda like roof of the Lysekil Sea baths, designed by Torben Grut in 1911, grace a promon-tory in the seaside hamlet of Lysekil.

◀ At 190 m tall, HSB's Turning Torso is one of Europe's tallest residential buildings. Structurally, it is based upon a series of nine cubes with five floors per cube and a floor in between each one. This amounts to a total of 54 stories. The frame consists of concrete columns. The 10.6 m wide central core, the walls of which gradually become thinner the higher it goes, is also made out of concrete. The foundations alone took nearly a year to complete, which is understandable when you consider that they are 7 m thick and consist of over 6000 m³ of concrete. Turning Torso is located in Västra Hamnen district, within walking distance of the sea and downtown Malmö.

▲ Riberborgs sea baths, popularly known as *Ribban*, are a much-loved symbol of Malmö. Erected in 1898 they are one of Sweden's best known and most popular sea baths and are frequented by bathing enthusiasts all year round.

Malmö

Sweden's doorway to Europe

For a long time Malmö was one of Sweden's leading industrial cities and many Malmöites fondly recall the days when local factories turned out the biggest ships and the best socks. Malmö has long been a place to fight for your rights, agree on your obligations, swim at the beautiful beaches of Ribersborg and have a beer in Möllevångs Square.

Over 270 000 people live in Sweden's third largest city. They speak over a hundred different languages and come from over 160 different nations. Hardly surprisingly Malmö has a definite continental feel about it.

The violence of the Medieval period left its mark on Malmö where blood often flowed in the streets. For many years the Danish held sway here but Swedish King Magnus Eriksson managed to claim the town in 1332. However, the Danes retook her under Valdemar Atterdag and it wasn't until Karl X Gustav forced the Treaty of Roskilde in 1658 that the southern county of *Scania* and the town of Malmö came under Swedish sovereignty once and for all. The two countries that have tussled over territory have now grown up into considerate siblings, holding each other's hands across an enormous concrete bridge. Not only is the population of Malmö growing, the city itself is rapidly expanding into the Öresund region. Things have changed and continue to change on many levels. Perhaps the most significant development is the shift from a working class town to a town of professionals. Many people now live in Malmö and work in Copenhagen or vice versa. Less and less relevant, the border between the two countries is fading into oblivion. New residential areas are constantly emerging. For example, the newly developed Västra Hamnen (West Harbour) area is a wonderful patchwork quilt of different architectural styles – a model of environmentally sound civic planning where the waters of the Öresund Strait lap soothingly below the apartment balconies. Sweden's most famous residential building, Turning Torso is also a magnificent example of the diversity of modern Malmö.

Turning Torso signified the beginning of a new age in Malmö – an age where art and architecture meet. This spectacular building has been the subject of endless discussion and the butt of many an angry comment. The comparisons have also been varied: is it a woman performing a classical dance or a man throwing a discus? Architect Santiago Calatrava often thinks of sun, wind, cold and fire when he designs buildings and the long stem of Turning Torso was inspired by the wind off the waters of Öresund Strait. The twisting form has certainly also been influenced by Antoni Gaudi's *Sagrada Familia*. Residents can wave to their Danish neighbours from their balconies. Talk about making borders obsolete!

Holidays and festivals

The four seasons

Swedish festivals have always been inextricably interwoven with the four seasons. It is actually only the far north and south of the globe that experience these distinct climatic variations. Temperatures in Sweden can vary by up to 80 degrees over the course of a year. Winters are long, bitterly cold and dark. In the north of the country, ice covers the lakes and snow blankets the land until May. Each day the sun pokes its sleepy head out for just a few hours before retiring for the night. In the spring, Jack Frost is chased off by Mrs Thaw although in the north he refuses to give up without a fight. When he finally relinquishes his grip the Swedes bathe in the light and warmth they have so desperately craved. Swedes are enthusiastic about their festivities and usually serve traditional food and spiced spirits. Snaps are served at Christmas, Easter, Walpurgis Night, Midsummer, crayfish parties, herring parties … Well, you get the picture. If something is to be celebrated, snaps will be involved.

Swedish drinking habits can be traced back to the Vikings, and many behaviourists have tried to identify just what it is in the Nordic character that often leads them to drink until they drop. Some claim that it is because the land is sparsely populated, winter is long and cold and that Swedes traditionally live in isolation. When they actually meet other people they need to compensate for under-developed social skills and loosen their tongues with a little alcohol. Does it depend on the climate? Who's to say? Cheers anyway! When it comes to drinking, the otherwise so sensible Swedes often throw the concept of moderation out the window leaving many foreigners to return home with "special" memories of Swedish parties. As a rule Swedish festivities are bound to the four seasons, the ancient farming calendar or religious holidays. Some traditions are so ancient that no one can recall their origins, which is hardly surprising given the amount of alcohol usually consumed on such occasions. After a while no one can remember what they were celebrating in the first place.

NEW YEAR'S EVE is celebrated in ancient Roman fashion on the last day of December, an evening that often coincides with record breaking temperatures. However, the Swedes always insist on welcoming in the New Year with fireworks and a glass of champagne, even if it is 30 below zero outside. They are so accustomed to this that just thinking of New Year's Eve will make most of them shiver a little. If there is one occasion when the Swedes really pull out all stops and indulge in lobster, foie gras, oysters, caviar and other delicacies, it's New Year's Eve. They may even go so far as to replace their usual sparkling wine with champagne.

SHROVE TUESDAY

Shrove Tuesday, or Pancake Day as it is known in some parts of the world, is the day one traditionally eats *semlor*. These are a cardamom-spiced, wheat flour buns filled with whipped cream and almond paste floating around in a bowl of warm milk. Tempted? Hardly something for those counting their calories, this much-loved pastry is consumed from January until March. It was originally eaten only on Shrove Tuesday as the last festive food before Lent, but with the rise of Protestantism Swedes stopped observing Catholic traditions and the *semla* became a traditional dessert eaten every Tuesday between Shrove Tuesday and Easter.

These days no one cares what day it is, they eat them as long as they can buy them. Every year the local press reviews the annual batch of *semlor* and their articles are closely followed by the public and bakeries alike. A favourable review can result in long queues outside a bakery.

In many countries Easter is the most important religious festival of the year. Easter is also celebrated in Sweden although quite few know why. "Err … something about Jesus and the cross …" will be the usual answer when you ask a young Swede. The Swedes are a secular people. Religion has little meaning in their day-to-day existence and statistically they are way down the list of regular church-goers, even though the numbers get a little better around Easter and Christmas. Most Swedes celebrate Easter with friends and family. On Holy Saturday Swedes paint eggs, enjoy salmon, lamb, herring, indulge in the obligatory snaps and give each other paper mache eggs filled with candy.

Modern Swedes make no distinction between *Lenten Twigs* and *Easter Twigs*. Once upon a time these twigs were used to whip each other either on Shrove Tuesday or Good Friday. It is said that the origin of Lenten twigs harks back to ancient mystical practices where they were thought to bring the *whipee* long life and happiness. *Flagellation on Good Friday*, a tradition in Sweden since the 17th century, was intended to remind the faithful of the suffering of Christ. In time this developed into a game where children were allowed to whip their parents, provided they got up early enough to catch them in bed. However, in the late 18th century these twigs took on a tame decorative function and were adorned with colorful ribbons, paper flowers and such. These days the birch twigs are crowned with dyed feathers.

MAUNDY THURSDAY

On Maundy Thursday children dress up as crones on their way to *Blåkulla*, the place to where witches flew to kick up their heels with the Devil. Despite their frightening appearance the kids actually have more innocent activities in mind – namely knocking on doors collecting candy or money in their baskets.

WALPURGIS NIGHT

Walpurgis Night (*Valborg*) is celebrated on 30th April. During the Middle Ages, this was the end of the financial year, a festival to pay homage to spring and the day livestock were once again put out to pasture. Bonfires were introduced in the 18th century to scare off wild animals. People also started firing guns and making a general racket. In modern Sweden, Walpurgis Night is the last night you are legally permitted to light bonfires before the customary summer fire bans are imposed.

SWEDEN'S NATIONAL DAY

Spring and summer in Sweden are as light as the winter is dark. Sweden's National Day falls on 6th June – the date Gustav Vasa was elected king in 1523 and a new constitution ratified in 1809. The Swedes are not very patriotic – almost the opposite in fact. This is a country where the word *un-Swedish* is actually used as a compliment. 6th June was declared a holiday a few years ago but as yet no one really seems to care. The proposal to make this day a holiday met with widespread opposition as it meant losing another established holiday. Sweden's National Day has always just been an ordinary day, so as yet there is no traditional food or drink associated with it.

Few occasions are so eagerly
anticipated as the annual Midsummer celebrations. The
raising of the traditional leaf and
laurel clad pole on the longest
day of the year is an ancient
one, the exact origins of which
are unknown. On this day everything is said to be brimming with
power; the dew, the flowers,
the branches of the trees and
water from the springs. In short,
Midsummer in Sweden is an
enchanted time.

When spring arrives it is as if the Swedes come out of hibernation. Winter clothes are stowed away and they emerge, beaming in their summer attire. The *Winter-Swede* is a completely different creature from the *Summer-Swede*. Summer in Sweden is short, but light and intense. Midsummer's Eve is celebrated on the Friday closest to the summer solstice, the longest day of the year, and usually lands around 20th June. Midsummer is a magical time – it is even said that plants are charged with healing energy at this time of year. When it comes to celebrating Midsummer the Swedes don't hold back. On this day the sun only pops down behind the horizon for a brief rest before returning to the sky to illumi-nate the landscape that has exploded into a sea of bright green foliage. Expatriate Swedes often try to time their visits home to coincide with Midsummer, the "holiest" of Swedish festivals. Most people choose to celebrate Midsummer in the countryside where they pick wildflowers and birch foliage to dress the maypole, a timber pole adorned with two large wreaths.

The maypole was originally a fertility symbol, which is one explanation for its phal-lic appearance. In many parts of Sweden people will dress in traditional regional costume in honour of the occasion. Each county and parish has its own particular variation, and to the foreigner these colourful costumes can seem quite exotic. In the middle of nowhere you will find groups of brightly clad people – children, adults and the elderly – all danc-ing around, singing at the top of their lungs "Small frogs, small frogs, what funny things they are …" The Swede takes Midsummer very seriously which may seem contradictory in this otherwise high-tech society. All of a sudden people are dancing around in folk dress with pom poms on their knees fanatically observing tradition. Traditional Midsummer food is sacred. Without it, it just wouldn't be Midsummer. Typical Midsummer fare consists of herring, new potatoes, snaps, sour cream, chives and strawberries – which absolutely, positively must be Swedish. A cold spring (which is hardly unheard of at these latitudes) can cause headaches for Swedish strawberry farmers and send shockwaves across the country. This is headline material; CATASTROPHE: SWEDISH STRAWBERRY CROP FAILS TO RIPEN IN TIME FOR MIDSUMMER! And if the annual potato crop also fails, the nation will be plunged into a black hole of despair. Midsummer is not an occasion for the sleepy. Most people stay awake for the few brief hours of darkness which last from around midnight to three in the morning. Those who absolutely must sleep pick seven types of flowers, lay them under their pillow and dream of their perfect match. In some parts of Sweden people jump over seven fences instead. Some revellers will have indulged a bit too heavily during the day and not dream anything at all. *Lagom* is a unique Swedish word that means *just the right amount*. Every Swede innately knows the exact meaning of this word, but when it comes to alcohol however they often seem to forget.

The traditional Midsummer celebrations in the village of Kynakulle in Dalarna. If you're looking for traditional costumes Dalarna is the place to go. This type of clothing ceased to be daily attire around 1850, although the fashion persisted in some areas, in particular Dalana. Each parish has its own style which is worn with pride during Midsummer.

CRAY FISH PARTY

The eating of crayfish has been a Swedish culinary tradition since the 16th century, however once upon a time it was only enjoyed by the upper class. Ordinary folk eyed crustaceans with suspicion. These days everyone eats crayfish, and special crayfish parties are held in the evenings in early August once the crayfish fishing season is under way.

Crayfish were once only available in the stores after the season had been officially opened, however imported crayfish are now available all year round. Swedish crayfish are fresh water creatures and are traditionally cooked with dill, salt, sugar and porter/beer. They are eaten cold. You may be surprised to hear that Swedes drinks snaps with their crayfish.

They also wear small paper hats and bibs while the tables are decorated with paper lanterns in the shape of the man in the moon.

Ideally crayfish should be eaten outdoors and, as usual, the snaps is accompanied by singing. Cheese, pie and bread are also served.

BOILED FRESHWATER CRAYFISH

Approx. 1 kg live crayfish
3 litres water
100 g salt
3–6 sugar cubes
1 bottle of good beer
or porter/stout
dill

Bring the water to the boil in a
saucepan with a steamer insert.
Place the crayfish in the water but
not so many at a time that the water
stops boiling. Place the dill in the
saucepan and then boil with the lid
on for about 7 minutes. Remove
the dill and lift out the crays.
This bright red Swedish delicacy
is now ready to eat!

SURSTRÖMMING

The tradition of eating rotten herring comes from the north of the country. It is actually fermented using a time-honored method of food preservation that originated in Asia and Northern Europe. This strange dish is eaten with flatbread, almond potatoes and onions. Fermented herring simply must be eaten outdoors – the smell makes eating it in enclosed spaces unbearable. Believe it or not but the odour of a latrine seems positively delightful in comparison. It may be of some comfort to know that it doesn't taste as bad as it smells. Some people actually put a peg on their nose when eating this Swedish delicacy. Fermented herring season starts at the end of August and is most popular in northern Sweden, although it has made some inroads further south.

EEL PARTY

Eels are fished during the late summer and autumn off the unique stretch of coast at Hanövik bay in southern Sweden. The eels only move under the cover of night or the *eel dark* as it is known in these parts. They have migrated all the way from the Sargasso Sea off the West Indies before making their way into Swedish rivers and lakes where they can live for up to 15 years. Why not stay in the West Indies? They just seem to prefer Sweden. All that remains is the return journey to their spawning grounds in the Sargasso Sea. On the way they sometimes pass Hanövik bay where the fishermen lie in wait, ready to supply southern Sweden with the local delicacy – female eels. Eel parties are held from the middle of August until the Middle of November.

MÅRTEN GÅS

Eating goose in November is a southern Swedish tradition. Practically all of the bird is eaten. Black soup is soup made from the blood whilst *krås* is made out of entrails and goose liver sausage. Dessert is traditionally *Spettekaka* – literally *Spit cake* – which sounds disgusting. Fortunately however *spit* in this context has nothing whatsoever to do with saliva. It actually refers to the stick that the cake is threaded over when being made. This local delicacy is a crisp meringue-like tower prepared using scores of eggs, potato flour and sugar. Sugar frosting is then drizzled over the entire creation forming beautiful folds and stalactites. One hundred percent simple carbohydrates, zero percent fibre.

About the same time as geese are being eaten in southern

ADVENT

The word *advent* means *to arrive*, and ever since the fifth century AD, Advent has been a period of preparation for Christmas and the coming of Christ. Each weekend in December Swedes light a new candle in a special four-candle candle holder, a tradition that started in the 19th century. They also hang large electric stars in their windows, something that alludes to the Star of Bethlehem. These days electric candles replace the real thing and are placed in as many windows as possible, even in enormous office buildings. The Swedish yearning for light at this time of year knows no bounds. This is a time when mornings and afternoons alike are impossibly dark. 21st December is the winter solstice after which darkness begins to relinquish its grip on the land as each day gets a little longer.

The herring that are used for fermentation are harvested during the spawning season in late spring and placed in open wooden barrels filled with brine. To get the fermentation process going they are rolled out into the sun. When the process is complete they are canned and distributed to herring-lovers across Sweden.

HOW TO EAT SURSTRÖMMING (FERMENTED HERRING):

Open the jar carefully, ideally under water! Rinse the fish in carbonated water. Gut them and remove the fins. Place on a well-buttered piece of flatbread with mashed new/almond potatoes and sliced/diced onions. Finish off with a large dollop of sour cream. Fold the creation and then eat while holding your breath. To make sure you survive potentially lethal nocturnal burps knock back a few shots of snaps.

Discussions are currently underway to decide whether or not the eel should be protected.

TYPICAL EEL PARTY MENU:

Smoked eel with scrambled eggs and dark bread

Eel soup

Boiled eel with mustard sauce and potatoes

Fried eel with mashed potatoes

Grilled eel with herb cheese

Apple pie and custard

Sweden, there are Lamb's head parties being held in Gotland and *Kroppkakor* – Body cakes – parties being held on the island of Öland. Once again the name Body cakes is slightly misleading. They are actually potato dumplings filled with pork and onions. However, lamb's head is exactly what the name suggests.

In the North they are punished for the gift of the Midnight Sun with a stubborn, black winter.

On 1st weekend in December children are permitted to open the first of the 24 flaps on their Advent Calendar. A TV and radio series usually accompanies this tradition. This series running up until Christmas is often the subject of much discussion among critics as well as the viewing public. "It always used to be better", is often heard across the country. *Glögg*, sweet mulled wine, also makes its first appearance for the year during Advent, and for once, believe it or not, there is no tradition of consuming snaps.

ALL SAINT'S DAY

All Saint's Day has been celebrated since the year 731 AD and
is dedicated to all the saints who
aren't fortunate enough to have
their own festival. These days, All
Saint's Day is observed on the first
weekend in November when it provides a much-appreciated break
in the autumn darkness. In a ritual
imported from the Catholic countries of the Mediterranean, Swedes
visit the cemetery and light a
candle for a departed loved one.
On the other hand, worshiping
saints at the beginning of autumn
is an ancient local tradition.

RECIPE FOR GLÖGG

**2 bottles of
unpretentious red wine
450 ml water
400 g sugar
2 cinnamon sticks
20 cloves
30 cardamom pods
6 blanched bitter almonds
The skin of three bitter oranges**

Combine the water, sugar and
spices in an aluminium or stainless
steel saucepan. Simmer for a while
and then add the wine. Remove
from heat just before it boils. Let
it cool and the spices draw for 1
hour. Strain the mixture and pour
into bottles. Warm the required
amount when needed. Add raisins
and almonds.

The *Lussekatt* saffron bun originated in Germany where it was originally known as the *Devil's cat*. The story goes that the bun was formed in the shape of a sun cross and coloured with saffron in order to entice the sun to return and drive off Lucifer, Prince of Darkness.

SAFFRON BUNS

50 g yeast
150 g butter
500 ml milk
1/2 tsp salt
150 g sugar
1 tsp cardamom pods (whole)
1 tsp ground cardamom
750 g flour
1 g saffron

Crumble the yeast into a bowl. Melt the butter and add the milk. Heat until it reaches a temperature of 37°C (use a thermometer!). Finely divide the yeast with a spatula. Add the salt, sugar, cardamom and saffron. Mix until the yeast has dissolved.

Add enough flour to make a smooth dough that doesn't stick to the edges. Pour a little flour over the dough, cover with a cloth and let it rise until around twice its original size (approx 50 min)

Place the dough on a lightly floured surface and knead. Form the dough into strings and then into shapes such as the traditional "s" or a braid. Bake at 225°C (430°F) for 8 minutes.

47

Lucia Day is celebrated on 13th December. Traditionally, one is awoken at an ungodly hour by a procession of singing women in white robes – one with candles in her hair followed by a bevy of maidens. All this is accompanied by the consumption of coffee and saffron buns. For the uninitiated, Lucia can be dramatic and a little frightening.

"In our dark houses, Lucia arises with lighted candles, Saint Lucia, Saint Lucia …"

Lucia was first performed at a manor house in western Sweden in the middle of the 18th century. It was adopted by the masses in the 20th century largely due to the efforts of the school system. It has even become an arena for equal opportunity. Once upon a time the most beautiful and often blondest maiden in town was usually chosen to be Lucia for the annual procession. This pattern was also followed at schools and day-care centres. In a modern politically correct society however, anyone who wants to be Lucia can; redheads, blondes or brunettes are all welcome.

But why is Lucia celebrated in Sweden? After all, she was an Italian saint. Exactly how Saint Lucia evolved into a Swedish Festival of Light is open for discussion, although there are several possible explanations. According to legend Lucia was born in 283 AD in Sicily. She was gifted with supernatural powers which apparently didn't win her any friends and led to her being tortured to death. First she was tried and sentenced to work in a brothel where it was thought the violation of her chastity would force the Holy Spirit to leave her. Then she would be paraded through town in an ox-drawn cart to be pilloried by the mob. However, one thousand men and oxen couldn't budge her. Instead they tried to burn her at the stake, where she just plain refused to burn. Somewhat peeved they poured boiling oil over her, but the beautiful and uncooperative Lucia remained unharmed. Finally she was sentenced to death – as if the previous ordeals were just playing around – and was killed by the executioner's sword.

The Swedish Lucia is a reminder of the Sicilian saint. The red belt around her waist is said to symbolise blood, and the candles in her hair may well be the bonfire to which she was subjected. In any case Swedes are the only people to honour her in this fashion. Her day is a celebration of light during the darkest month of the year.

GINGER BISCUITS

300 g butter
400 g sugar
100 ml light syrup
1 tbsp ground ginger
2 tsp cinnamon
1 tbsp ground cloves
2 tsp cardamom
1 tbsp bicarbonate of soda
200 ml water
750 g flour

Let the butter come up to room temperature. Mix the butter, sugar and syrup into a smooth mixture, ideally using an electric mixer.

Add the ginger, cinnamon, cloves, cardamom and bicarbonate. Then add the water and flour. If you don't have an electric mixer, knead the dough on a flat surface.

Wrap the dough in aluminum foil and let it rest in the fridge for at least an hour.

Taking a bit at time, roll out the dough with a rolling pin. Cut the dough into shapes with biscuit cutters and place on a cold, greased baking tray or use baking paper/pan liner. Bake in the middle of the oven at 200–225°C (390–430°F) for 4–5 minutes.

After a month of warming up with sticky *glögg* parties, Lucia and Advent candles, it is finally time for the grand finale – Christmas. Celebration of the winter solstice was a time honoured tradition in certain places in Europe long before the birth of Jesus, and is thought to be the origin of Swedish Christmas celebrations. Christmas is probably the most important family holiday in Sweden even though there are those who think it is over the top. Many Swedish households start preparing for Christmas way in advance; they clean, bake, make candles, stuff sausages, make toffee, bring out Christmas ornaments, curtains and table-cloths and decorate the Christmas tree. Once again, the oh-so-Swedish concept of moderation takes a holiday.

The traditional Swedish Christmas buffet, or "Christmas table" as it is called, is graced with pork in a variety of forms; hams, terrines, sausages and ribs. Farms usually slaughtered most of their livestock in the autumn although they saved a few animals so they could enjoy some fresh meat a little later in the year. It worked out well to slaughter these animals a few days before Christmas, which is why pork has become a Christmas tradition. The Christmas ham has pride of place in the buffet. Another must is *Lutfisk* – dried cod that has been soaked in lye to create a gelatinous, rather tasteless dish. The modern Christmas buffet also includes salmon. Christmas is supposed to be a festive occasion so Swedes often eat food that was traditionally considered exclusive. However, certain other Christmas dishes are more prosaic such as old bread dipped in the broth left over from boiling the ham. This traditional delight usually turns into a soggy mess, which, if you ask yours truly, is slightly disgusting. Christmas beer, *Must* (a soft drink made from hops and malt) and snaps are all obligatory in the Swedish Christmas buffet.

Three p.m. on Christmas Eve is a magical hour of great significance in Swedish Christmas celebrations. At this time a medley of Disney cartoons is shown on TV – a tradition since 1959. All other festivities are timed around this event, which may seem slightly bizarre especially when one considers that the same cartoons are shown year after year. Prior to the introduction of commercial and cable TV in the early 1990s Swedes had a choice of two government-run TV channels. Christmas was the only time that Swedish children (and adults for that matter) got to enjoy cartoons of this type, which explains why the likes of Donald Duck and Ferdinand the Bull have become much-loved Christmas figures.

The Swedish Christmas is slightly frenetic, expectations are high when it comes to food, presents and staging. The Swedish variation of Santa Claus – *Jultomten* – turns up on Christmas Eve to present the gifts to the family. He is most likely an amalgamation of three different characters; St Nicholas, the Christmas Goat and the Garden Gnome. Once upon a time gifts were distributed by a straw goat, but he has now been relegated to a decorative function beside the tree.

Snow is always more than welcome at Christmas. Shame on the meteorologist who fails to find the low pressure system that will guarantee a white Christmas.

The Garden Gnome is an ancient figure in Swedish folklore – a small, quiet person, often dressed in grey, who watched over people and animals on the farm. To keep him placated he is given porridge at midnight. The Garden Gnome was actually on duty all year round and not specifically associated with Christmas. In certain parts of Sweden people eat rice porridge with almonds and cinnamon. A single almond is placed in the porridge and, according to superstition, the person lucky enough to find it will be married within a year. Left over porridge is given to the gnome.

At the end of the 19th century author Viktor Rydberg wrote a famous poem about a gnome. Many people know the words by heart. It starts thus:

Hard is the cold of Midwinter's night, stars sparkle and gleam.

In the lonely town at this midnight hour, all are sleeping.

The moon wanders its silent way, snow shines white on fir and spruce, snow shines white on roofs.

Only the gnome is awake.

CHRISTMAS HAM

1 lightly salted ham 1.5-4 kg

Mustard coating:
4 tbsp mustard
1 tbsp sugar
1 egg
breadcrumbs

Heat the oven to 125°C (250°F). Rinse the ham well under running water. Leave the net on. Place in a baking dish or tray with the rind side up. Insert a meat thermometer so that its tip is at the centre of the thickest part of the ham. Place the ham on the lowest rung in the oven. When the thermometer shows 70°C (160°F), take out the ham. Let it cool somewhat and remove the net and rind. You can also bake the ham at 175°C (350°F) provided you wrap it in foil.

Coating: Heat the oven to 200°C (390°F). Place the now rindless ham in a baking tray. Mix the egg, mustard and sugar. Brush the mixture onto the ham and then sprinkle with breadcrumbs. Leave in oven until golden brown (about 15 min). Baste occasionally with meat juices to give the coating an extra crispy texture.

FATHER-IN-LAW'S HERRING SALAD

2 herring fillets
3 boiled potatoes
5 pickled beetroot
2 apples
1 gherkin
2 tbsp chopped onion
100 ml juice from pickled beetroot
100 ml whipped cream

Soak the herring in water overnight. Cut all the ingredients into small chunks and mix gently. Place in a bowl and carefully fold in the whipped cream. Garnish with chopped hard-boiled egg and parsley.

SWEDISH MEATBALLS

300 g ground beef
1 egg
3 tbsp flour
100 ml milk or cream
grated onion
salt and pepper

Mix the ingredients well, roll into small balls and fry. Serve with mashed potatoes, gravy and lingonberry preserve. Bon appetit!

The average diameter of a Swedish meatball is between 25 and 35 mm.

JANSSON'S TEMPTATION

1 kg potatoes
2 onions
1 can anchovies
300 ml cream
small piece of hard cheese
breadcrumbs
50–100 g butter

Set the oven at 225°C (430°F). Peel and cut the potatoes into pieces resembling very thin French fries. Peel the onions and cut them in half. Slice them thinly and separate the slices into rings.

Grease a baking dish. Combine the potatoes and onions and place them in the dish (ideally 4–5 cm deep). Pour the liquid from the anchovies and the cream over them.

Cook for about 30 min. Remove from oven and sprinkle the grated cheese, breadcrumbs and thin slices of butter on top. Cook for a further 30 min. Before serving check that the potatoes are soft and the crust is golden brown (not burned). The oven must be sufficiently hot to cause the cream to "bubble up". If the crust turns too brown too quickly, cover with aluminium foil (this will also help the liquid to bubble up)

Serve with bitter lager, snaps and crispbread.

CRISPBREAD, a type of hard bread that originated in the Nordic region, is often considered something quintessentially Swedish. Rolled out into flat, thin biscuits, pricked with a special multi-pronged fork and then baked briefly at high temperatures, the crispbread is then dried. A moisture content of less than 10% means that crispbread can be stored in dry environments for long periods. This low perishability was vital in times when other methods of conserving food were questionable or non-existent.

Crispbread is usually made using whole grain rye but other grains are also used. Crispbread comes in both rectangular and round shapes.

These days most crispbread is made in large scale commercial bakeries. 85% of Swedish households stock crispbread compared to 45% in Germany and 8% in France.

54

GRAVLAX WITH MUSTARD SAUCE

2 kg fresh boneless salmon filet with skin (ideally the middle section of a 4–6 kg salmon)
100 g sugar
150 g salt (ideally half rock salt)
8 tbsp chopped dill
1 tsp coarsely ground black pepper

Divide the fillet into two equal parts. Rub the pepper into the meat side of each piece. Combine the salt, sugar and dill. Rub half of the mixture into the meat. Place the pieces together, meat against meat with the rest of the spice mixture in between. Place the entire package in a large dish, preferably glass, and just large enough to accommodate the fish. Cover with foil. Place a small weight on top and leave in the fridge for a couple of days. Turn the package over after one day.

Best enjoyed with crispbread although it also goes well with boiled potatoes. Serve with beer and snaps!

MUSTARD SAUCE

2 tbsp mustard (ideally one of sweet Swedish mustard and one of Dijon)
2 tbsp lemon juice or one tbsp white wine vinegar
1 tbsp honey or sugar
4 tbsp finely chopped dill
200–300 ml cooking oil (flavour-neutral such as canola, corn. i.e. NOT olive oil)
salt and pepper

Mix together the mustard, lemon juice and honey thoroughly.
If you are just using unsweetened mustard you may require a little more honey. If you are using sugar be sure to mix until the sugar has thoroughly dissolved. Gradually add the oil in a thin stream while beating the mixture. Mix in the dill and add salt and pepper to taste. For more bite, add a little extra vinegar or lemon juice.

**SWEDEN MUSSELS IN ON
INTERNATIONAL CUISINE**

In the past few years, Sweden
has distinguished itself as one of
the most gastronomically progressive nations. Despite this, the
most famous Swedish chef in
the world is still a Muppet …

FIKA – SWEDISH FOR COFFEE BREAK

Fika (pronounced fee-kah) is a Swedish word that is difficult to translate into English. *Coffee break* is perhaps closest. The word exists in various descriptive forms such as morning-fika, afternoon-fika, evening-fika and fast-fika. It can also be used as a verb as in *I'm just going to go and fika*. Nobody fikas like the Swedes, but what they really mean is to take a BREAK.

Foreigners have been known to sum up their visit to Sweden with the phrase, *The country where you fika*. It is a sweeping term that may include just about anything that you can imagine consuming during a break: coffee, tea, milk, juice, buns, biscuits, rusks, sandwiches and even cake.

The Swedes can even turn spirits into fika material by lacing their beverages with something a little stronger. Hey Presto! With a flick of the wrist coffee is magically transformed into something called *kask*. In Norrland the expression *go' fika* (god=tasty) is used and indicates that the break includes sandwiches.

The Swedish passion
for snaps

"40 thousand sober people are a greater
danger than 40 million drinkers" **August Strindberg**

Spirits first seem to have appeared in Sweden in the 15th century when they were mixed with gunpowder, although exactly when soldiers first realised they could be used for another type of shot is unclear. The idea of flavouring spirits originated in the 16th century. One of the pioneers of this noble art was the Princess Anna of Sachsen, who is reputed to have taken 200 delicious recipes for spirits flavoured with everything from bones to pike eyes to elk hooves with her to the grave. And even though these varieties are thankfully no longer commonly served at Swedish tables, they have been complemented with an endless number of other flavours. Large quantities of snaps are sold year round in Sweden with three sales peaks: Midsummer in late June, the end of August when all the Crayfish parties are underway, and the ultimate peak in December when the traditional Yuletide fare absolutely demands the presence of spiced spirits.

Spirits have always been considered medicinal and many people still regard them as such. Once upon a time, an ailing Swede might cure his earache by pouring spirits into his ear or delouse himself by washing his hair with it. Spirits were thought to be beneficial for the lungs, spleen and liver (!?), and spirits poured into the navel were believed to cure stomach aches. Because they were seen as a general cure-all and tonic, they were often taken to prevent illness and keep one fit as a fiddle. It was also common to take a shot to wake up, one at morning tea, one at lunch, afternoon tea, dinner and finally one as a night cap. Just why people felt it necessary to be cured when they weren't even sick is open to discussion, but there seemed to be no limit to the magic drink's curative properties. It was even used to curb excessive drinking, but first a corpse had to be soaked in it for a few days until the flavour had been absorbed.

The concept of spirits as medicine is a venerable one, and the notion that it may actually be unhealthy is a relatively recent idea. A French doctor by the name of *Le Cat* had issued warnings in the early 18th century. He defined a disease that he christened *Combustino Spontanea* – spontaneous combustion, distinguished by the hapless victim suddenly bursting into flames or flying into the air. He assumed that this condition arose when the patient's body heat caused the temperature of the alcohol in their system to rise to dangerous levels. Obese women were at greatest risk, he claimed.

In the 19th century the average Swede drank 46 litres of spirits per year. As long as spirits have been in Sweden there have been peculiar rules governing its consumption. In 1914 a rationing system was implemented where people were issued with a bank book like *motbok* containing coupons, and in which all alcohol purchases were recorded. Interestingly, historical evaluation of the system showed it actually increased consumption rather than moderated it. Rationing may well have contributed to the way Swedes glorify the properties of alcohol. Sweden's first referendum was on the question of whether or not to

Only spirits containing at least 37.5 percent alcohol and that are spiced with cumin or dill may bear the name *aquavit*. Everything else is classified as flavoured sprits of which there are countless varieties using every imaginable combination of spices.

Once upon a time each family or farm had its own recipe. These time-honoured traditions give the Swedes every right to be as proud of their flavoured spirits as the Scots are of their whisky and the French of their wine.

There are a few simple rules to be observed when drinking snaps:

Drink in moderation. Snaps have an alcohol content of around 40 percent. Traditionally one empties the glass in one go although these days many people sip more demurely.

Make sure you have someone to drink with.

Snaps should not be served colder than fridge temperature. Many pundits claim that it should be served at room temperature because chilled snaps anesthetize the taste buds. However, for many people this is the only way to get it down.

introduce a total alcohol ban. For once, Swedish politicians followed the will of the people and they were allowed to keep drinking.

For many foreigners Swedish snaps drinking is an exotic experience. And what exactly do they say? That's right, *Skål!* (pronounced *sko:l*). The word skål means bowl in modern Swedish but its use in this context harks back to the Viking Age when people drank beer out of wooden bowls. Others claim that it stems from when mead was drunk out of a skull bone that was passed around the table as the gods *Thor* and *Oden* were toasted. The experts may disagree but who cares? *Skål* anyway!

These days the Swedes are slightly more civilised drinking their snaps out of small long-stemmed glasses. But before the *skål* comes the song. Show a Swede a jar of herring and he will have to fight the reflex to burst into a drinking song. One almost never eats herring without snaps. The dish is a good excuse to have a few shots and is obligatory at all Swedish festivals and holidays.

Swedish cuisine has become trendy both abroad and at home. This has also stimulated interest in Swedish snaps. The combination of food and snaps is something genuinely Swedish and amongst the finest Swedish cuisine has to offer. The right choice of snaps to accompany a meal can create a fantastic gastronomic experience. Snaps has been a vital element in the rediscovery of Swedish culinary culture and is a given ingredient for festive occasions. There is a huge variety of snaps so some guidance is required when combining food and drink. Creating exciting dining experiences should be uncomplicated and inspiring.

RECIPE FOR DILL SNAPS

2-4 bunches of dill,
depending on their size.
350 ml plain spirits

Place the dill in a carafe or glass jar with a large opening. Pour the spirits over the dill and allow to draw for 4-5 hours (no longer as the dill can start to taste a little rotten).

Serve icy cold ideally with herring.

Do not make more than you need as the flavouring agents in dill will spoil after a while.

The herb dill plays an important role in Swedish folklore and traditional medicine. Its pungent smell was said to ward off witches and trolls and its curative properties were believed to aid indigestion, colic and insomnia. Nursing mothers were also encouraged to use dill to increase their lactation.

Dill grows wild in Sweden but has been cultivated since the Middle Ages. It is a common herb in Swedish cuisine and is used to season herring, new potatoes, conserves and crayfish. Midsummer celebrations without new potatoes and dill would be as catastrophic as a Midsummer without snaps. Well, almost. If you asked a Swede to rank herring, potatoes and snaps, snaps would most likely come in first place.

And of course, you can flavour snaps with dill. In fact in Sweden you can flavour snaps with practically anything. You are only limited by your imagination.

In addition to herring, snaps and dill there is one more thing that Swedes are passionate about – potatoes. Swedes probably consume more boiled potatoes than anyone else on earth. Herring must be accompanied by new potatoes, even if they happen to cost several hundred crowns per kilo, which can actually happen if the spring has been a cold one.

The potato arrived in Sweden in the 18th century with the help of industrial and agricultural pioneer Jonas Alströmer, but first become popular in the 19th century when people began to realise that it could be used to distil spirits.

The Swedes eat potatoes in a variety of ways: mashed, potato patties, potato cakes, au gratin, potato salad, French fries, baked – just to name a few. However the most popular way is still boiled. And the most popular type is new potatoes, harvested in late spring and served with herring, dill and snaps.

SKÅL!

The Swedish passion
for herring

The Swedes have always eaten prodigious amounts of herring and it is available in just about as many varieties as snaps. Herring has had pride of place on Swedish tables as long as anyone can remember. In the Middle Ages, salted, smoked and dried herring were amongst the country's primary exports. It was said that when the herring were running in the Öresund Strait you could chop into the school with an axe. Up until the end of the 1800s herring was considered poor man's food, but it has slowly swum into favour at the other end of the socio-economics spectrum and is now mandatory at all Swedish celebrations. Naturally herring is also said to have medicinal properties. For example, herring milk was believed to kill bedbugs and was used to treat corns, while herring skin was used to cure tooth ache. There were many other ailments that could be treated with this humble fish, in fact too many to be listed here. Suffice it to say, if a Swede had enough snaps, herring and dill at home he could cure just about anything.

The herring is also a recurrent character in the Swedish language figuring in many expressions. *Stupid as a herring*, *Mute as a herring*. The Swedish equivalent of a *crybaby* is a *cryherring*. A coward may be called *herring milk*. One can say someone is *as pale as herring milk*, a bus or tram conductor is a *herring packer* while a lazy or lifeless person is a *dead herring*. When things are crowded together they are *packed in like herring*. When something is worthless Swedes say *I wouldn't give you many rotten herring for that,* and when things don't turn out as you had hoped they might say *there'll be no herring out of that mackerel. A lovely herring* is a beautiful young maiden and if a women goes to sleep with a herring tail on her bedside table she is bound to dream of her future love.

THE GLASS MASTER'S HERRING

2 cans of herring fillets
1 medium sized carrot
2 red onions
10 allspice corns
2 bay leaves
50 ml white distilled vinegar 12%
150 ml water
400 g sugar

Mix the water, sugar and vinegar and bring to the boil. Cool the mixture by immersing the saucepan in cold water. While it is cooling rinse the herring fillets under cold running water. Cut them into 1 cm squares.

Slice the onion as finely as possible. Slice the carrot into slightly thicker pieces. Lay out the herring in a dish alternating it with pieces of carrot, onion, the bay leaves and allspice. Pour over the cooled mixture making sure it covers the herring.

Let it stand in the fridge for at least one day, ideally two. Serve with boiled potatoes.

Sweden's national drink

Sure packs a *punsch*

Snaps is not the only drink that gets the Swedes singing. Tradition also dictates that one breaks into song when the punsch bottle appears. *Here comes the punsch, here comes the punsch, delightful and cool …*

The Swedes have been making punsch since 1773, the year the Swedish East Indiaman *Fredericus Rex Sueciae* docked in Göteborg with its first cargo of arrack. The name punsch is thought to stem from the Hindi word *panch* which means *five*, as five ingredients are used: arrack, pure spirits, sugar, water and wine. When punsch arrived in Sweden it became a drink for festive occasions. Wealthy families even had their own punsch service, often ordered from China. This consisted of a very large bowl and accompanying plate and small china mugs decorated with the family's initials. To make punsch, a sugar loaf was first placed in the bowl and boiling water poured over it. A punsch ladle was then used to stir the mixture until the sugar dissolved. Arrack was added, followed by pure alcohol, before the mixture was rounded off with a little wine from the Rhine valley. Arrack was of great importance to the crew of the East Indiamen. Strict rules applied: each man paid export duty himself in Canton and was not allowed to consume more than half of the precious cargo on the trip home to Sweden. The remainder was sold at auction. In the years 1799 – 1806 over 20 000 litres of arrack were shipped to Sweden.

Few drinks have been lauded as much as punsch and poets and troubadours have long sung its praises. Older Swedish houses often have a *punsch veranda* where one spent warm summer evenings enjoying the cool drink.

According to Swedish tradition, on Thursdays one eats pea soup and drinks warm punsch. Why Thursdays? Who knows. But even today there are many restaurants and schools that serve pea soup and pancakes on Thursdays. Punsch however is conspicuous by its absence. At lunch at any rate.

PEA SOUP – 4 portions

500 g dried, split peas
1 ham bone
1.5 l water
2 onions
1 tsp thyme
1 tsp marjoram
Salt
1/2 leek, chopped
2 vegetable stock cubes
1 slice fresh ginger

Put the peas in a large bowl. Cover them with water and allow them to soak overnight.

Drain the peas and then boil them in fresh water with the salt added. Remove any rind from the ham and boil until it is tender. Remove it before the peas are cooked. Remove the scum that is formed on the surface and boil the peas until they are soft – usually around one hour.

Peel and chop the onions. Add the onions and ginger. Add the spices and leeks towards the end of the boil. Dilute with water if necessary.

Dice the ham and serve as a side dish or mix it into the soup prior to serving.

Serve with mustard and fresh bread.

Melody: THE MERRY WIDOW

Here comes the punsch,
here comes the punsch
Delightful and cool

Glasses clink and voices ring
In the room

Cheers for happy memories
Cheers for each new spring

Our sorrows dispelled by the joy
that punch brings

Nina Jobs, *Barbara* carafe/vase

The best glass
in the world

The crystal that makes Sweden famous

Erika Lagerbielke, *Difference*

Swedish glass first came to the attention of the world after the World Exhibition in Paris in 1925. Even at this time, works by the biggest names commanded prices exceeding a year's wages for the average worker.

Sweden was a late bloomer in the art of glass blowing, especially when compared to countries such as Italy and Germany. The first evidence of domestic glass making appears in the 16th century when Gustav Vasa brought foreign, probably Venetian, glass blowers to Stockholm.

The Swedes may have enjoyed fantastic success in the field for most of the 20th century, but there was a time when they were ridiculed for the quality of their glass. When the Swedes display their traditional cut crystal at the Stockholm Exhibition in 1897 it becomes a laughing stock, dismissed out of hand as stale and out of fashion. At this time the French were way ahead, as was the rest of Europe, and were forging ahead with revolutionary new techniques. One such method was creating layers of different coloured glass from which a pattern was etched. The technique is used in Sweden and local glass manufacturers realise they will need help from foreign artisans. In the early 1900s Orrefors find artists Simon Gate, Edward Hald and Edvin Ollers, who are actually painters, and secure their services. When they arrive at the hut in Småland they have never worked with glass, which is perhaps why the trio is so innovative. Unconstrained by convention, they approach the medium from a completely new angle and revolutionise the Swedish glass industry. At the Paris World Exhibition in 1925, they display an impossibly beautiful engraved cup designed by Simon Gate. The cup is a gift from Stockholm to Paris and will place Sweden firmly on the international glass map. Suddenly the world is crying out for engraved glass. Orrefors creates an engraving school which attracts students from far and wide, including one Sven Palmqvist. Many of you will be familiar with Palmqvist's centrifuged bowls *Fuga* and *Colora*, but he is perhaps best known for his *Ravenna*, inspired by the mosaics from the Italian town of the same name.

When newly graduated sculptor Erik Höglund arrives at Kosta as a designer, he brings with him a completely new approach to glass blowing, even going as far as throwing potatoes into the mix! This produces a cloudy, imperfect glass that resembles glass from bygone eras. There are those that regard the technique as blasphemy, but just as many that appreciate a more rough-and-ready type of glass.

◀ Simon Gate, *Paris Vase*

Sven Palmqvist, Vases in the *Kraka* technique

Ingeborg Lundin, *Apple*

In many ways glass has become a calling card for Sweden, where the vast, white winter landscapes provide an endless source of inspiration for artists. Indeed, one does not need to stretch the imagination too far to see the similarities between the magical crystal sculptures and the icy formations created by Mother Nature.

Lena Bergström, *Starline*

Ingegerd Råman, *Slowfox*

Bertil Vallien, *Dreams*

Mirjana Kos-Frithiof, *Peacock* platter

Mats Jonasson, *Atle II*

Rune Strand, *Scandinavian*

Berit Johansson, glass light

The Kingdom of Crystal is the name given to the glass making region in Småland, where every glass works has its own history, character and style. A place where you can browse amongst unique works of art and choose a beautiful and timeless memento to take home from the land of ice and lakes.

Ulrica Hydman-Vallien, *House Gods*

Göran Wärff, *Seaside*

Erika Lagerbielke, *Soft Spot 1*

Elegant simplicity

The world famous minimalism of Swedish design

Monica Förster, *Cloud*, portable room for resting, meeting and contemplation.

Sweden has a reputation as a world leader in design. For centuries Swedish designers have been inspired by international trends, although once imported into the "poor man's country" these influences have taken on their own unique form – a form that can perhaps best be described with the words *elegant simplicity*. Ostentatious, extravagant and gaudy furniture is rarely encountered in Sweden, not even in stately homes where one may expect the more grandiose expression often seen in equivalent European settings. Sweden's poverty has cultivated uniquely innovative sensibilities which are particularly evident in the field of design. Sensibilities embodied in the motto *use what you have at hand*. Swedish design is characterised by clean lines – minimalism without austerity – a design ethos that was as apparent in the 18th century as it is today.

Swedish design and architecture first received international attention in the 1920s when Swedish Classicism, under the name *Swedish Grace*, launched the National Romanticism movement. In keeping with the *Gustavian* spirit, this style is characterised by an uncomplicated and expressive form skillfully crafted from high quality materials. At around this time Swedish glass and china works, such as *Orrefors, Kosta, Rörstrand* and *Gustavsberg* began using gifted designers and thereby transforming Sweden into a major international presence. Elegant, cool and pleasant designs in a light palette took over.

The 1930s saw the emergence of Functionalism, particularly in the field of architecture. *Funkis* as it is affectionately referred to in Swedish, embraces smooth, light exteriors, flat roofs and generous windows to make the most of the available light. Swedish functionalism is governed by three main concepts: beauty should be available to everyone, everyday items should be as attractive as well as functional, and art and industry can meld. In 1939 Sweden participated in the World Fair in New York under the banner *Swedish Modern* and took America by storm. Three heavyweight designers weighed in with their furniture – Josef Frank, Carl Malmsten and Bruno Mathsson.

The term *Swedish design* has a positive ring to it, both in Sweden and abroad, and almost acts as a brand in itself denoting something that is modern and of high quality. Swedish politicians and businessmen are more or less compelled to show off Swedish design when travelling. Most people also associate the term with safety, especially when it comes to the car marques *Volvo* and *Saab*. Throw in *IKEA's* roll in championing the idea of good design for the masses and the circle is complete.

SEVERAL FAMOUS SWEDISH DESIGNERS:

Josef Frank, 1885–1967. Architect and designer who founded *Svenskt Tenn* together with Estrid Ericson. Perhaps best known as a designer of elegant furniture and brightly coloured textiles.

Carl Malmsten, 1888–1972. Inspired by the free forms of the natural world and his own moods, Malmsteen created many magnificent pieces of furniture that clearly own their heritage.

Bruno Mathsson 1907–1988. Designer who built his formidable reputation on chairs made out of bent wood and strapping. Aside from chairs, couches and tables, Mathsson also designed unique glass houses.

Stig Lindberg, 1916–1982. Best known for his work as a designer at ceramic manufacturers Gustavsberg. Lindberg is one of the pre-eminent designers of the Swedish *people's home*.

Karin Björquist, born 1927. One of Sweden's most famous potters, popular for her dinner services. Has even designed the Nobel and Royal dinner services.

Jonas Bohlin, born 1953. Raised eyebrows and created headlines when he launched *Concrete*, a chair in concrete and steel. One of Sweden's leading furniture designers and interior decorators, both at home and abroad.

Mårten Claesson, born 1970, Eero Koivisto, born 1958, Ola Rune, born 1963. Architect trio that tackle everything from interior design to building a cultural centre in Kyoto, Japan, to product and furniture design. Their résumé is long and varied.

Pia Wallén, born 1957. Textile designer best known for her work in felt. The famous *Crux blanket* is just part of her portfolio.

Nina Jobs, born 1965. Internationally recognised product and textile designer renowned for her uncomplicated, functional expression.

Mats Theselius, born 1956. An interior designer, artist and designer, Theselius has designed some of the most renowned furniture of the 1990's.

Margot Barolo, *Lampel*

Anna Kraitz, *Fire*

Thomas Bernstrand, *Do Swing*©

Louise Hederström,
Grace floor

Pukeberg *Original*,
table lamp

Country style bridal chair from
Öland (1852)

Jonas Bohlin, *Concrete*

Mats Theselius, *Norrsken*

Thomas Bernstrand, *People*

Yngve Ekström, *Lamino*

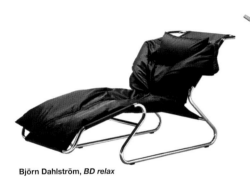

Björn Dahlström, *BD relax*

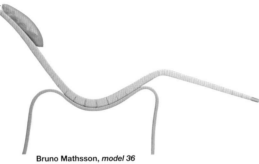

Bruno Mathsson, *model 36*

Mårten Claesson, Eero Koivisto and
Ola Rune, *Pebbles seating island*

Carl Malmsten, *Lilla Åland*

Anna von Schewen, *Hug Armchair*

Johan Erik Höglander (1750–1813),
Odenslunda, replica

A&E design, *Vitemölla*

Monica Förster, *Glide*

Thomas Eriksson, *E-seat*

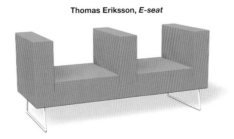

Thomas Sandell,
Vågö

81

Stig Lindberg, *Lustgården*/Garden of Eden

Märta Måås-Fjetterström, *Röd flossa* rug

Josef Frank, *Tulpan*

Dagmar Lodén, *Tistlar*

Nina Jobs, *Jungle*

Jonas Bohlin, *Trädgård vid Havet*

Åsa Lockner, silver bracelet

Vivianna Torun Bülow, *Vivianna*

Caroline Lindholm, *Lövdosa*

Sigvard Bernadotte,
The Bernadotte pot

Folke Arström, *Focus de luxe*

Annika Jarring, *Tenn Pewter*

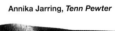

85

Knee tassels, painted wooden horses and Swedish handicrafts

Symbols of Sweden

Tradition is often preserved through local handicrafts where centuries of knowledge of patterns and materials help create a picture of bygone eras. Each country has its own traditional handicrafts that are often transformed into souvenirs for tourists. Visiting a souvenir shop in any country can be exciting as it usually gives a fairly good indication of the local traditions and symbols.

In Sweden we have the *Dalahäst*, which has been unchallenged in the number one spot for many years. This simple wooden horse painted in bright colours with a simplified *kurbits* pattern is a Swedish icon, more strongly associated with its country of origin than the Swedish flag. Its international breakthrough came in 1939 at the World Fair in New York, but it first came into existence long, long ago, whittled in front of an open fire after a hard, cold day's work in the forest. The horse was a natural choice, a friend and workmate and a symbol of strength. At first they were intended as toys – something that could be sold to bring in a little extra cash – but these days they are a decorative object and tourist memento. But a handicraft nevertheless. Hundreds of thousands of them are made every year in the town of *Nusnäs* in Dalarna. Tourists from around the world flock there every year to see them whittled and decorated and to take one home with them. Every fifth horse finds a home somewhere other than Sweden.

The self-taught, wandering painters from Dalarna had their heyday from 1780 to 1870 leaving a legacy of naïve, colourful and unique works behinds them. Kurbits was contemporary graffiti. These painters were in demand – real Dalarna painting on the walls and especially the ceiling were high status. They often took their motifs from the bible, dressing biblical characters in their own regional costumes. These were then framed with bright, elaborate floral embellishments – kurbits – intended to fill in empty spaces and create a decorative balance

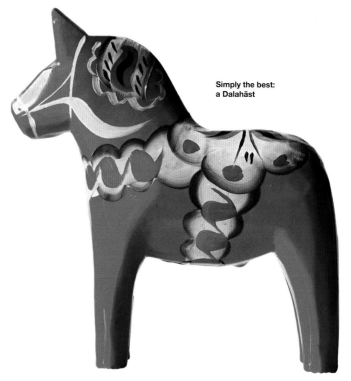

Simply the best: a Dalahäst

◀ *Sámi* handicrafts: Traditional Sámi handicrafts originated in the nomadic environment of the Sámi and are created from the materials they had at hand; reindeer horn, bone and skin as well as wood and roots from the forest. A life where camp was often broken required lightweight and practical household items. The original shape of the material and the nomadic lifestyle have been two of the major influences on Sámi design. The recurrence of round items is noteworthy. Objects are seldom excessively decorated – tasteful moderation and balance between shape, colour and decoration are considered to be the signs of a master artisan. Reindeer horn knives are prized by collectors around the world and fetch high prices at auction.

▲ Plate from *Nittsjö* decorated with a traditional *kurbits* pattern.

◀ Clogs; robust, heel-less foot-wear consisting of a wooden sole and leather upper. These have been in use in southern Sweden and Denmark since the 17th century. Today they are primarily a summer shoe that remarkably enough manages to survive all prevailing fashion trends. Some of them are painted with the same *kurbits* pattern as the wooden horses from Dalarna.

▼ Another typically Swedish tourist souvenir is the *cheese slicer*, an item that is found in every Swedish kitchen. Available in a variety of models and price classes, you can buy them in gold, silver, reindeer horn or birch wood – you name it. This ingenious device produces even slices and makes the cheese last a bit longer. It is sometimes known as a *Cheap-scrape* by true cheese lovers who crave thicker slices.

▼ Modern high-heeled clogs designed by Åsa Westlund.

▲ Glass from one of the many Swedish glass works is a powerful symbol of Swedish craftsmanship of which Swedes are justifiably proud.

Lovika mittens are an example of an ancient Swedish handicraft that keeps the hands warm when it's cold out. Lovika is a heavy woollen yarn from which Swedes knit mittens, hats and socks. All of these are then decorated with brightly coloured embroidery around the edges and a tassel.

91

Gustav Vasa, King of Sweden from 1560 until his death, is assumed to have been born on 12th May, 1496 and died on 29th September,1560 in the Royal Palace in Stockholm. He introduced the hereditary monarchy into Sweden and is considered to be the founder of the modern Swedish State. The sixth of June, the date he was elected King by Parliament in 1523, is now Sweden's National Day. He developed a strong centralised government and efficient administrative apparatus. In more modern times, particularly from the late 19th century onwards, he has ascended to the status of founding father and as such has become an important national symbol.

Modern historians however, have since cast a more critical eye over the reign of Gustav Vasa, in particular questioning the ruthless way in which he dealt with opposition.

TAFVEL SAMLINGEN

Painting by Carl Larsson:
Gustav Vasa entering Stockholm in 1523 is a gigantic work by Carl Larsson that was started in 1891 and completed in 1908. It currently graces the stairs at the National Museum in Stockholm.

Gustav Vasa

The celebrity king

Gustav Eriksson Vasa, the son of King's Counsel Erik Johansson (Vasa) and Cecilia Månsdotter (the Eka family) is believed to have been born in 1496. Legend has it that he emerged wearing a *victory hood* – the contemporary term for remnants of the amniotic sac – and a red cross on his chest. These were interpreted as signs that this child would lead a charmed life, which indeed he seemed to do. After all, he did become King of Sweden.

Gustav Vasa is one of the most colourful monarchs ever to sit upon the Swedish throne. Most Swedish school children are familiar with his exploits of which there are many. For example, hiding in a hay cart to elude Danish soldiers and raising an army in Dalarna to wrest the throne from the Danish King, *Kristian the Tyrant*. When news of Kristian's flight from Denmark reached Gustav Vasa, he decided to hold a meeting of the nobility to elect a king. The meeting was held on 6th June 1523, and around the time of Midsummer he marched triumphant into Stockholm. Gustav Vasa was an exciting monarch whose memory is kept alive through the annual *Vasaloppet* ski race and the salvaged warship in Stockholm that bears the name of his royal house.

Quite a lot of correspondence from Gustav Vasa's era has survived. He appears to have been personally involved in the development of the nation's agriculture. His political skills, capacity for work and grasp of the prosaic is impressive. As a person he was said to be both loveable and humorous. He was also interested in music and singing but was rumoured to be highly suspicious with an explosive temper. Apparently Good King Gustav was a man with two sides.

Gustav Vasa died of severe intestinal inflammation in autumn of 1560. His legacy was a Sweden united under a strong centralised leadership and on the path to modernisation. He is interred in Uppsala Cathedral. Nobleman Per Brahe described him in this way:

"He was a fitting height for a man … had a roundish head, whitish yellow hair, a large, long beard, piecing eyes, small, straight nose, a well-shaped mouth, ruddy cheeks and red-brown body, so well formed as to delight any painter, and so whole that there were nary a blemish the size of a pinhead. A lover of manly and royal attire he wore clothes well, regardless of their cut. He possessed such astute judgement that he, despite not having time himself to indulge in the bookish arts, oft surpassed those who had studied. He could with great accuracy adjudge proportions and qualities of paintings, portraits and buildings, landscapes, animals, herbs and trees. God-fearing, he led a righteous life and even unmarried was never rumoured to keep the company of concubines. Nor was there talk of bastard offspring and his marriage was well kept. Fortunate in all he undertook, in games – should one ever succeed in enticing him thither, in raising crops and animal husbandry, in fishing and prospecting, yay, even uncovering treasures in the earth."

▼ Situated on a promontory on Runn Lake in Dalarna, Ornässtugan is a perfect example of a medieval Swedish timber house. Legend has it that Gustav Vasa, dressed only in his nightshirt, jumped out through the outhouse to elude the Danes. He then made his escape across the frozen lake in a sled driven by a farmhand.

Damen med slöjan, 1768
(*The lady in the veil)*, is unquestionably Alexander Roslin's most famous painting, betguiling observers with her secretive expression. Roslin was born in 1718, a period of reconstruction when Swedish people had little time for the "extravagance" or "vanity" of the fine arts. For this reason artists often travelled abroad. Roslin was no exception settling in France.

Swedish art

Touched by northern light

▼ Carl Gustaf Pilo's unfinished monumental painting of the coronation of Gustav III from the 1770s. This work is noteworthy for several reasons. Firstly, even though Pilo was not at the ceremony he can be seen in the painting. Secondly, both the King and the artist died before it was completed and as if that wasn't enough, in an attempt to produce the required depth of colour, Pilo used a type of asphalt that disintegrates when exposed to sunlight.

▶▼ Urban Målare "aka Urban Larsson", Vädersolstavlan *Sun dogs*. In the year 1535, the skies above Stockholm put on a spectacular show consisting of halos, arches and extra suns circulating around the sun. We now know that these phenomena are caused by the sun reflecting off air borne ice crystals, however in the Middle Ages they were seen as an ill omen. Rumours spread that God or the Church were warning of retribution for the brutal politics of Gustav Vasa. In order to allay these fears the artist was commissioned to commit the phenomena to canvas.

Attempting to paint a general picture of Swedish art is a treacherous undertaking, but if one really must, then perhaps the first two things to come to mind would be melancholy and northern light.

Internationally speaking, Swedish art was relatively unknown until the end of the 1800s when a few artists were suddenly recognised abroad. Almost without exception, these artists had spent time in France and had been tutored by one of the masters. The two leading stars in Swedish art history are undoubtedly *Anders Zorn* and *Carl Larsson*, both of whom were active in the latter part of the 19th century and in the early 20th century. Zorn became known primarily for his portraits although he also painted rustic scenes from Dalarna. He further developed his relationship with light in the Stockholm archipelago placing his models outdoors where they could resonate with nature. Zorn's ability to capture the sea and the play of light on water is uncanny.

Carl Larsson is probably the most famous of all Swedish artists. Few Swedes are unfamiliar with his work and many own copies of his idyllic scenes from Dalarna and *Sundborn*. Carl Larsson motifs have been reproduced on everything from place mats to coffee mugs. He displayed an uncommon artistic talent at an early age and was accepted into the Royal Swedish Academy of Arts when just thirteen years old. In his twenties, he travelled to France where he painted light, airy watercolour landscapes. Watercolour was always his medium of choice.

One of the greatest Swedish painters of the 19th century was Ernst Josephson. He is perhaps best known for his painting *Näcken* (*The Water Sprite*) 1882–83, a depiction of the water sprite of folklore. Seen in a wider context Josephson exerted great influence on the development of Swedish art, particularly through his expressionism. Just like his contemporary Carl Fredrik Hill, Josephson experienced many setbacks in his life and finally succumbed to mental illness.

Anders Zorn was awarded a first
class medal at the World Fair in
Paris in 1889 for his watercolour
Une Premiére. The painting
was sold at auction in 2007 for
8.4 million Swedish crowns!

▲ The Daniels Manor is a classic example of Dalecarian painting at its best that came to fame through Carl Larsson's watercolour *Vinterstugan*, *(Winter cottage),* from 1890. Larsson admired the old farm paintings and depicted the cottage in several of his works.

◄ In an image that clearly reflects middle-class life at the end of the 19th century, Hanna Pauli's painting *Frukostdags*, *(Breakfast time),* depicts a laid table in a garden setting. Hanna Pauli was another Swedish artist who travelled to Paris where she was inspired by impressionism and met her husband artist Georg Pauli. Unlike most women of her time, Hanna successfully combined life as a working artist and mother.

◄◄ Sigrid Hjertén struggled against the prejudices of her time for her entire working life and first reached a broad public in 1936. Today she is considered one of the founders of the Swedish modernist movement. In *Studio interior* (1916) her radical approach is evident. The painting depicts her various roles in life – artist, woman, and mother – and their different worlds. Hjertén sits on a couch between her husband and fellow artist Isaac Grünewald and Einar Jolin while they converse over her head. Meanwhile she sits staring into space with her big blue eyes. Sigrid died as a result of complications arising from a lobotomy performed at a mental institution.

◄◄ *Den Döende Dandyn (The Dying Dandy)* 1918, by Nils von Dardel is one of the 20th century's most famous Swedish paintings. In the late 1980s it fetched 13 million swedish crowns at auction! Influenced by Cézanne, Braque, Henri Rousseau and even cubism, Nils von Dardel was long considered one of the leading figures of modern Swedish art. He also became renowned as a portrait painter in the 1920s, particularly for his beautiful likenesses of upper-class Swedish women. Dardel's work is distinguished by its primitive oriental palette.

▲ Ola Billgren's *A Mediterraneo* (1966) combines two images in one; a couple in a hotel room and a beach promenade somewhere out in the world. Painted in a warm filmic palette, this ironic work questions the utopian images presented in travel brochures. "It is not reality that I want to deal with, it is uber-reality" as he himself describes it.

Both of Ola's parents were artists so he learned to paint early. It didn't take long for him to develop a technical vocabulary that enabled him to move freely between different forms of expression. His paintings demonstrate exceptional skill.

100

▲ Olle Baertling became the great Swedish concrete artist, experimenting his way to innovative new ideas. During the 1950s he started working with open acute angles to achieve open form. Sharp black lines are used to separate the fields of colour and bear the weight of the work. Baertling was first recognised for his strict concrete art in the 1950s, its powerful abstract form treating observers to a visual knock-out.

▲ *Första mötet, (The First Meeting).* In just a few short years Karin Mamma Andersson has succeeded in becoming one of Sweden's most internationally recognised artists, inspiring a new wave of interest in the endless possibilities of painting. Born in 1962 she grew up in Luleå close to the forests. Her paintings, which magically reflect the joy of storytelling, have depicted mountains, trees and plains, usually Nordic. However, in recent years landscapes have often been replaced by interiors.

Carl Milles' *God's Hand* from 1953. A small man stands in a huge hand and look towards the sky. His body is tense, his fingers spread as if he had received a message, presumably from God. Elevating the sculpture thrusts him into the heavens.

At the end of the 19th century Milles was awarded a scholarship to study in Paris. Once there he supported himself as a carpenter while studying anatomy at the Ecole des Beaux-Artes under Auguste Rodin.

Carl Milles was one of Sweden's greatest 20th century sculptors. Many of his works can be seen at Millesgården just outside Stockholm, the property he and his artist wife left to the Swedish people in 1936.

▲ Dan Wolgers is perhaps best known for designing the cover of the Stockholm telephone directory. This version of the book, with Wolgers' own telephone number printed on the cover, now commands high prices at auction and is on display at the Museum of Modern Art in New York. Wolgers' work has always evoked strong reactions. His Duchamp-inspired bottle dryer, a contribution to Absolut Vodka's art series, has been displayed at the Louvre. The crucifix bible speaks for itself.

Mining operations at
Dalhalla ceased in 1990.
Dalhalla is 60 m deep,
400 m long and 175 m wide.
It is open June–August.
The Opera Festival in August
is an annual highlight.

Dalhalla

Music in the most dramatic of settings

In the middle of the forest several kilometres north of Rättvik in Dalarna lies one of the world's most beautiful outdoor arenas. An enormous amphitheatre with an emerald green lake, fabulous acoustics and the sky as scenery, Dalhalla offers an incomparable theatrical experience.

Once upon a time a star fell to earth and created the Verona of the North. 360 million years ago, a meteorite crashed into Dalarna forming the Silja basin and its beautiful surroundings. Traces of the impact are clearly visible in the walls of the disused limestone quarry, Dalhalla, where colorful layers of rock create a fascinating backdrop. Dalhalla was once the site of thriving mining operations, so prosperous in fact that an enormous natural amphitheatre was created. Who would have imagined that a quarry could be turned into such a magnificent natural theatre?

The slumbering giant was brought back to life in 1991 when opera singer and radio producer Margaretha Dellefors began looking for an arena for the performance of opera and classical music. She knew that a disused quarry in Avignon, France had been used as a venue and began searching for a similar site in Sweden. Her quest ended in Dalarna in a magical place that could easily have been lifted straight out of a Wagnerian opera – Dalhalla.

The ABBA story

Evergreen stars that conquered the universe

ABBA's road to stardom began at a party in Linköping in 1966 where Björn and Benny's paths cross for the first time. A few years later the two *B*s each fall in love with a beautiful songbird, Anni-Frid and Agnetha. Two *A*s. So it was love that created ABBA. The more they perform together the more attention they attract.

Presenting themselves as a group consisting of four names proves too complicated, so they simply combine their initials. However, before deciding on ABBA they ring the famous Swedish seafood company of the same name and ask their permission. The company perceives the young group to be a clean cut bunch that is unlikely to affect their reputation, so they agree. Little could they know that their pop group namesake would go on to be considerably more famous than their herrings. It would be interesting to know if their share of the seafood market grew as a result of consumers' positive associations with the name.

ABBA's victory in the 1974 Eurovision Song Contest in front of an audience of 600 million viewers would prove to be the fuel that would rocket them to international fame. They prepare for the contest by sending tapes to all the leading radio stations in Europe as they know that commercial success depends largely upon repetition. A song simply has to receive a lot of airplay in order to become a hit. For some reason ABBA seem to have the unique ability to appeal to fans in all age groups. Everyone from tots to grannies seems to like them. Their music still seems fresh after thirty years – a remarkable achievement for a pop group and music genre. The key to their success is the ability to present melodic music without a political agenda or pro-drug stance to a world longing to fill the vacuum the Beatles left behind them. Ask just about anyone, anywhere on the planet and they are likely to be able to sing an Abba hit. *Dancing Queen*, *Mamma Mia*, *Money, Money, Money, Fernando* – there are a lot to choose from. The last ABBA single to be released is *Under Attack*. By this stage the group is beginning to feel that it's time to take a break and pursue other projects. Besides, the bonds of love between (A+B) x 2 are beginning to fray.

The compilation album *ABBA Gold* is released in 1992, 10 years after their break up, and tops the charts around the world becoming their best selling album. And as with all the great bands of the past, speculation is rife as to whether or not they will ever reform. They have been offered staggering sums of money to do so but so far have not been tempted.

POLAR MUSIC PRIZE

THE ROYAL SWEDISH ACADEMY OF MUSIC AWARD

THE POLAR MUSIC PRIZE – THE *NOBEL PRIZE* OF MUSIC

Stig *Stikkan* Anderson, publisher and owner of Polar Records, is perhaps best known as manager of pop super group ABBA. However, he is also famous for founding the music world's most prestigious prize, the Polar Music Prize. Awarded for the first time in 1989, the prize is presented to people, groups or institutions, regardless of nationality, that have made exceptional contributions to the world of music.

The prize has been awarded to a Swede on one occasion only when conductor and choir master Eric Ericson received the award for his ground breaking contributions as a conductor, educator and source of artistic inspiration in the sphere of Swedish and international choral performance.

Alfred Nobel –
the peace-loving king of dynamite

The man who tamed nitroglycerine

Alfred Novel was an incomparably successful innovator and businessman. However his life was also tinged with accident and misfortune. His list of accomplishments makes impressive reading: taming the explosive power of nitroglycerine, inventing the blasting cap, dynamite and ballistite, and founding a global empire.

Alfred Nobel was born the youngest of three brothers in Stockholm in 1833. His father Immanuel is an inventor and builder, constructing mobile timber houses and tooling machines. The year before Alfred was born, his family's house is ravaged by fire and his father's business goes belly up. All of a sudden the well-off family is poor. A few years later Immanuel establishes a business in St Petersburg, manufacturing naval mines, casters and machinery, and the whole family moves to Russia.

As a child Alfred is frail and sickly, suffering from a constant runny nose and frequent headaches. He is however, exceptionally academically gifted and by the time he is a teenager can speak five languages fluently. At the age of 17 he travels to Paris where he serves an apprenticeship in the laboratory of Professor of Chemistry, Pelouze. It is here that he encounters pyroglycerine, a highly explosive substance that spontaneously combusts at 180 degrees. Chemists of the day consider it useless but Alfred sees a business opportunity in the offing – if he can just tame it.

Immanuel is delighted when Alfred returns with pyroglycerine, which they rename nitroglycerine, as it has the potential to dramatically improve his mines. Times are good – Alfred is given an important position in the company laboratory and with the Crimean War in full swing orders from the Russian armed forces just keep rolling in. However, when peace finally descends upon Russia demand for their products evaporates.

The Nobel family move back to Stockholm, but Alfred and his brother Ludwig remain in Russia where they set up a laboratory in the kitchen of their apartment. Alfred experiments with nitroglycerine and discovers that he can ignite it by packing gunpowder around it and inserting a fuse. The neighbours complain loudly about the constant explosions, and you can hardly blame them. It can't be easy living with the knowledge that your house could be blown out from under you at any time. As a result the brothers become rather unpopular and eventually return to Stockholm where they continue their experiments. Unfortunately their explosions continue to be unpredictable – sometimes they are too powerful and sometimes too weak. After around 50 unsuccessful attempts and in an act bordering on desperation, Alfred constructs a detonator out of a copper capsule filled with fulminate of mercury. To get it to explode he attaches a fuse and lowers it into the nitroglycerine.

Alfred is awarded a total of 355 patents during his lifetime. Some of these such as the blasting cap and dynamite, are considered to be technological milestones that heralded new ages of development for humanity. His blasting oil plays a vital role in the development of mining and subterranean construction. Alfred continues his work on a farm near Långholmen in Stockholm. By now he has mastered the art of detonating his blasting oil under controlled conditions, so he turns his attention to improving nitroglycerine manufacturing techniques. During one of their experiments, the area is suddenly rocked by an enormous blast as their house is blown to smithereens. His much-loved little brother Emil and several friends are blasted into oblivion.

In the aftermath, Immanuel is overcome with grief from which he never recovers, and Alfred seriously considers abandoning the explosives business altogether. However when the worst of the sorrow has passed, he rolls up his sleeves and manages to persuade one of Sweden's richest people, j.w. Smith, to become a partner in the company Nitroglycerin Aktiebolaget. The injection of funds from Smith enables manufacturing to continue and expand. This is timely as the world is becoming very interested in explosives. Alfred spends a great deal of time travelling to

Alfred Nobel was a multi-faceted character; creative, generous and somewhat peculiar. He is renowned for his will which formed the basis for the prizes bearing his name that are presented annually on the anniversary of his death. At the time of his death, his estate was valued at 33 million Swedish crowns – 100 billion crowns in modern money.

In the 63 years of his life, Alfred Nobel lodged no fewer than 355 patent applications. Several of his innovations are considered to have heralded the beginning of new ages in human development. Dynamite is probably the most famous among them and also formed the basis for his immense fortune.

demonstrate his products and opens manufacturing plants in Germany and Scotland.

He travels to the USA to defend his patent interests there – a visit that arouses considerable interest and its fair share of terror as things have a way of blowing up around Mr Nobel. Alfred is convinced that his blasting oil is harmless; however guests at a hotel in New York would be justified in claiming otherwise when his luggage suddenly explodes. A number of embarrassing misadventures follow where several boat loads of blasting oil spontaneously detonate. Alfred is under pressure to improve the substance. The American government is on the verge of banning it and to add insult to injury his factories in Germany have inconveniently begun blowing up.

Alfred is all too well aware that unplanned explosions cost lives, money and goodwill. He simply must improve the safety and precision of blasting oil. At his factory in Hamburg, he mixes nitroglycerine with an array of substances in an attempt to stabilise it without diminishing its power. He tries sawdust, wood meal and cement but nothing seems to work. He is about to give up when he casts a glance out over the river and suddenly gets an idea. Why not make a dough by mixing it with diatomaceous earth – a chalky powder that his high in silica? He tries it, attaches a fuse and detonates it. Nitroglycerine has finally been tamed and dynamite has been born.

Nobel's business skyrockets and as his empire grows he continues to work on improving his explosives. He soon stumbles upon a more sophisticated form of explosive he calls blasting gelatin. One day he cuts his finger and coats the wound with collodium, a gel that is used to form a protective film over wounds in much the same way as a modern surgical plaster does. Suddenly, in the middle of the night he gets an idea. Could this mixture of cellulose and ether be combined with nitroglycerine to form an explosive gel? Yes it could! Alfred invents blasting gelatin which is more effective than dynamite and can even be used under water. This innovation was used in 1880 in the construction of one of the world's longest tunnels, the St Gotthard Pass through the Alps.

Naturally Alfred's inventions were of great interest to weapons manufacturers. Personally he was a man of peace who believed that the best way to prevent war was to deter it; to produce a weapon so destructive that no one would dare use it. He held very firm beliefs on world peace. Amongst other things, he proposed the creation of an international peace keeping authority that would settle conflicts around the world and thereby avoid war an idea not unlike the modern United Nations which wasn't founded until 50 years after his death.

By the age of 50, Alfred is living alone in his mansion in Paris. The woman he loves, Bertha Kinsky has rejected his proposal of marriage and married another man. He abandons all hope of having a family and devotes all his time to his beloved company. His entrepreneurial endeavours live on today in the form of 300 companies located in over 30 countries.

On 10th December 1896, his greatest fear becomes a reality. He dies alone as a result of an aneurism. His financial legacy is a staggering 33 million Swedish Crowns. His will drops a final bomb on his family. Most of the money is to go to the creation of a foundation that will award an annual prize to the person in each of the five specified fields that has conferred the greatest benefit on mankind.

Nowadays Albert Einstein is seen as a symbol for genius and an obvious candidate for a Nobel Prize. But this wasn't the case in his day. Einstein was a contentious choice when he received his prize in 1921 and was no doubt a little surprised to discover that his diploma included a little additional introductory text: "Regardless of whether the theory of relativity proves to be true or false", before continuing with "Albert Einstein is awarded the Nobel Prize …". The Nobel Committee were afraid that the theory of relativity would be disproved; something that would naturally cast them in a bad light. Of all the diplomas that have been presented throughout the years, Einstein's is the only one to begin in this way. The identity of the cautious person responsible for the inclusion of the unprecedented text remains unknown.

The Nobel Prize

A party where the whole world is invited

The Nobel Prize celebrations on 10th December always commence with the Awards Ceremony in the Stockholm Concert Hall where around 1 500 guests witness the Laureates receiving their medals and diplomas from His Majesty the King. The appearance of the Medicine diploma differs somewhat from the others in that the Nobel Medal is depicted and the calligraphy is by Susan Duvnäs. The other diplomas are graced by the work of various other artists.

At the time of his death Alfred Nobel's estate was estimated to be worth in the vicinity of 30 million Swedish crowns, which, at the end of the 19th century was an enormous sum of money. Some of it was bequeathed to friends and relatives, but his will stipulated that the major part of his fortune was to be invested in safe securities. The interest from these investments would then constitute a fund from which an annual prize would be awarded to those in the fields of physics, chemistry, physiology/medicine, literature and peace who had conferred the most benefit on mankind during the previous year. The Nobel Prize for peace was to be awarded by five people chosen by the Norwegian Parliament. The reason for this was that at this time Sweden and Norway formed a united kingdom. The union between the two nations was dissolved in 1905, however the Nobel Peace Prize remained in Norway.

Alfred Nobel began drawing up his will as early as 1889 at which point he had already decided to give away most of his estate. In a letter to friend Sofie Hess he wrote, "The thought of all the shocked expressions and expletives of those missing out on the money gives me great pleasure." He had no regard for lawyers, calling them "formality's parasites" and re-drafted his will twice himself. His last will and testament was read five days after his death and the scene he had envisaged became a reality. His relatives were shocked and angry and felt that they had been robbed. They instigated legal proceedings in an attempt to acquire a larger portion of the estate, and to some extent they succeeded. Swedish King Oscar II thought the idea of awarding prizes to foreigners was unpatriotic while Hjalmar Branting, a Social Democrat politician who later became Prime Minister, declared the donation "deception of the highest order". However, thanks to several loyal and persistent colleagues, Alfred finally got his wish.

The thing Alfred feared most was dying alone and forgotten, and as fate would have it this is exactly what happened. On 10th December 1896 he collapsed over his desk in his villa in San Remo, Italy and died – alone. However, another even more dreadful scenario had apparently plagued his thoughts; that of being buried alive. To make sure this didn't happen, his will gave explicit instructions that once he had been declared "dead" both his wrists be slit, an operation that was duly performed during the autopsy.

Each year on 10th December, countless people around the world spare a thought for Alfred Nobel. He may have died alone but his legacy has been skillfully managed and lives on in the form of the world's most prestigious prizes

and one of the world's most spectacular parties. In 1968 the existing prize categories were joined by a prize for economics, inaugurated by the Swedish Central Bank which was celebrating its 300th year of operation. This particular award is still financed by the bank.

The Nobel Prize has become synonymous with the highest level of human endeavour. Few people in the world are unaware of its existence but few know that it is the legacy of a brilliant and generous Swedish inventor and industrialist.

Traditionally the Nobel festivities get under way with the Awards Ceremony at the Stockholm Concert Hall where guests are greeted by the Swedish Royal Family, the Stockholm Philharmonic and a breath-taking array of floral arrangements. Once the Laureates have received their medals and diplomas, dinner is served in the Blue Hall at Stockholm City Hall – one of the world's biggest, most glamorous banquets. This spectacular feast is enjoyed not only by the Laureates and their families, but also the Royal Family, members of parliament, the business elite, and honoured guests from all corners of the globe. Everyone is kept in suspense as to what will be placed in front of them on the famous Nobel dinner service. The menu is always kept secret. Three different menus are tried during the autumn and when one is chosen it is then polished and refined and combined with suitable wines. Twenty of Sweden's top chefs plus 200 waiters and waitresses work together to make sure guests are treated to an unforgettable evening. If you ever happen to be in Stockholm on 10th December try to avoid eating out as most of the best chefs and serving staff will be otherwise engaged.

A spectacular event with distinguished guests dressed up to the nines, this is an event where pomp, elegance and grandeur are the order of the day. Where dignitaries dress up to the hilt and dance the night away in the glittering Golden Hall. Fortunately the sun is on vacation in Sweden in December which means the guests can practically dance forever … Many Swedes dream of attending this party, if not as a prize winner then at least as a guest. However, the gilt-edged invitations are received by few so most of them have to settle for watching the proceedings from the comfort of their living room couch – homemade Nobel supper and bubbly at hand.

There is always speculation, particularly in the tabloid press, about who was the centre of attention at the party. One year Princess Madeleine's décolletage was the subject of many column feet in local newspapers.

When Soviet Authorities prevented Boris Pasternak and

Alexander Solzjenitsyn from attending the awards, a wave of protest reverberated around the world. The Nobel Prize never fails to cause some sort of stir and the party has been the source of many noteworthy anecdotes, often involving the authors. The elderly Anotole France arrived in 1921 wearing three winter coats and then promptly fell asleep on stage serenading all present with his cacophonous snoring. Italian Salvatore Quasimodo chose to bring his mistress to Stockholm instead of his wife which created enormous headaches for the arrangers; exactly what was protocol in such cases, what status should she be given and where should she be seated?

Norwegian author Knut Hamsun received the Nobel Prize in 1920 and in honour of the occasion put away copious amounts of drink. During the banquet, he staggered up to Selma Lagerlöf, Literature Laureate in 1909 and at the time a member of the Swedish Academy, rapped his fingers on her corset and exclaimed, "It sounds like a buoy!" When he finally returned to the Grand Hotel he left both his diploma and prize check in the lift. Fortunately, such indiscretions are not possible today as the prize money is electronically transferred directly to the Laureates bank. And a good thing too.

▲ THE NOBEL DINNER SERVICE

Guests were first given the pleasure of eating off designer Karin Björkquist's exquisite bone china service in 1991 in conjunction with the Nobel Prize's 90th birthday. This dinner service from Rörstrand is a wonderful example of Swedish design where the colours represent the four seasons, the continents of the world and the leading Nobel prizes.

Tablecloths and napkins are designed by Ingrid Dessau for Klässbols Linnen Mills. Glasses are from Orrefors and cutlery from Gense, courtesy of Gunnar Cyrén with his unmistakable design sensibilities – elegant, strict lines with the occasional bold or even impudent detail.

▼ The inaugural Nobel Banquet was held in 1901 in the Hall of Mirrors at Stockholm's Grand Hotel. 113 guests were invited, all of them male. Today over 1300 guests attend the Nobel Party which is held in the Blue Hall at Stockholm City Hall.

470m of linen table-cloths are draped over the 63 tables on which are placed 7000 pieces of china, 5000 glasses and 10000 pieces of cutlery. The surroundings are adorned with 10000 flowers and 5000 pieces of foliage, all donated by San Remo in Italy, the town where Alfred Nobel spent the last years of his life.

◀ Carolina Klüft, a track and field athlete who mainly competes in the heptathlon. By the age of 22 she had become the youngest person ever to win gold medals at all five international competitions, namely the Olympics, World Championships (indoor and outdoor) and European Championships (indoor and outdoor).

▼ Annika Sörenstam is one of the most successful female golfers ever. By 2006 she had bagged 69 LPGA tournaments including ten majors.

▲ Björn Borg won the Wimbledon singles title five years in a row, an unprecedented achievement, especially for someone who was actually a clay court specialist. Borg, who recently turned 50, won a total 11 Grand Slam titles.

◀ Zlatan Ibrahimović is one of Sweden's most famous soccer players. Several glowing years with Italian clubs Inter and Juventus have earned him the reputation as the most successful Swedish A series player in modern times.

◀◀ Jan-Ove Waldner is a legend in table tennis circles. In China he is known as *Lao Wa* or *Chang Quing Shu* – The Evergreen Tree. Waldner is considered of the greatest ever table tennis players with six World Championship and several Olympic medals under his belt.

Cold faces, warm hearts

Different impressions of Sweden

"To regard all things Swedish as exceptional, or at least better than everything else in the world, is not at all Swedish."

– Carl Jonas Love Almqvist

Here is a selection of results from a worldwide survey commissioned by the Council for Promotion of Sweden Abroad to gauge how Sweden-savvy the rest of the world is. Please note that the list presented here is by no means comprehensive or scientific.

Sweden is most famous for its welfare system. After this come ABBA, Astrid Lindgren and Ingmar Bergman. Gorgeous women and liberal sexual attitudes are also something widely associated with Sweden. Beautiful unspoiled landscapes and cars are also high on the list. In most countries Volvo is better known than SAAB but Scania also places. IKEA is also popular, with many non-Swedes naming it as something they recognise as Swedish.

Sweden is also known for its sporting achievements with Björn Borg topping the list. Most people are aware of the *Ice Borg's* dominance of international tennis and his cool disposition. He won the Wimbledon singles title five years in a row, an unprecedented achievement, especially for someone who was actually a clay court specialist. Borg, who recently turned 50, won a total of 11 Grand Slam titles. The fact that he is vividly remembered by people so many years after his retirement is an indicator of just how great he was.

The other Nordic countries often describe Sweden as a good neighbour. Other things that are included in the rest of the world's picture of Sweden are the cold climate; that it is sparsely populated, highly regulated and neutral, as well as meatballs, spirits, the Nobel Prize and high taxes.

According to the people surveyed, the best things about Sweden were its openness, transparency, ability to solve problems and sensible governing regardless of which party was in power. Other positives were its economy and welfare system, stability, neutrality, liberal stance in the EU, lack of corruption and that it is a well-ordered, modern society. That it is a reliable business partner and very beautiful were also highly appreciated.

On the down side, we have the climate and darkness as well as the taxes, the amount of regulation and the hypocrisy concerning alcohol. One stereotype that is perhaps more resilient than most is that of the blonde-haired, blue-eyed nymphomaniac – although this may well be considered a positive thing by some. For some inexplicable reason the myth that Swedish women are *easier* than their sisters abroad persists. Everyone who lives there however knows that this is not the case. Not all Swedes are blonde or promiscuous and the idea that Sweden is a paradise of constant nude bathing and free love is an extreme exaggeration. But the myth of sinful liberated Sweden lives on, perhaps not as prevalent as it once was, but alive and kicking nonetheless.

Another misconception about Sweden is that it has the highest rate of suicide in the world – a myth based on statistics. The thing is that Swedes have always been good at keeping statistics, even when it comes to suicide. Suicide is not officially recorded in other countries which therefore gives the appearance that Swedes are more likely to kill themselves than other peoples.

One of the finest compliments you can give a Swede is to say, "You are so un-Swedish!" Name another country where you could do that without getting into a fight.

Lagom

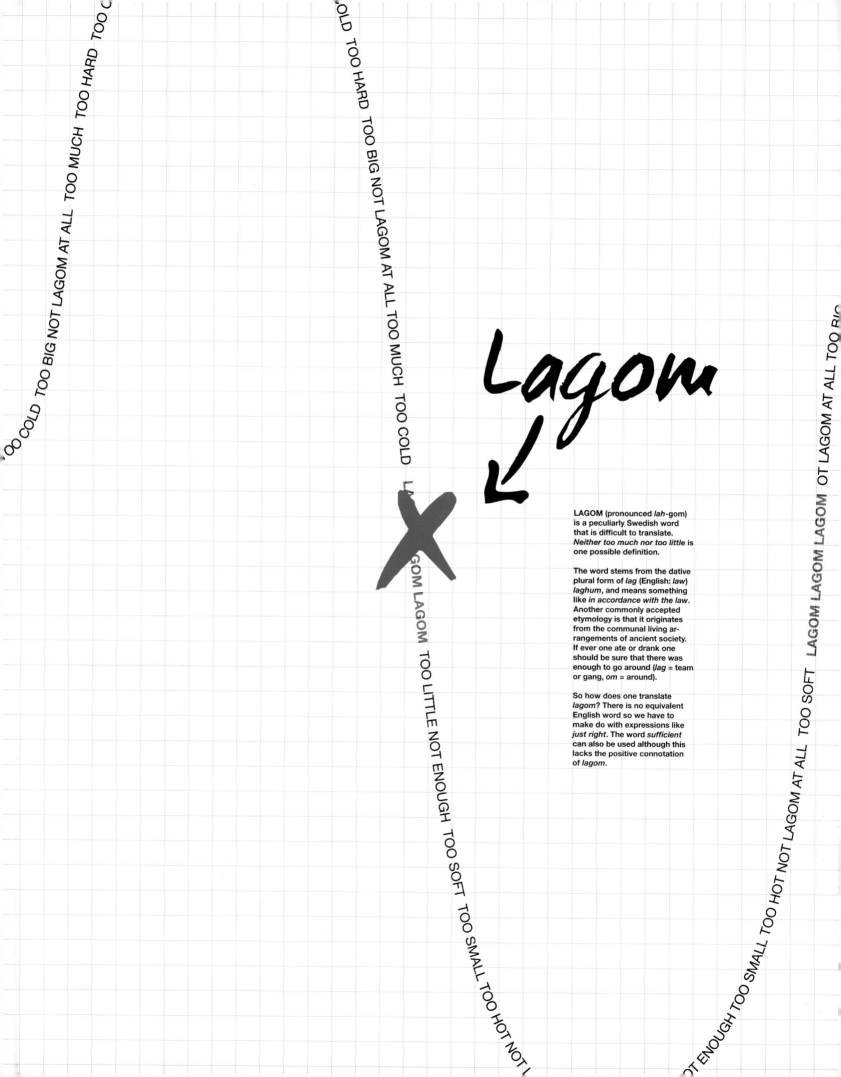

LAGOM (pronounced *lah*-gom) is a peculiarly Swedish word that is difficult to translate. *Neither too much nor too little* is one possible definition.

The word stems from the dative plural form of *lag* (English: *law*) *laghum*, and means something like *in accordance with the law*. Another commonly accepted etymology is that it originates from the communal living arrangements of ancient society. If ever one ate or drank one should be sure that there was enough to go around (*lag* = team or gang, *om* = around).

So how does one translate *lagom*? There is no equivalent English word so we have to make do with expressions like *just right*. The word *sufficient* can also be used although this lacks the positive connotation of *lagom*.

"THE SWEDISH SIN"

A myth that largely owes its origins to the occasional nudity of Swedish films from the 1950s and 60s, but which has little to do with reality. While it may be true that Swedes generally have a fairly relaxed attitude towards nudity and sex, when it gets down to cold hard statistics Sweden is usually at the bottom of the list of international comparisons in things such as teenage pregnancy and sexually transmitted diseases. Most Swedish women are well and truly fed up with the fact that blonde, promiscuous air-heads in films are often portrayed as Swedish. And that they invariably wear the leather shorts characteristic of the Alps. But then again, Hollywood never has been able to tell the difference between Sweden and Switzerland.

"Summer with Monika",
Ingmar Bergman

Snuff

Wad's that under your lip?

Swedes consume the most snuff in the world – close to 7 kg per user per year. Over one million of them regularly walk around with a strange bulge under their top lip. And this little wad of moist ground tobacco has even transcended traditional gender barriers with a fifth of all users being women.

Those who try to quit know how hard it is. The main reason is that snuff contains a lot of nicotine. Another aspect is that Swedish society is tolerant towards snuff whereas it generally frowns upon smoking. The question of snuff was a crucial issue when Sweden sought EU membership and resulted in an exemption clause that allowed its continued use. Smoking is banned in most workplaces and is no longer permitted in bars and restaurants but snuff users can pack their lip wherever and whenever they please.

Snuff found its way to Sweden via Columbus. Europeans first encountered tobacco on the island of Hispaniola – modern day Haiti in the West Indies – and the Portuguese and Spanish sailors took the plant home with them. In the middle of the 16th century, Portuguese doctors began using the herb as a medicine believing it could cure both cancer and syphilis. It would be interesting to know if anyone actually survived the cure.

Jean Nicot, French ambassador to Lisbon, played a large part in the spreading of snuff when he introduced the tobacco plant to Paris – a contribution that was acknowledged by Linné when he christened the tobacco plant *Nicotiana tabacum*. At that time trends that were set in Paris were mimicked by the rest of the continent, so it didn't take long for a wave of snuff sniffing to sweep across Europe. References to the use of snuff in Sweden first appear in 1637.

By the 18th century the use of smelling (dry) snuff was all the rage amongst the aristocracy, and all gentlemen of breeding owned a snuff box which was fashioned out of exclusive materials and handled most elegantly. These small masterpieces of gold, silver or other precious metal became prized gifts. Tobacco was even planted in Sweden where none other than Jonas Alströmer, the father of local potato production, commenced large scale cultivation.

The French Revolution put an end to smelling snuff and the upper classes that had enjoyed it. Napoleon however was a heavy user, and the drug experienced a new wave of popularity during his reign. Once he had been deposed it fell out of fashion, as using it was definitely no longer considered "politically correct".

Over a million Swedes emigrated to the other side of the Atlantic between 1846 and 1930. Naturally their traditions accompanied them, including the use of snuff. In fact, snuff was so common that the main street in Swedish-American parts of towns was often called *Snuff Boulevard* by the Americans. Moist snuff has become a symbol of Swedish identity.

The use of snuff is on the rise in Sweden in spite of health concerns, and the number of women users has trebled in the last ten years. Snuff has worked its way up the social ladder. Once popular only in country regions, it has now found its way into the nightclubs of central Stockholm. The most blatant "girl brand" is Mocca – a soft little package of smaller portions that resembles a make-up compact. Emma in this picture however has snuff powder under her lip.

A bulging back pocket worn thin where the material has rubbed against the snuff box is about the most Swedish of all things. Snuff is practically a trademark for being a Swede and many strange expressions are associated with it. *As elegant as snuff* is a common expression that probably originates from the 18th century when the drug was considered exclusive. Interestingly Sweden has the lowest rate of lung cancer in the EU, which may have something to do with the fact that more people use snuff than smoke.

A passionate tribute to Swedish nature

Majesty and silence.

The Swedish landscape dazzles with majestic shifts in mood. Enjoy an unforgettable adventure in a brilliant winter wonderland or when the spring explodes in an orgy of green. Summer invites you to bask on sun drenched granite islets or bathe in warm forest ponds before Mother Nature changes into her fiery fall attire. Sweden is unique, presenting four distinct seasons and innumerable possibilities in pristine natural settings. These sections from the different parts of Sweden are without captions. We could never put into words what they manage to express so eloquently, namely Sweden is fantastic.

◀ Lake in Lappland

Vindelälven, Lappland

Watercourse, Trappstegsforsen,
Saxnäs, Västerbotten

◄ Jämtland

◄◄ Faldreven at Höksfalan,
Västergötland

◄ Vargkitteln, Kilsbergen
Bergslagen

◄◄ Ramsjön, Bergslagen

Sea-stack, Fårö, Gotland

Gotska Sandön

Yttre Huö, Bohuslän

The Stockholm archipelago

Katterjåkk, Lappland

Låktatjåkka midnightsun,
Lappland

Lapporten, Abisko, Lappland

It's cold in Sweden.

As a child in early 18th century Sweden, Anders Celsius soon shows himself to be a mathematical genius. The legal studies he later commences at Uppsala University are soon abandoned in favour of mathematics and astronomy. He becomes Professor of Astronomy at the ripe old age of 29, but achieves eternal fame for his 100 degree temperature scale. Initially he deems the boiling point of water to be 0 degrees and its freezing point to be 100 degrees. However, Carl von Linné does not approve, at least according to 18th century rumours, and wants to invert the scale. And so it comes to pass. The boiling and freezing points of water are easy to identify and reproduce which leads to the widespread use of the Celsius thermometer. In fact the whole world uses the Celsius scale every single day …

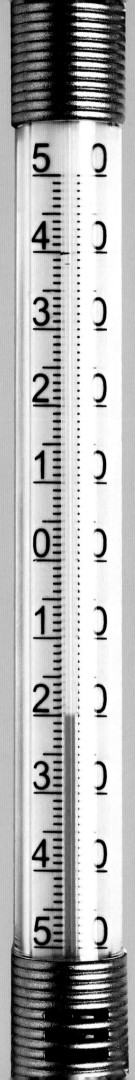

Off track

Swedish snow

Every Swede has their own particular relationship with snow. The Swedish language has several words for different types while the *Sámi* have several hundred expressions that describe the amount, consistency, load-bearing capacity, surface and resistance to skis and sleighs. They even have words for fresh snow cover, different types of tracks, frost in all its forms, snow on trees and bushes, bare ground, melting snow and patches of snow that remain throughout the summer.

Snow consists of transparent ice crystals that are formed when condensation in the atmosphere freezes around small particles in the air. Snow flakes are formed when partially melted crystals collide with each other and refreeze. In extreme cases these flakes can be up to 10 cm across. Snowflakes are hexagonal in shape and their appearance is determined by temperature. Common crystal shapes include needle, column, flat and star. Endless variations in temperature mean that no two snowflakes are alike. It's amazing to think that every tiny snowflake is absolutely unique.

Snowflakes are highly reflective which is why they appear to be white. Snow depth is measured in centimetres although it can sometimes be given in terms of precipitation i.e. how much water would it be if it melted straight away.

In Sweden, winter is synonymous with skiing. Nearly all Swedes ski, either alpine or cross-country and many do both. The real test of your man or womanhood is competing in the annual *Vasaloppet*, a 90 km cross-country ski race. Of course the more often you manage to complete the course the more man/woman points you earn. The origins of this slightly bizarre event hark back to the year 1520. After many years of fighting, Danish King Kristian II – commonly known as *Kristian the Tyrant* – had finally conquered Sweden. He promises members of the Swedish nobility who had opposed him an amnesty. However, once he is sworn in as king he promptly rounds them up and has them killed in what became known as the Stockholm Bloodbath.

A few magic moments in Madonna di Campiglio, Italy in 1974 would forever change alpine skiing in Sweden and put the little mountain village of Tärnaby on the international map. This is when Tärnaby native Ingemar Stenmark won his first world cup victory – the beginning of one of sporting Sweden's greatest success stories. In total Ingemar won 86 world cup events. Whenever he competed, Sweden would literally come to a standstill as the nation nervously congregated around its TV sets. Work stopped, school classes took a break and university lectures were postponed.

The story continued in the shape of Anja Pärson, currently one of the best women skiers in the world, who happens to come from the very same village as Ingemar. Her victory in the World Championship Downhill in 2007 saw her become the first woman ever to win the World Championship in all five events.

A young Swedish nobleman by the name of Gustav Vasa loses his father in the massacre and swears to avenge him. Alone and in disguise he travels up to the county of Dalarna to organise an army to strike at the Danes. In the town of Mora, he tries in vain to inspire the men of Dalarna to rally and liberate Sweden, but unfortunately nobody believes his grisly story of the massacre and he is forced to leave alone. Bitterly disappointed, he dons his skis and heads off for Sälen and Norway.

Shortly after his departure, news of the Stockholm Bloodbath reaches the men of Dalarna. Outraged they change their minds and immediately send two men on skis to find Gustav Vasa. They find him in Sälen and promise the support of Dalarna if he returns to Mora. Gustav Vasa's peasant army wages war on the Danes and eventually succeeds in liberating Sweden from Danish oppression. On Midsummer's Day 1523, Gustav Vasa rides into Stockholm as King of Sweden.

172

◀ The first 90 km *Vasaloppet* race is held in 1922 in memory of Gustav Vasa's journey in 1520 and attracts 119 competitors who tenaciously fight their way through winding forest roads to see who can get to Mora first. These days the route is prepared. In addition to the original event there are now seven other races including one for women, one for skaters and even several for kids. Each year a total of 50 000 skiers gather on the first Sunday in March to compete. A record 16 139 skiers entered the 80th Vasaloppet.

Slightly stiff snow is that which has good load-bearing properties and produces a really rough, hard crust. Fluffy new snow, powder snow, sleet, lumpy snow, untouched winter snow … each type has its own word in Swedish. The Sámi way of classifying snow is even more complex and detailed.

Ice – friend or foe?

Gliding through Sweden

Tour Skating is enormously popular in Sweden and most people planning a tour will check the ice reports before heading out. Every type of ice has a name which means that these reports can be totally incomprehensible to anyone other than an experienced skater, e.g. *mostly good black ice or snow ice. Some pack ice and pressure ridges*. Snow ice (sometimes called grey ice) softens quickly when the temperature increases. Black ice is affected by the sun whose rays penetrate deeply weakening the bonds between the pillar-shaped crystals. As a result ice that appears to be thick and supportive can actually be weak. Other types of ice include spring ice, which is the most treacherous of all, and sea ice which is weaker than fresh water ice due to the presence of salt crystals.

The season is long, often stretching from October to April. Virgin black ice that is free of snow and cracks is skater heaven.

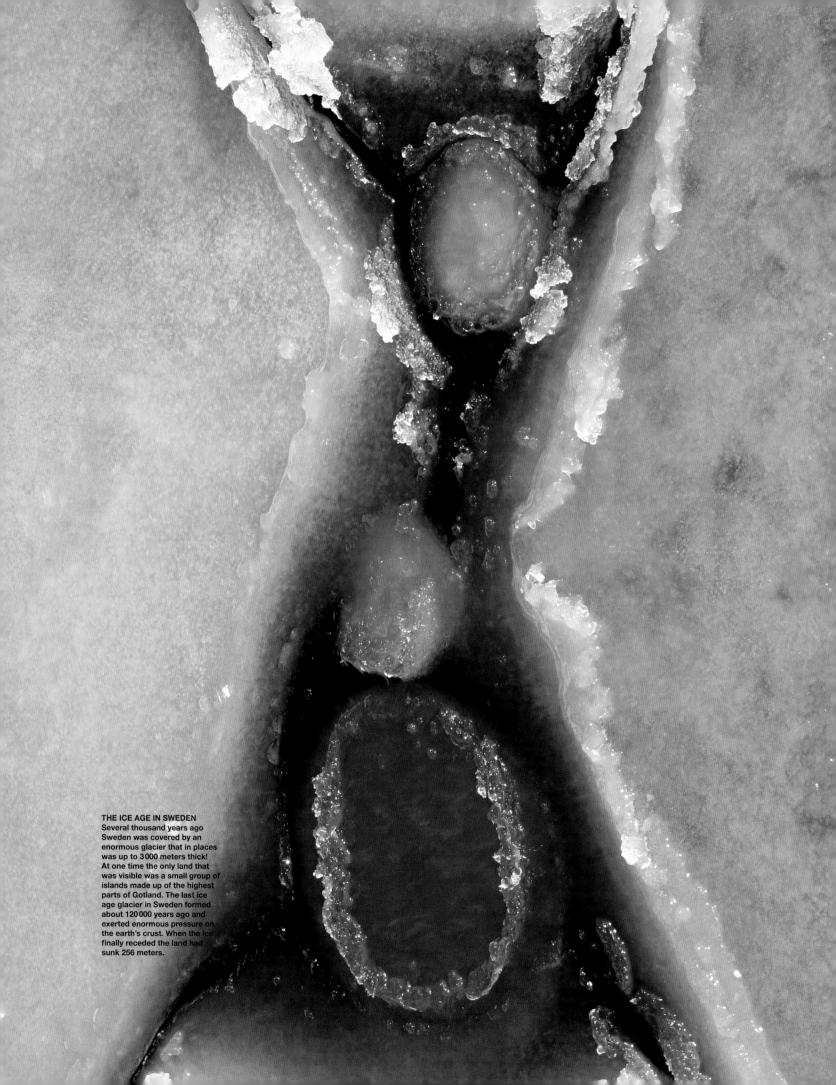

THE ICE AGE IN SWEDEN
Several thousand years ago
Sweden was covered by an
enormous glacier that in places
was up to 3000 meters thick!
At one time the only land that
was visible was a small group of
islands made up of the highest
parts of Gotland. The last ice
age glacier in Sweden formed
about 120000 years ago and
exerted enormous pressure on
the earth's crust. When the ice
finally receded the land had
sunk 256 meters.

The Swedish winter is ideal for skating as there is always a snow-free, stretch of natural ice somewhere. Gliding across a mirror-like surface on a beautiful winter's day is a magical experience combining rhythm, speed and the great outdoors with the occasional surprise. Perhaps it is the element of the unexpected that excites the most – one never really knows if the ice will hold or fold. It lives its own life offering pleasure and excitement. The Swedes say that experienced skaters and winter fishermen can read the ice – a skill only acquired through long, occasionally wet experience.

Tour skating (often known as *Nordic skating*) is best done in groups, primarily for safety reasons, however the experience is no doubt more pleasurable when shared.
Ice is rarely the same thickness over an entire lake or archipelago. The various phases of ice formation are often quite distinct, however there can be treacherous exceptions and every season experienced and inexperienced skaters alike fall through the ice. In southern Sweden the sun is the ice's main enemy, even in the middle of winter. On occasion however the ice can reach as far south as the Danish isles – like in the winter of 1658 when Swedish King Karl x Gustav was able to march his army across the ice and conquer part of Denmark.

The intimate relationship between Swedes and ice is reflected in their language. For example *there's no cow on the ice* is a common Swedish expression which means, there's no reason to panic. At first this expression may not seem to make any sense, but it is actually perfectly logical given the country's climate and history. A cow falling through the ice would have been a catastrophic event for any farm – not to mention the cow.

There are three simple safety rules; knowledge, equipment and company.
A skater should always have the following with him; a backpack containing a change of clothes in a waterproof bag, ice claws, a whistle, lifeline and a mobile phone in a plastic bag.

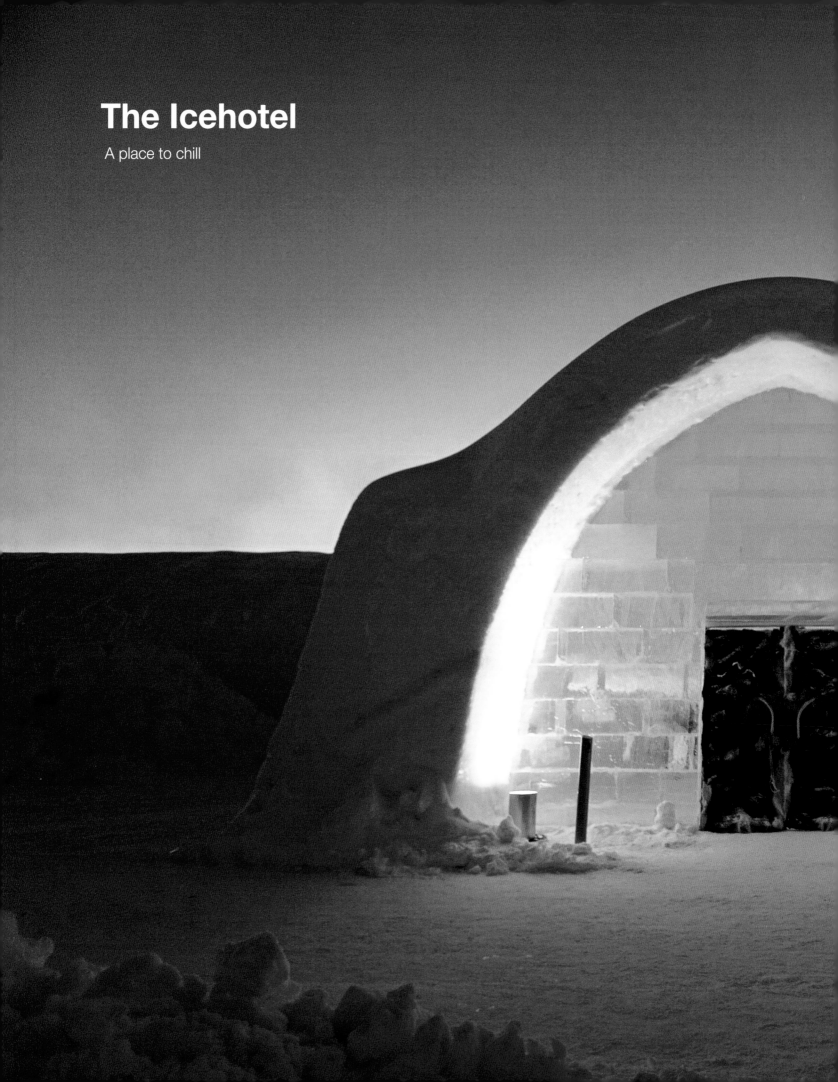

The Icehotel

A place to chill

The Torne river was born of glaciers 10 000 years ago and its crystal clear waters have flowed freely ever since, cutting a swathe throughout the landscape on their long journey to the sea. The Icehotel in Jukkasjärvi in northern Lappland is built out of thousands of tonnes of ice and snow borrowed from the richly flowing river, where, in the warmer months, fish are seen battling the currents, living their life as part of a thundering, foaming torrent.

The Land of the Midnight Sun can offer fantastic outdoor experiences during the brief summer, which is why

▼ The main hall.
Sculptures by artist
Jörgen Westin.

Jukkasjärvi had always focused on attracting summer tourists. However, during the long winter the river slumbered, the population of the small town went into hibernation and earnings fell as rapidly as the temperature. And winter up there is unbelievably long. By the end of the 1980s, a group of locals had decided to make the most of the hand they had been dealt – to look upon winter as an asset and create experiences from the natural materials they have in abundance; the cold, the darkness, ice, snow and the magical northern lights. Inspired by Japanese ice artists, they invited French artist Jannot Derid to visit them. Derid held an exhibition in a purpose-built igloo, the Artic Hall, placed in the middle of the Torne River. People travelled from far and wide to view this curiosity, many shaking their heads at the insane notion.

One night, a couple of foreign guests slept in the cylinder-shaped igloo, snuggling up in sleeping bags on outstretched reindeer skins. They loved it and couldn't wait to tell all their friends about this incomparable experience. Suddenly, the concept of the Icehotel had been born. A lot has happened since then and the modern hotel is now world famous for the magical cultural experience it provides. Astounded visitors are overcome with child-like wonder as they enter the magical realm of the Ice King and often return home feeling as if they have been part of a fairy tale.

Construction of the hotel begins each year in November to make sure that they are up and running in time for the winter season which starts in December. Each year a legion of artists, architects and ice builders fashion a unique hotel out of the crystal clear Torne ice. The spectacular building has become one of Sweden's major tourist attractions – an insane idea that has become internationally renowned.

The Icehotel may have exclusive suites and double rooms but it has no heating. The temperature indoors is usually between minus 4 and minus 9 degrees Celsius depending on the temperature outdoors. Outside the mercury can plummet to minus 40 Celsius. That's plenty cold. Fortunately guests are spared chattering teeth as they are bedded down in cosy sleeping bags guaranteed to keep them warm. The hotel includes a lobby, a pillared chamber, cinema and the famous Icebar, where people from all the corners of the globe mingle until the ice melts. And melt it will, because when spring arrives the hotel will glide inexorably into the Torne River, once again uniting the reception area, rooms, suites and bars with the mighty river flowing out to sea.

If you feel the need to contemplate the natural order of things you can leave the bar and visit the ice church – an experience that can be even more poignant when you consider that the church itself is transient.

Couples from around the globe visit the ice church to promise eternal fidelity – vows that can take on a special meaning when the church in which they were exchanged soon becomes nothing but a memory. One could also speculate as to whether marriages forged here turn out to be frosty, or even frozen, in which case they might last much longer.

The medicine bottle
that conquered the world

The Absolut Story

The story of Absolut Vodka starts with *Absolut Renat Brännvin* (Absolut Distilled Spirits) which was launched in 1979 as a more up-market type of spirit. Today Absolut is the fourth biggest brand of spirits in the world as well as being one of the best-selling Vodkas in the USA. The reasons for this are twofold. Firstly the distinctive design of the bottle which is inspired by old fashioned medicine bottles. Add to this an award-winning advertising campaign placing the bottle in various well-known settings from around the world and you have the key to international success. Designers Lars Börje Carlsson, Gunnar Broman and Hans Brindfors' choice of bottle was certainly no accident. The Swedes have more or less always considered spirits to be medicinal.

The originals for the revolutionary advertising campaign consist of a collection of art works commissioned from some of the late 1990s greatest artists. The collection, which is known as the *Absolut Art Collection,* currently consists of over 500 works. The first artist to be commissioned was Andy Warhol and he has been followed by a number of internationally famous artists such as Keith Haring, Ed Ruscha and Chris Ofili. The Absolut story is one that created art and advertising history. Placing a value on the collection is difficult as the brand connection is both a strength and limitation on the art market.

Who is coolest clutching an ice tumbler? A hot bar for cool types at the Icehotel in Jukkasjärvi where a cosmopolitan clientele indulge in Absolut Vodka drinks specially created for the hotel. Beyond the crystal walls reality is another world away, which is exactly how it has been since 1994 when Absolut Vodka and the Icehotel joined forces to create the world's first bar built out of ice. Here revellers can enjoy a dreamlike ambience created by skilled artists and craftsmen. The hotel and bar melt into the waters of the river each spring only to be recreated following winter.

Geographically, the distance between Absolut Vodka in Åhus in southern Sweden and the Icehotel in Jukkasjärvi in Lappland is great. However, when it comes to an appreciation of fine craftsmanship, creativity, design and unique raw materials, they are definitely neighbours. Each possesses their own crystal clear trademarks; the autumn wheat and fresh spring water from Åhus in the south, and the pure ice of the Torne River in the north.

ABSOLUT PERFECTION.

ABSOLUT ADRENALINE.

ABSOLUT BANGKOK.

Absolut Vodka is the fourth biggest brand of spirits in the world. V&S Absolut Spirits' facility in Åhus are currently shipping more Absolut Vodka than ever before to the 126 markets around the world where it is on sale. USA is the biggest market whilst China is the biggest in Asia.

Absolut Vodka is available in more than ten different flavours. When Absolut Vodka was launched in the USA in 1979, its sales figures went through the roof and they have been on the rise ever since. Nowadays little Åhus in Skåne County produces over 90 million litres of vodka each year.

The indigenous people of Sweden

The Sámi – one people, one land, four countries

The *Sámi* (once widely known as *Lapps*) are Sweden's indigenous people and have inhabited the land they call *Sápmi* since time immemorial. Like all peoples classified as indigenous, they have continually inhabited the same area prior to being invaded or colonised. There are approximately 20 000 Sámi in Sweden. They speak their own languages and have their own flag.

References to the Sámi first appear in 98 AD in Roman historian *Tacitus'* book *Germania* where he describes a people he calls *fenni*: "They eat herbs, clothe themselves in animal skins and sleep on the ground. The only things they trust are their bone-tipped arrows. Men and women accompany each other and seek nourishment on the same hunt".

The Sámi were perceived as an unusual and exotic people as the men and women shared hunting duties. Remains of prehistoric settlements in Upper Norrland testify to a hunter-gatherer society that eventually domesticated and farmed reindeer. Reindeer farming is still a primary source of income amongst the Sámi. In addition to the commercial aspects it is part of the Sámi's cultural heritage and central to their sense of identity. What started as hunting has become a modern form of animal husbandry where helicopters and snow scooters are used to muster the animals. However, Mother Nature still governs the natural cycles of the herd as they graze in the wild all year round. The Sámi are permitted by law to run reindeer on around one third of Sweden's territory which currently supports a total of around 230 000 animals.

In an interesting example of equality of the sexes, the reindeer is the only species of deer where both males and females grow horns. However, a bull may assemble a harem of up to 30 cows, which immediately seems to dispel any ideas of equality. The cows take to the fells in May in order to calf and during the summer will eat copious amounts of food to build up the fat reserves necessary to survive the bitter winter. A number of the bulls will be slaughtered in the autumn just before they come into heat and when they are at their fattest. The reindeer slaughter is a spectacular event that is unlike anything else in the world – a highly exotic ingredient in the otherwise technologically advanced Swedish society and by no means a quaint remnant of a bygone era recreated for the benefit of well-heeled tourists. This is the real deal. This is their daily bread.

Nomadic peoples have always had difficulty asserting their right to the land they live on. Governments have rarely been familiar with their way of life and have often claimed that they have no right to the land that supports them. When Sápmi first came to the attention of the surrounding nations it was considered a wasteland. There was no government here, no common chief, and no state apparatus. Sámi society was based on groups of families called *sijdda*. Surrounding states all tried to take control of the region and its riches arguing over who was the rightful claimant of the land in the north and, just as in other

Modern Sápmi stretches across four countries and is populated by approximately 60 000 Sámi. There are around 20 000 in Sweden, 35 000 in Norway, 5 700 in Finland and 2 000 in Russia.

parts of the world, the Church supported the government in an attempt to extend their own sphere of influence. As God's instrument on earth they believed they were fully entitled to repress the pagan Sámi religion and "encourage" conversion to Christianity. Karl IX, Swedish regent from 1604–1611, wanted access to the rich fishing grounds of the North Sea at any price. In a sly move he started calling himself *King of the Lapps* and started taxing the Sámi. However, this gesture in itself was not enough to assert Swedish sovereignty in the area – the Danes, Norwegians and Russians all excised taxes from the hapless Lapps. The best way to claim the area was to populate it with Swedes. The Sámi were neither Swedes, Norwegians nor Russians, but if they converted to Swedish Christianity, paid Swedish taxes and lived amongst Swedes then surely the land could be called Swedish. The architects of this strategy no doubt thought they were being particularly clever.

Despite slight regional religious differences, the Sámi share a common belief system that stretches across the whole of Sápmi, all the way from the Kola Peninsula in Russia, across northern Finland, and into Norway and Sweden. They divide the cosmos into three strata: an upper, middle and underworld, each with their own gods and spirits. Man is considered both a heavenly and terrestrial being.

Traditional Sámi fare can be summed up in two words – meat and fish, and has remained practically unchanged despite outside influences. They still eat reindeer meat, fresh, dried or preserved. Dried reindeer in particular is considered a delicacy. No part of the reindeer goes to waste – the head, hooves, bone marrow and blood are all used.

Traditionally men were responsible for food preparation, butchering the meat and cooking the stew. The men have also been the artisans, using their handicraft skills to create lightweight, practical household items out of hide, sinews, timber, roots, horn and bark. This tradition has developed into an exclusive art form prized by collectors around the world. A well-made Sámi knife by a famous carpenter is to be considered an investment.

According to certain ethnographers, the Sámi style of singing known as *yoik* is the oldest form of music in Europe. There was a time however when it was not even considered music. In the early 17th century, Christian IV, King of Norway and Denmark, declared that anyone practicing Sámi witchcraft, including *yoik*, should be put to death.

The four elements have played a central role in Sámi folk medicine. The practice of stone baths has been used by forest Sámi since time immemorial. A stone is taken from

the water, one from in the earth and one that has lain on the ground. A small pit is dug, the stones put in it and a fire lit. This way the power of the four elements is united. Once the stones are hot, a tent is pitched over the pit, and water poured on the stones to produce a primitive steam bath. The ailing person is brought in and, hey presto, is cured. Magic was also of great importance, expressed in fundamental principles such as *like cures like*, *evil expels evil*. Birch splinters could be used to cure a toothache by first poking the tooth and then hammering them back into the tree. In this way the pain was transferred to the tree. Unfortunately, the unsuspecting person who eventually chopped down the tree would be afflicted by the toothache. The spring sap of the birch was also used to prevent illness during the coming year. The thin layer under the bark was used as a dressing for wounds and to stop bleeding. *Birch-whipping* is a time honoured tradition in Nordic countries that survived well into the 20th century. People gathered in the spring sun and whipped each other until their torsos were red, driving winter out of their bodies allowing the power of the birch to infuse them with health and vigour. Birch is still used medicinally in northern Sweden and Finland, and birch branches are used in the sauna where bathers whip each other red or until they scream – a Sámi practice that is considered very healthy. Apart from its medicinal and recreational uses birch still plays an important role in Swedish life and is often used as decoration at weddings, graduation parties and at Easter.

Burning tinder involves placing birch tinder on the skin and lighting it. The idea is that the "evil" that is ailing the patient will seep out through the weeping burn created by the heat. This practice resembles Chinese moxibustion and as it happens both cultures use the same points and meridians. Amazing!

Animals also play a vital role in Sámi medicine where they have powerful symbolic value. The bear could relieve pain and in the case of a toothache, for example, it may have been sufficient just to place a bear paw (presumably from a dead bear) against the cheek of the patient for the pain to subside.

The reindeer, the traditional livelihood of the Sámi, was naturally also an important part of their domestic drug store. The fat that was boiled down from hooves worked wonders for constipation and a broth made out of horn was used as a miracle cure for heavy colds. These days Japanese men use the horn to improve their potency which has turned reindeer into a lucrative export product for the Sámi. Does it work? You'll have to ask Japanese women …

Land of contrasts

Black velvet nights and the Midnight Sun

This may come as a shock, but polar bears do not wander the streets of Stockholm. They live in the polar region which is further north. A lot further. The only polar bear in Stockholm is the one at the outdoor museum *Skansen*, which, by the way, is the world's oldest. The weather in Sweden varies widely during the course of the year depending of course on the season. This variation makes the Swedish climate unique; this is one of the few countries on earth where you can experience four distinct seasons across the entire land.

Sweden is habitable thanks to the warm waters of the Gulf Stream surging up from Mexico and the westerly and south-westerly winds flowing in from the Atlantic. These phenomena make Sweden much warmer than it should be given its latitude. Without the Gulf Stream, Stockholm would no doubt be home to those infamous polar bears. Sweden is a long, thin country. The distance between the southern most point *Smygehuk*, and the northern most, *Treriksröset*, is 1600 km as the crow flies. The further north you go, the shorter the summer and the longer the winter. The beginning of each season varies greatly between the south and the north. According to meteorologists spring has arrived when the daily average temperature is on the rise and is somewhere between 0 and 10 degrees Celsius. In the north this happens at the beginning of May, whereas in the south it is at the end of February.

The coldest temperature ever recorded in Sweden is minus 53 degrees Celsius and the hottest, 38 degrees. The northern summer is characterised by intense daylight around the clock. If summer is yang, full of brightness and energy, then the northern winter is yin, dense and dark – as if a black velvet cloak had been swathed over the countryside. Days are so short that they go by practically unnoticed. The payoff however is two distinct seasonal peaks. The polar circle traverses the counties of *Norrbotten* and *Lappland*. North of this line lies the Land of the Midnight Sun, where it hangs tenaciously in the sky from the end of May until the beginning of July. The result? No night. This spectacular backdrop provides the opportunity for many unique activities. How does skiing in a bikini at midnight sound? An unforgettable, slightly bizarre experience that can really mess with your head.

Winter on the other hand is the realm of darkness. It is bitterly cold and the sun only briefly manages to drag itself into the sky before dropping behind the horizon. So if you want to experience some daylight at this time of year, you will have to hurry. On the plus side however is the sublime *Aurora Borealis – the Northern Lights* – a dazzling heavenly display that has always enchanted mankind. The spellbinding sight of twisting curtains of light swirling and shifting colours against the night sky is seldom forgotten by those fortunate enough to witness it. This phenomenon was once known as *Herring Lightning* as the people in the north though it to be the reflection of schools of herrings in the sea. The Northern Lights occur when solar flares bombard the earth with charged particles. These particles travel at great speed and some of them are captured by the earth's magnetic field and guided towards the north and south magnetic poles. The particles collide with gas molecules in the atmosphere and kinetic energy is emitted as photons, or light particles. Colours can vary from yellowy-green to red and even violet depending on the type of molecule colliding with the particle, the speed of the collision and the charge of the particle. Some claim that the Northern Lights emit a crackling sound, whilst others insist that this is a scientific impossibility. True or false? The best thing to do is to witness it for yourself and draw your own conclusions. Either way you are guaranteed to be enthralled by one of Sweden's greatest natural wonders.

▶ The Northern Lights is a spellbinding sight of twisting curtains of light swirling and shifting colours against the night sky.

A scientific revolution

God may have created, but Linnaeus organised

Carl von Linné – often known as *Carolus Linnaeus,* the Latin name under which he published his scientific work – was a visionary. A man of revolutionary ideas he is without doubt the most famous of all Swedes. Stories from the 18th century portray him as a charismatic figure with a keen sense of humour. Self-assured yet humble. There are innumerable descriptions of this botanical superstar. Some of them portray him as a self-important and boastful diva but we choose not to give credence to these stories here.

After an intensive courtship where he uses every possible means at his disposal to impress his intended, including dressing up in Sámi costume, he eventually marries Sara Lisa. Standing a mere five feet tall (154 cm) he is forced to use every trick in the book to convince her of his manliness. He succeeds, and they go on to have four daughters and a son.

Linné classifies the natural world according to a system that comes to be known as *Systema Naturae.* To simplify things flora and fauna are given international scientific names. This system, which uses two Latin names for every plant or animal, is still in use today and allows communication between botanists, zoologists and gardeners from around the world. The language of Linné is truly universal.

Carl Linnaeus was born in Råshult in Småland in 1707. His father Nils is a priest and a recreational gardener. Carl develops an interest in nature at an early age, but is forced to follow in his father's footsteps and become a clergyman. However, he hates school and often plays truant so he can be outdoors. He much prefers to sit under an oak tree and smell the flowers than to sit at his school bench. His teachers are less than impressed and summon Nils to an audience. What he hears shocks and surprises him, however a natural history teacher suggests that young flower-loving Carl may actually be more suited to being a doctor.

In the 18th century, anything concerning natural science fell under the heading *Medicine.* This suits Linné to a tee, but at this time the profession of doctor was a lowly one and his mother is distraught. "Is poor Carl to be no more than a simple field surgeon?" she exclaimed.

When Linné arrives at Uppsala University in 1728 he finds a medical faculty that is deficient to say the least. Only 10 of the university's 500 students are studying medicine. But Carl has come to the right place and writes the paper *Praeludia Sponsaliorum Plantarum* in 1729. His work shocks many as it refers to the sex life of plants, using terms such as house, bedchamber, wedding, bed, procreation, men, women, hermaphrodites and mothers. Printed plant pornography à la the 18th century.

At this time in Sweden, one could not become a doctor of medicine so Linné travels to Holland where he publishes the book *Systema Naturae.* This work presents a new system for the classification of the Kingdoms of Nature - flora, fauna and minerals – and arouses the interest of contemporary scientists. It presents many changes amongst which the reclassification of the flora is seen as particularly revolutionary. Linné uses a system based on sex where species with the same number of stamens are grouped together. Even fauna is reclassified, and for the first time humans are placed in the same group as the apes – a bold move in the 18th century and one that causes an outcry in many circles.

Over time Linné refines his system, for example moving whales from the fish family to the mammal family. When the 13th edition is released, it is 3 000 pages long and describes 20 000 species. The first version had been a little over 10 pages. There is no modern equivalent to *Systema Naturae* as no single work could describe all of the over 1 413 000 species that are currently known to science.

During his time in Holland, Linné becomes the first person in Europe to cultivate bananas. He claims that the fruit offered to Adam by Eve in the Garden of Eden was a banana and therefore christens the banana *Musa paradisiaca.* We can image what the church thought of his throwing out

apples for bananas.

On the subject of bananas … Linné even worked as a doctor for a while in a clinic in Stockholm. Most of his patients were young men and, according to his autobiography, most of them were suffering from some sort of "social" ailment. Linné prescribed a cure of a bottle of wine a day for two weeks apparently with great success. Interesting when you consider that in most cases the affliction was raging syphilis. Perhaps it was Linné's charisma that produced so many satisfied clients or maybe it was just the wine.

Linné produced more than 70 books and 300 scientific papers including *Praeludia Sponsaliorum Plantarum* which is usually translated into English as *Prelude to the marriage of the plants*. Here he explains how he came up with his system based on the sexuality of plants. The number of stamens determines the class of the plant whereas the number of carpel or pistils is used to build sub-groups. In order to emphasise the similarity between the sexual organs of plants and of man he uses a picture of the hermaphrodite *Dog's Mercury – Mercurialis perennis –* flower on the cover.

Linne's work left an indelible mark on Swedish society and is no doubt at least partly responsible for the reverence with which Swedes regard the natural world. You would be hard pressed to a find a people that appreciate the great outdoors more. Few people cherish flowers and foliage like the Swedes. And we are not talking about neatly cultivated gardens. Swedes worship Mother Nature in all her natural glory. Linné has often been portrayed as simply being interested in plants. Indeed his contribution to the world of botany was enormous and his system is still studied today. However, few stop to consider the breadth of his work.

He studied the entire natural world and categorised all known flora, fauna and minerals. What was known in his day as natural history has since developed into the contemporary fields of botany, zoology and mineralogy. One can wonder if the man ever slept or when he got to meet his wife and children, although 18th century rumour had it that he was a devoted husband and father.

In 1741 Linné is appointed Professor of Medicine at Uppsala University. One of his first projects is to revamp the ailing academy garden where he enlists the help of two celebrities; Danile Nietzel from Holland and Carl Hårleman from the Swedish Royal Court. Linné's vision is to transform the garden into a "living textbook" where students can stroll around and experience plants from the various classes in his system. He also introduces animals; parrots that mimic his voice demanding that visitors blow their noses, monkeys that steal the hats from cowering students and even a raccoon. In effect he creates his own little Utopia. He acquires plants and animal, via a variety of methods. He purchases some of them but coming from Småland, traditionally a very poor part of Sweden where the inhabitants are known for being – shall we say – "careful" with their money, he is frugal by nature. When an animal catalogue arrives from Holland he is astonished by the prices. "When I look at this catalogue the hair on my head stands up and the lice nibble at its roots. 300, 100, 50 guilders!!! The sum of a pair of riders, horses without jockeys. Animals may be beautiful but alas not as beautiful as money."

Linné remains close to his beloved garden. In fact the professorial residence is located in one corner. Here he lives happily with his flowers until he dies.

Trespassers welcome

Provided they don't disturb or damage

There is a law in Sweden that is one of a kind. Its origins can be traced back to the Middle Ages when pizzerias were scarce and travellers braving the vast Swedish forests had to make do with what they could forage along the way. Common law stated that every man was entitled to take a handful of nuts to sustain him on his journey. This practice survives under the name *Allemansrätten* – the right of common access – and has even been enshrined in Swedish law.

So what exactly is *Allemansrätten*? Whereas most other societies go to great lengths to protect private property, this law is exactly the opposite. In short, the right of common access exists to guarantee that everyone in Sweden has access to nature. In return for access one is expected to be considerate towards flora and fauna, as well as property owners and fellow visitors.

Although *Allemansrätten* is sometimes invoked to defend oafish behaviour, it is not intended to allow a free-for-all. Its freedoms come with certain responsibilities. Fortunately most people see it as an opportunity rather than a right; a unique chance to enjoy the riches cherished by the average Swede.

The right of common access even applies to waterways. Anyone wishing to swim at the beach, or to travel just about anywhere by boat and spend a day or two on private land is entitled to do so, provided they maintain an appropriate distance from private dwellings and do not disturb local residents.

Considerate campers are welcome although larger groups must seek the permission of the property owner – a courtesy that prevents the local circus from pitching their tents in your flower beds. One is even allowed to cycle on roads running through private property, although not over someone's plot or through cultivated or sensitive land. Most Swedes know this. Those who don't are usually promptly informed.

Camp fires are a wonderful part of life outdoors, but make land owners a bit edgy. Every year productive forest is destroyed by careless campers – all in the name of the right of common access. Lighting a fire is permitted provided the usual safety considerations are applied. For example, a suitable site must be chosen. Total fire bans are common in Sweden in the summer and in such cases open fires are not even permitted in fire places.

Dogs are welcome outdoors but the rules that apply are many and strictly enforced. Owners are expected to maintain control at all times, but unfortunately many are lax. The regulations primarily exist to protect sensitive ecosystems; however a large loose dog can negatively impact upon the local population of *Homo sapiens*. Unsympathetic owners usually say "Oh, Fido is the gentlest dog in the world! He just wants you to throw his stick" – words that are of little comfort to the unwitting mushroom picker with the image of a charging beast, jaws agape, all too fresh in their memory.

The Swedish right of common access is a unique law that states what is forbidden and loosely defines the boundaries of acceptable behaviour. However it is not simply a case of everything that is not expressly forbidden being allowed. The wording of the law is archaic and common sense still needs to be applied. For example, moss and lichens are not specifically mentioned, however one is not permitted to harvest them in large amounts. Certain plants are protected and nature reserves and national parks are often governed by special regulations. Fortunately, even though the right of common access is a remnant of the Middle Ages, most Swedes have an innate appreciation of what it entails.

Legislation intended to ensure the right to move freely outdoors on foot or skis was proposed in the early 1960s. It was never passed, which in reality had little effect as one is already granted access practically everywhere. In Sweden, nature lovers – *nearly* always have right of way.

WHAT YOU CAN DO:
• You may walk, cycle or ride almost anywhere outdoors as long as it is not too close to a private dwelling. If you open a gate you must close it behind you.
• You may walk, cycle or ride on private roads.
• You may camp overnight. If you wish to stay longer you must ask permission from the landowner.
• You may bathe, travel by boat and go ashore anywhere but not too close to a private dwelling.
• You may pick flowers, berries and mushrooms.
• You may fish with rod and reel along the coast and in the five major lakes (Mälaren, Vänern, Vättern, Hjälmaren och Storsjön)
• You may light a small fire, provided the customary safety precautions are taken. You may not light a fire directly on rocky surfaces as these may crack.

Ånnaboda, Kilsbergen in southern Bergslagen. Bergslagen is a rather diffusely defined area in central Sweden where mining and metal smelting have long been of vital significance. Here, Mother Nature offers enchanted forest environments and crystal clear lakes brimming with delicious fish.

Despite the fact that each of the
office blocks around Hötorget
Square in Stockholm was
designed by a different member
of the Swedish architectural
elite of the 1950s–60's, they are
all quite similar. The idea was to
create a homogenous expression and as such the architects
were only given free reign when
it came to the design of the
facades.

Little red cottages

Swedish architecture

It would be difficult to find a better, more humane model for modern architecture. The excesses of the late 19th century have given way to a more manor-like, classic style with harmonious rooms and a relatively low ceiling height of around 250 cm. Light-coloured, wide plank flooring, thinly painted walls in a warm grey tone plus painted ceilings and moldings all contribute to this style which is loved by the Swedes.

By and large Sweden has been spared the ravages of war. One of the benefits of this is that Swedish architectural heritage has been uncommonly well preserved. The country is dotted with countless remnants of the ancient peasant society and the evolution of Swedish building practices is evident in an unbroken chain up until the post WWII period. And if Swedish politicians had been less meddlesome, there would be even more ancient architecture that could be enjoyed in the present day.

It is not just the absence of war that is to be thanked for the well-preserved state of Swedish buildings. Buildings here have traditionally been built using the best natural materials available. Country houses often testify to differences in local building practices, architectural trends, social patterns and economic conditions. *You use what you have* has been a credo in Swedish building. If the local area is rich in stone, that's what you build your houses out of. It is no coincidence, for example, that Gotland is peppered with limestone houses. One thing that all historic country buildings have in common is sensitivity to the surrounding environment.

The oldest type of Swedish building is the one-room house. The entrance to these houses was usually situated on the gable as the roof reached almost all the way down to the foundations. Swedes started painting their cottages with the traditional red emulsion as early as the 17th century. This colour would go on to become a characteristic feature of the Swedish countryside. The classic image of Sweden is still a red timber cottage with white corners nestled in a landscape of cultivated fields and forest with a small lake nearby. A small, flat-bottomed row boat lies tethered to the jetty waiting to glide out amongst the water lilies and the pike that spawn in the reeds. This, Ladies and Gentlemen, is Sweden. For many Swedes the ultimate pleasure is spending time at their summer house and a surprisingly large portion of the population actually own a little red piece of paradise somewhere in the country.

The 19th century was the golden age of the Swedish farmer. As he prospered, a powerful symbol of his wealth was built in the county of Hälsingland.

Over the years the Swedish architectural language has primarily been influenced by European trends, however inspiration and technical innovations have also been imported from the East. Just as in every art form, inspiration is found in different cultures and eras and each work of art reflects contemporary movements. Architects of each generation have cast an eye in various directions and then transposed what they see into *revolutionary* architecture. The architect translates the style and material into Swedish, where it becomes Swedish. So what exactly is Swedish and what is imported? This is impossible to say. The carved timber ornamentation often seen on older houses is considered typically Swedish, but can be found in many places around the world including the West Indies. Decorative *kurbits* painting on ceilings and walls is another feature traditionally associated with Swedish interiors, although similar patterns can be seen in places like Bhutan. A utilitarian approach to design often characterises Swedish design. No frills, using whatever is at hand. At any rate, red timber cottages are undeniably Swedish and their prevalence is a result of the natural materials available in the country. If there is one thing that there is plenty of in Sweden, it is trees.

By the middle of the 18th century Sweden had become a melting pot of foreign influences. France, Italy and Germany all exert their influence on local architecture but it is the Orient which draws the gaze of contemporary architects in search of inspiration. The rich ornamentation of Persia and India is all the rage and the distinction between art and architecture becomes blurred. Ideas are also harvested from the Moorish architecture of North Africa and Spain.

It didn't take long for the Swedes to realise that money could be made out of the contemporary interest in all things Asian. The East India Company was formed in Göteborg in 1731 and over the years made a total of 132 trips, primarily to China and Canton. The majority of their import trade was in porcelain and works of art, although they also shipped tea and coffee. The ideas and styles they brought to Sweden left their mark on Swedish furniture and architecture.

▼ Elements of Far Eastern design are also evident in Swedish architecture of the period. The extraordinary Chinese Pavilion at Drottningholm Palace is a wonderful example of the Chinoiserie that was so popular at the time. Rumour has it that King Gustav III would have given anything to be a "real" Japanese but had to settle for dancing around the palace theatre dressed in Japanese clothing.

The Chinese Pavilion at Drottningholm has been deemed a site of outstanding value to humanity by UNESCO and placed on their World Heritage list.

FALU RED PAINT

Falu red paint is one of Sweden's oldest and most popular types of paint. During the 1600s red timber houses were a sign of wealth emulating the red brick houses of the continent. It wasn't until the 1800s that the fashion spread to the countryside. Prior to this, houses were often unpainted.

Falu red contains natural mineral pigments from the Falu mines. In addition to copper, it consists of a rare combination of iron ochre, silica and zinc which together act to preserve timber. This paint provides a beautiful matt finish where the silica crystals delightfully refract light. In the evening sun a house painted with Falu red takes on an intensive, almost glowing tone. Red cottages with white corners are strongly associated with Sweden.

Closest NCS colour:
S5040–Y80R

Domargården, Pershyttan

Villa Karlsson, Tidö–Lindö.
By Tham, Videgård, Hansson
Arkitekter AB. Built: 2002–2003.

A Falu red, pitched roof, long
house inspired by traditional
timber house construction.
The house is clad in robust
timber panelling punctured by
freely placed windows in two
sizes. The house's exterior character is enhanced by the fact
that both the façade and roof
panelling are tarred in the same
colour. This type of roof is often
found on older Swedish building
and is laid in such a way that the
panells exert tension on each
other forming a seal.

Stockholm City Hall (1911–23) is Östberg's most famous work. Here he succeeded in combining national romanticism, exoticism and embryonic classicism in one monumental building.

RAGNAR ÖSTBERG

One of the biggest names in modern Swedish architecture is Ragnar Östberg. A professor at the Royal University College for Fine Arts, he was the leading architect in what is known as the national romanticist movement. Östberg started his professional life designing furniture, interiors and private dwellings, and together with Carl Westman turned contemporary ideals on their head. They advocated lighter, less pretentious interiors, quality craftsmanship and sensitivity to the natural surroundings as seen in Villa Ekarne on Stockholm's Djurgården.

Stockholm Stadium was built for the 1912 Olympic Games making it the oldest arena still in use today. The stadium was built during a turbulent historical period with many opposing forces asserting themselves. Many Stockholmers believe that the stadium was designed by Ragnar Östberg, the man behind City Hall, however it was actually designed by the bath house architect Torben Grut. An accomplished architect, his experience as an athlete was decisive in his being chosen, as contemporary politicians believed he would know exactly what was needed to create the perfect arena. The stadium was designed in the shape of a horse shoe magnet pointing towards the northern hill. Adorned with two decorative towers it was completed with a beautiful arcade facing Valhallavägen, inspired by the Colosseum in Rome.

Runner crossing the finish line at Stockholm Stadium, by sculptor Carl Eldh (1873–1954). The artist's studio, located in idyllic Bellevue Park in Stockholm, was designed by Ragnar Östberg in 1919 and has been preserved in its original condition.

207

◀▲ *Skogskyrkogården*
(The Woodland Cemetery) in
southern Stockholm was built
between 1919 and 1940 by
architects Gunnar Asplund
and Sigurd Lewerentz. Here,
on a pine covered ridge, they
created a sacred environment
where several smaller chapels
harmoniously interact with the
natural surroundings. The entire
complex is considered a seminal
architectural work.

Skogskyrkogården is a
large-scale expression of the
prevailing architectural ideals
of the years preceding and
immediately following WWII.
Society demanded solutions
that were both functional and
beautiful, and this applied even
to peoples' final resting places.
An international architectural
competition was held in 1915 to
find the optimal design for the
cemetery. Asplund and Lewerentz emerged victorious.

ERIK GUNNAR ASPLUND

was one of the pioneers of the
functionalist movement and
is considered to be one of the
leading Swedish architects of
the interwar period. Stockholms
stadsbibliotek (Stockholm
Public Library), Skogskapellet
(The Woodland Chapel) at Skogskyrkogården and Karlshamns
läroverk (Karlshamn Teacher's
College) are amongst his most
famous works.

Stockholms stadsbibliotek,
which opened in 1928, is considered a milestone in modern
Swedish architecture. Ground
breaking both in design and
fittings, this library was the first
to be fitted with shelves that
were accessible to the public.
Strange as it may seem today,
this was the first time borrowers
could actually browse amongst
the books – something that may
have contributed to the fact that
Swedes borrow and read so
many books.

Stockholm Public Library

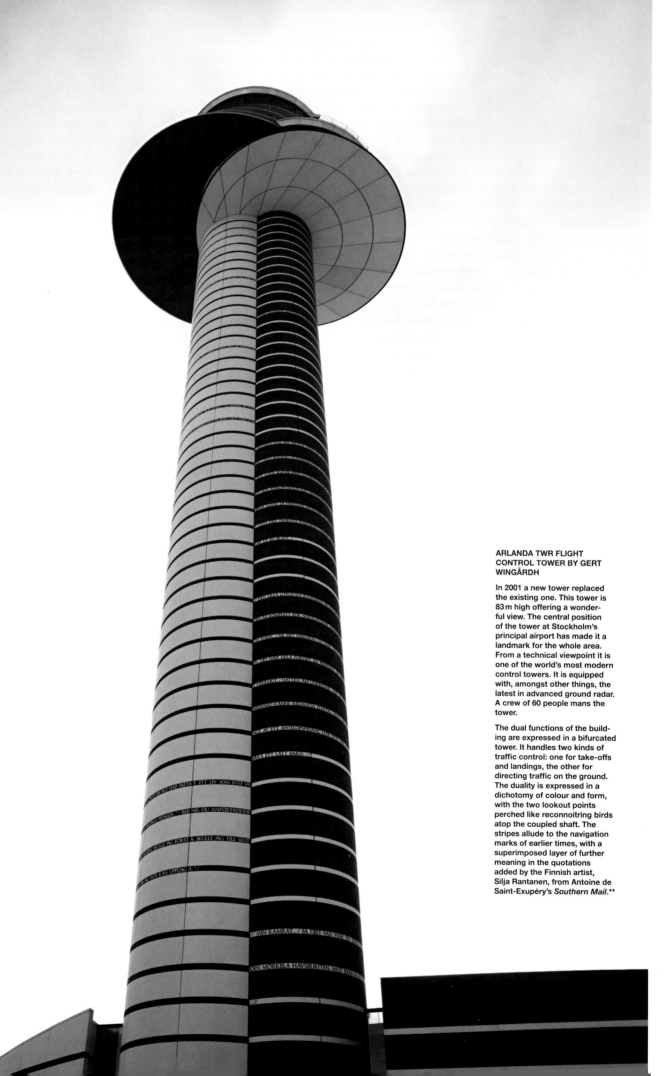

ARLANDA TWR FLIGHT CONTROL TOWER BY GERT WINGÅRDH

In 2001 a new tower replaced the existing one. This tower is 83 m high offering a wonderful view. The central position of the tower at Stockholm's principal airport has made it a landmark for the whole area. From a technical viewpoint it is one of the world's most modern control towers. It is equipped with, amongst other things, the latest in advanced ground radar. A crew of 60 people mans the tower.

The dual functions of the building are expressed in a bifurcated tower. It handles two kinds of traffic control: one for take-offs and landings, the other for directing traffic on the ground. The duality is expressed in a dichotomy of colour and form, with the two lookout points perched like reconnoitring birds atop the coupled shaft. The stripes allude to the navigation marks of earlier times, with a superimposed layer of further meaning in the quotations added by the Finnish artist, Silja Rantanen, from Antoine de Saint-Exupéry's *Southern Mail*.**

GERT WINGÅRDH

Even as a newly-graduated architect in the 1970s, Wingårdh was considered a slightly odd figure at odds with the prevailing leftist establishment. He succeeded in pre-empting the 1980s feeling of opulence and called himself a Post-modernist. His breakthrough came after his Scandic Hotel project with Slussen in Stockholm and the Club house at Öijared golf course (1988). The club house was placed underground with an enormous glass wall facing the course and a tee on the lawn covered roof. This spectacular building has been likened to an uprooted tree.

Gert Wingårdh's work cannot be ascribed to any particular school or trend. On many occasions he has used unexpectedly bold solutions on prosaic projects. The air traffic control tower at Stockholm Arlanda Airport is just one project that has aroused interest. He often uses glass and stone but also treats timber with great respect. Lately he has even begun designing interiors, often with an industrial feel like the well-known reception area where the counter is coated in rubber. His work is often unconventional and has paved the way for new ideas and approaches to materials.

▲ The Mill House

▶ Citadellbadet, Landskrona

Tham Videgård Hansson,
Semi-detached in
Danderyd

Robert Such and Marge
Arkitekter, Weekendhouse
Arkö

Sandell & Sandberg,
Gåshaga, Lidingö

THE GUSTAVANIAN STYLE

No style is as beloved in Sweden as the Gustavian. Gustav III was extremely interested in the new style and would prove to be an influential figure in its popularity. Mid-18th century France had begun to tire of the excesses of rococo and had become inspired by the recent archaeological excavations of Pompeii and Herculaneum. A new more austere, light and graceful style emerged. Swelling surfaces were flattened out, legs were straightened and decoration took the form of symmetrical swirls and borders. No other period can boast as many types of chair, practically all of them with a stuffed seat.

At the height of the period furniture was painted pearl grey, light pink or grey-blue while a few were gilded. Beautiful gilded and bronze wall clocks were popular, many of them with sconces. Even mirrors were gilded and adorned with sconces.

The Gustavian style remains popular in Sweden, something that is reflected in the fact that IKEA has designed several series in this vein. Traces of Gustav III can be seen in many modern Swedish homes, both in the form of genuine antiques and copies.

Light, elegant and minimalist. Qualities that have made Swedish design world famous. One of Swedish porcelain's biggest icons is the Zebra cup from Gefle Porslinsfabrik; its black and white motif, a clear echo of the 1950s, seems to express a widespread yearning for pieces characteristic of a particular era. Classic pieces are often the work of famous designers, although Eugen Trost, the man behind the Zebra cup, is relatively unknown.

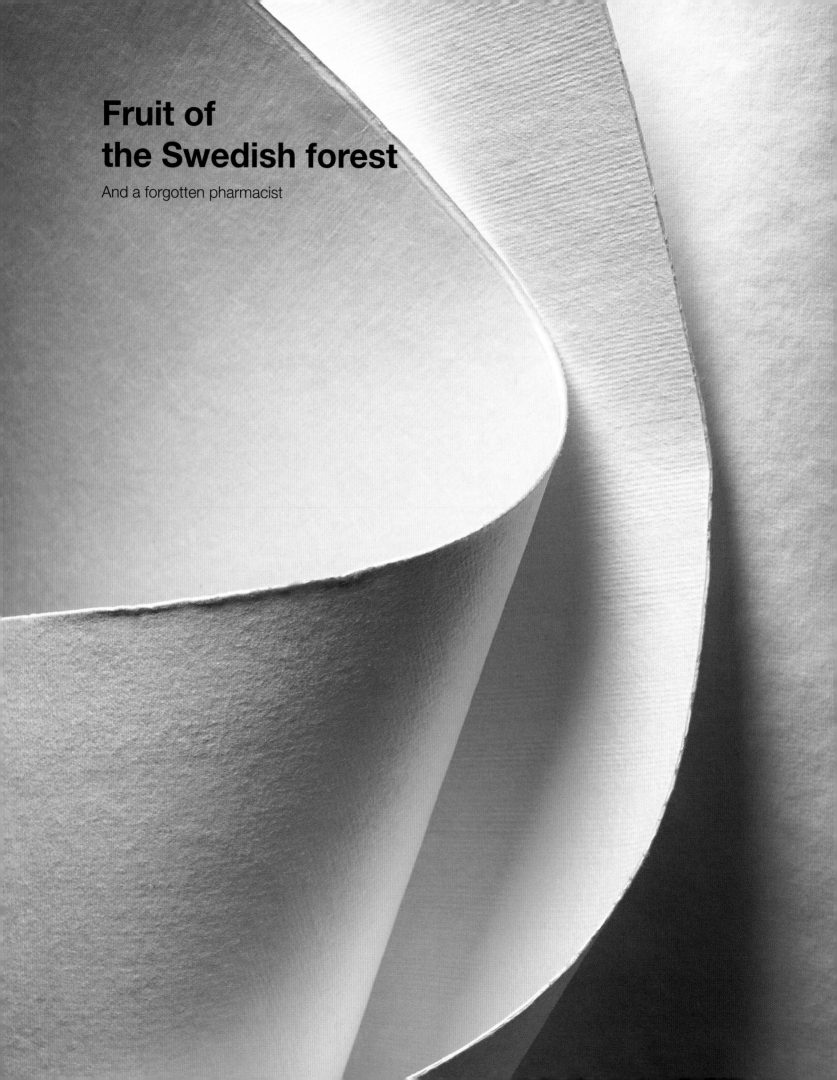

Fruit of
the Swedish forest

And a forgotten pharmacist

SÖDRA SKOGSÄGARNA

The dense Swedish forests are often privately owned. 50 000 Swedish forest owners have banded together to form an organisation to help them manage their natural resources – *Södra Skogsägarna* – Southern Forest Owners.

Operations are divided into five segments. *Södra Cell* is one of the world's leading producers of paper pulp. *Södra Timber* is the group's manufacturer of timber products for the construction industry. *Gapro* produces interior building products and fittings while *Södra Skogsenergi* primarily produces bio fuel from the waste products generated by the other *Södra* companies. *Södra Skog* trades in forestry raw materials and supplies the group with timber.

SVENSKA CELLULOSA AKTIEBOLAGET

SCA was founded in 1929 by businessman Ivar Kreuger who amalgamated ten forestry companies into a single entity. Kreuger's suicide and the Great Depression resulted in *Svenska Handelsbanken* taking control of the company. During the 1960s and 70s, *SCA* was restructured and pulp production was concentrated in fewer factories. Today they are a global consumer goods and paper company, divided into four major segments: Personal Care, Tissue, Packaging and Forest Products which includes printing paper, pulp and timber and solid wood products. Tissues, toilet paper and napkins account for almost one third of their turnover.

FROM WEAPONS TO PAPER

Holmen's history spans five centuries starting when the Duke of Östergötland built an arms factory on an island in the Motala River. Like many other companies, Holmen's origins lie in a completely different business based on an abundance of water, ore and timber. Today Holmen manufactures printing paper, cardboard and has significant holdings in forests and power production.

Mo and Domsjö AB, *Holmens Bruk* and *Iggesunds Bruk* merged in 1988 and formed the *MoDo Group*. In 2000 they changed their name to *Holmen AB*.

FROM IRON TO PAPER PULP

Rottneros' origins hark back to the 17th century, and like many other Swedish forestry groups they have their roots in the iron industry. Today they are a global supplier of high quality paper pulp produced by five mills in Sweden and Spain. Pulp products are sold under the brand *Rottneros* while their food packaging products are marketed as *SilviPak*. *Rottneros'* business concept is to supply high quality, customised pulp.

In the autumn of 1874, a ship casts off from a wharf in northern Sweden bound for England. Onboard is the first paper pulp manufactured using the sulfite method – a process developed by a young chemist called Carl Daniel Ekman. The load that is forging out into the Baltic is the first of what will become one of Sweden's biggest export products.

The story of Swedish forestry is one of a poor, sparsely-populated nation on the fringe of Europe developing into a wealthy welfare state. Forestry has been one of the main motors driving the Swedish economy through this transition. When it comes to the amount of timber produced per capita, Sweden is second only to Finland. Each year the Swedish forest grows to the tune of 100 million cubic metres and as long as there is sunlight, water and carbon dioxide it will continue to do so.

Timber-related industries in Sweden consume 5 million cubic metres of timber annually and employ over 50 000 people. A further 50 000 are indirectly involved working with things such as transportation. Many of these jobs are located in sparsely-populated areas close to the forests.

But let's get back to Carl Daniel Ekman who started off as a pharmacist and then went on to become a chemist. After completing his chemistry degree he is given full access to his school's laboratory where he puts his pharmacy skills to good use and experiments by bleaching sanded timber. By the middle of the 19th century, literacy rates are improving dramatically which results in increased demand for books and newspaper, and a worldwide paper shortage. The only raw material available for the production of high quality paper is linen or cotton rags. Rags are in sort supply and are therefore very expensive. Experiments making paper from wood begin in the 1840s although the quality of the paper is poor, often being discoloured. Carl Daniel Ekman is employed by *Bergmans Paper Pulp factory* in 1871 where he is given the assignment of developing a process for bleaching the pulp. The chemist throws himself into his work, shunning help and company. In fact he regards anyone who tries to get too close to his work with great suspicion. After a few months he makes a test batch of what would later be called sulfite cellulose. It's difficult to say how much he knew about similar methods in use abroad at the time, although his process was the first that could be used in a production environment. He is reluctant to reveal his secret and waits until 1882 to patent the process.

Unfortunately he never gets to enjoy the fruits of his labour. Paper pulp prices fall taking his income with them. He moves to England where he marries Rosina Noble and

devotes his life to two main passions: collecting Sevres china and making sherry out of beer. He dies penniless at the age of 49, however his technological legacy would eventually lead to Sweden becoming the world's third largest exporter of paper and fourth largest exporter of pulp.

The oldest corporation in the world is Swedish. The story of *Kopparberget* (Copper Mountain) is one of the enormous riches at Tiskasjöberg that were discovered by a goat named *Kåre* (Kor-eh). This famous goat was out grazing and happened to scrape his horns in the vitriol-rich ground turning them red – something that did not escape the attention of his owner. Kåre had discovered what would become Sweden's greatest treasure chest. Just when this horny character made his fortuitous discovery is unknown, although there is evidence that operations were underway in the 11th century and it is likely that copper ore was being mined as early as the 8th century. Operations were well organised early on; a document from 1288 describes the share held by each of the "mountain men" and how the business will be run. This makes Kopparberget the world's oldest corporation.

Sweden's rise to superpower status during the 16th and 17th centuries can be partly attributed to the natural riches of Kopparberget. "The Kingdom stands or falls with Kopparberget" as the contemporary rulers in Stockholm bluntly put it; a statement that was largely true. In the middle of the 1600's the mines at Falun accounted for two thirds of the world's production of copper. A unique culture developed in the area around the Great Copper Mountain which in its heyday was the biggest employer in Sweden. The mine has exerted great influence on the technological, social and political development of Sweden and has therefore been listed as a World Heritage Site by UNESCO.

The mine in Falun eventually gave birth to the *Stora* group of companies, who commenced their forestry operations in the saw mill business. Paper production started around 1900 with an annual output of approximately 30 000 tonnes – ten times as much as any Swedish paper mill had previously produced in a year.

Stora has been part of Finnish *Enso-Gutzeit Oy* since 1998 and has since traded under the name *Stora Enso*. The company is active in 40 countries and produces paper pulp, paper and processed timber products with a total value of 135 billion Swedish crowns annually. They employ over 44 000 people. Kåre the Goat's discovery of copper ore started a chain of events that led to Sweden's super-power status and the formation of one of the biggest forestry companies in the world.

Hidden riches

The safest mining operations in the world

Swedes learnt the art of mining from German mountain men who followed in the wake of Hanseatic traders. The first ore was extracted on the island of Utö in the Stockholm archipelago and forged in Gotland. In the 12th century ore was extracted by first heating then cooling the rock causing it to crack.

It wasn't until the 17th century that gunpowder came into use, and once again it was the Germans who led the way with the first mining taking place in Lappland in 1635. Unfortunately gunpowder was expensive, sensitive to moisture and its blasting power rather limited. It took many years for the technique to become effective and it actually wasn't until the 1870s that it became economically viable. It wasn't until Alfred Nobel's inventions at the end of the 19th century – first nitroglycerine, then dynamite and finally blasting gelatin – that blasting could take place under controlled conditions deep underground. Swedish ore extraction literally exploded into a new age, and finally the ingenious Thomas process that creates steel from phosphor rich ore could be used. When the railway found its way to the mines the steel could be transported from the ore fields of Gällivare and Kiruna, to the port of Narvik in northern Norway. Electricity followed hot on the heels of the railway and with it new steelworks and industries.

That the mountains of the north were a treasure trove of mineral riches was hardly a surprise to anyone, although even in their wildest dreams no one could have imagined the extent of the ore fields. Mining company *Luossavaara-Kiirunavaara AB*, LKAB, was formed in 1890 and to this day the ore produced in the mines of Kiruna and Malmberget remains the lifeblood of the entire region, even benefiting the Finnish side of the Gulf of Bothnia. Iron ore extraction has been the motor that has propelled the development of northern Sweden, transforming it from a sparsely-populated fell and woodland region into a modern industrial centre.

However, not only Kiruna and Gällivare/Malmberget depend on the mines. The arrival of the ore trains also

PERSHYTTAN

The foundry that is the heart of Pershyttan houses one of Europe's best preserved charcoal burning blast furnaces. Two foundries were operational until the beginning of the 18th century while the blast furnace was in use as recently as 1953. Historians agree that the foundries were running as far back as the second half of the 14th century, a conclusion that is supported by chronicles of the canonisation of Saint Bridget.

Bergslagen, the mining district in central Sweden, is afforded particular status not just in Sweden but throughout Europe. Rich in magnetite, hematite, hydropower and forests, Mother Nature blessed the area with all the necessary raw materials so it is no coincidence that Pershyttan is located here.

As in many other places the foundries here were built beside a stream in an idyllic setting. However, unlike many other mining hamlets, Pershyttan has survived, largely thanks to the efforts of its last owner, Avesta Ironworks. The goal is to keep this invaluable historic site intact thereby honouring its part in the industrial heritage of Sweden. Evidence of the years of hard work put into unearthing the earth's hidden treasures can still be seen in the surrounding landscape. Pershyttan is the site of Sweden's largest working water wheel which drives a 200 m long *stånggång* – a device that mechanically transmits the power generated by the wheel – and a preserved Medieval mine.

▲ A view of the ore mountain
Kiirunavaara.

In the ore fields, it is said that
many babies were born in a
mine shaft, rocked to sleep in
a dynamite crate and that their
first rattles were snuff boxes.

allowed the ports of Luleå and Narvik to flourish. Kiruna is the site of the most modern iron ore mine in the world. The use of the latest information technology and remote controlled transport systems not only result in optimal yields but also help to create a remarkably safe work environment. The system from Åkerströms Björbo AB has been likened to an enormous spider web that handles all communication and makes sure that the remote control locomotives work without a hitch, even deep underground. The heart of the communications system is a master placed deep in the tunnels and then connected to a central computer. To run the trains the "driver" sits in front of a computer screen and uses a joystick, making sure that each car is filled with ore. Seven trains per hour chug around underground, each carrying a load of 550 metric tonnes of ore. The trains can be driven both forward and in reverse while dumping their loads, which keeps human operators out of the danger zone. All operations are run and monitored from a suitably safe distance.

Above ground things are strangely peaceful. If they didn't know better, no one would ever guess what goes on a kilometre under ground, 24/7.

▲ LKAB in Kiruna extract ore with the help of cutting edge technology. Mining machinery 1000 meters underground is monitored and driven by joysticks, cameras and computers seven stories above ground.

◀ Pig iron.

From rock to worldwide chock

A businessman dealing in ship building and maritime trade, with no technical training, works out how to drill bigger holes in an oven that turns iron into steel which leads to the inexpensive production of high quality steel. Swedish super steel!

Swedish steel bites

A true man of steel

Bessemer – Göransson's salvation –
Sandvik's future

Sandvik is a high-techno-logy, engineering Group with advanced products and a world-leading position within selected areas. Worldwide business activities are conducted through representation in 130 countries. The Group has 47 000 employees. Sandvik's business concept is based on a unique competence in materials technology. This has resulted in a world-leading position in three core areas:

Cemented-carbide and high-speed steel tools for metalworking applications, and blanks and components made of cemented carbide and other hard materials.

Machinery, equipment and tools for rock-excavation.

Stainless and high-alloy steels, special metals, resistance materials and process systems.

Göran Fredrik Göransson is neither an inventor nor engineer but nevertheless manages to harness the Bessemer method and transform iron into high quality steel. He works as a consul and business man in the mid 1800s but is the first person in the world to use the Bessemer method for large-scale steel production. The method reduces the carbon content in molten pig iron, transforming it into steel or wrought iron without using any fuel. Air is blown through the molten iron causing impurities such as silicon and manganese to oxidize and escape either as a gas or solid slag. The process is terminated when the iron's carbon content has reached the desired levels.

In the early 1850s Henry Bessemer decides that he will try to develop a simpler way of producing steel. At this time steel is in short supply and its production is highly labour intensive. Smelters are small and mixing is done by hand which leads to high prices. Henry realises that iron that has been exposed to an air stream is free of carbon, which is exactly what he hoped to achieve. When temperatures are raised to between 1 500 and 1 600 degrees Celsius, steel is formed. Bessemer patents his process in 1851 despite the fact that it is not fully developed.

Businessman Göran Fredrik Göransson visits London a few years later intent on buying a steam engine but instead returns home with a fifth of Bessemer's Swedish patent. He starts experimenting with the process at Edsken's blast furnace but only manages to produce blistered steel which, of course, nobody wants.

After several years of persistent experimentation he succeeds in producing his super steel. Just how does he do this? He works out that enlarging the air intakes on the Bessemer converter raises the temperature which, in turn, speeds up the process and results in steel without blisters: the Swedish steel that becomes so famous. The Swedish steel industry and Sandvik owe their success to an ingeniously simple innovation discovered by a layman. His idea rocks the world, is adopted around the globe and reduces the price of steel by 75 percent! All of a sudden steel can be used where it had previously been considered too expensive; railway tracks, construction materials, tools, machines as well as countless other applications.

In 1862 Göran Fredrik Göransson founds the company *Högbo Stål & Jernwerk*, which is later restructured to form *Sandviken Jernverk*. Göransson is Financial Director and his son Henrik Refinery Manager. Göransson is also a pioneer in many other areas. Amongst other things he is way ahead of his time in what is known today as relationship marketing.

A century of brilliance

And the story of the three phase guy

Jonas Wenström first became interested in technical innovations as a teenager. He dreams of constructing a self-magnetizing DC generator or dynamo, a machine that converts kinetic energy into electricity, better than the one produced by Werner Siemens in 1867. Unfortunately his finances are limited so he decides to invent a light bulb, but Edison and Swan beat him to the punch with their own type using carbon fibre inside a vacuum.

He graduates with a degree in Natural Science in 1887 and becomes a technical consultant in his father's construction company. However, his thoughts continually turn to electricity. He has a lot of good ideas but just doesn't have the money to develop them.

In 1881 Jonas Wenström visits the Electricity Fair in Paris where the latest in dynamo technology is on show. He realises two things: firstly, that these would never work in an industrial setting and secondly, that he is actually well ahead of his competitors. Upon returning home he presents a new drawing to mill owner Engelbrektson who likes the idea. The device is shaped like a turtle in order to create as little resistance as possible to the magnetic field.

Around this time, businessman Ludvig Fredholm was negotiating to purchase the Swedish rights to the dynamo machine from an American company. Wenström offers him the rights to his dynamo instead. Fredholm agrees on one condition: that it is better than the competition. And it is, producing more light per horsepower. The company *Elektriska Aktiebolaget i Stockholm* is founded in 1883 with a view to primarily manufacturing DC lighting plants using Wenström's dynamos. Manufacturing occurs in a 40 m³ attic and the office is run out of Fredholm's apartment. Ironic to think that what eventually became ASEA and then ABB once had their Head Office in somebody's kitchen and their factory in a draughty little room in Arboga. But no company has ever started off as a global concern. They have all commenced operations with limited resources, but determined innovators and entrepreneurs have somehow managed to

convince investors to finance their ingenuity. This is perhaps the secret behind the success of the great Swedish companies: both inventors and financial backers have had the foresight to commit to a vision of the future. One shudders to think how many great ideas have never gone beyond the stage of a patent application.

Within two years operations in the attic expand from seven employees to 69. Wenström manages to further refine his dynamo and produces a better version known as *The Corset* on account of its shape. This model with four double-wound magnetic poles sells well and goes on to be ASEA's first successful product. DC machines have several advantages: their motor speed can be adjusted and they can be adapted to a variety of applications. They are used in lighting plants and the electrochemical industry while DC motors are used in trams and power tools.

Other Wenström inventions are the electromagnetic ore separator and the electric arc furnace. He always offers his inventions to Fredholm first but he usually declines, deciding to concentrate on electric lighting which he believes will be the next big thing. Sure enough, the company soon gets its first major order – to light the town of Västerås. The following year Arboga puts in their order.

Wenström travels to Europe together with mining engineer Gustaf Granström in order to study how others solve the problem of long distance electricity transmission. Inspired by the myriad of possible uses for electricity, they once again try to convince Managing Director Ludvig Fredholm to branch out into the area of power supply. Once again he says *no*, he wants to focus on electric lighting. His refusal leads them to form their own power company *Wenström & Granströms Elektriska Kraftbolag* using Wenström's own three phase system of generators, transformers and motors. This invention, which combines three different phases of alternating current into the one system, is patented by Wenström in 1890 and is still the main system for the distribution of electrical power. However, as with

**HIGH-VOLTAGE DIRECT
CURRENT (HVDC)**

ABB is the market leader in
high-voltage direct current
(HVDC) systems like the one
pictured here in China. HVDC
increases transmission capacity
while stabilising networks.

229

▶ The third generation of ABB's computer-aided distribution operations system (CADOPS) now provides the control information utilities need in real time.

many inventions, several inventors around the world were working on similar systems at the same time, so claiming that Wenström was solely responsible for the three phase system is a bit bold.

Wenström & Granström receive large orders for things like electrical railways and power supplies for mechanical workshops and it soon becomes unwieldy having two separate companies. In 1890 the companies merge to form *Allmänna Svenska Elektriska Aktiebolaget* which is abbreviated to ASEA. The name ASEA soon becomes widely known although not many Swedes know what the letters actually stand for. Head Office is transferred to newly built premises in Västerås where they can use hydroelectric power from the River Svartån. ASEA builds Sweden's first three phase power systems in 1893! ASEA is truly unique in their field.

In 1932 they build the world's first self-cooling transformer and expand operations by acquiring *AB Svenska Fläktfabriken* (The Swedish Fan Co.). In 1953 they become the first in the world to produce synthetic diamonds and seven years later they build Sweden's first nuclear power plant. They go on to build nine of the country's 12 stations. The list of their accomplishments is way too lengthy to be included here.

The 1980s see ASEA develop into one of the world's leading engineering companies. They become market leaders in HVDC technology: High Voltage Direct Current, a revolutionary power transmission technique where in principle, water functions as the return cable.

ASEA + BBC = ABB. In 1987, ASEA and BBC Brown Boveri announce that they will form a company called ABB – ASEA Brown Boveri Ltd. The new entity, whose Head Office will be situated in Switzerland, will be owned in equal shares by ASEA and BBC Brown Boveri. The company has an annual turnover of around USD 24 billion in 2006 and employs more than 110 000 people around the world. The result of a Swedish man of limited means who believed in his ideas.

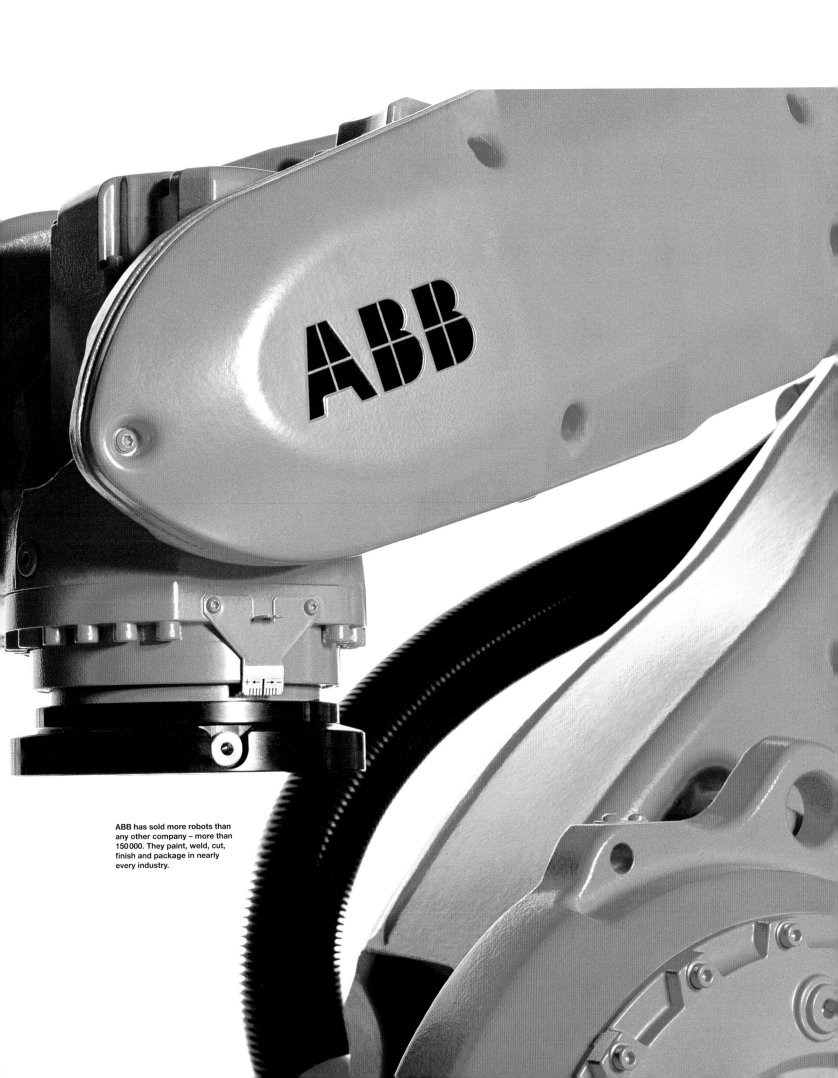

ABB has sold more robots than any other company – more than 150 000. They paint, weld, cut, finish and package in nearly every industry.

Drill and fill

Everyone recognises the yellow compressor

Atlas Copco has played an essential role in Sweden's industrial development. The company *Atlas* was founded in 1873 by engineer Eduard Fränckel who had previously worked for the government railways. The initial business concept was to construct and sell railway equipment, but also iron construction materials for bridges, buildings and church steeples. Magnate A.O. Wallenberg, owner of *Stockholms Enskilda Bank*, initially shouldered the financial burden, and the relationship with the Wallenberg family has continued to be a cornerstone of the company ever since. In the beginning the company was owned by an unusually large number of shareholders, 50 of them in fact, none of whom aside from Wallenberg, held more than ten percent of the stock. These days most sales and production takes place outside of Sweden, and a little over half of the company is owned by foreign interests, however the Wallenberg family and their company *Investor* are still the main stockholders.

Even though the future of the fledgling company seems bright, it doesn't take long for dark clouds to appear on the horizon. It soon becomes apparent that they had started off on too large a scale and had sorely underestimated their competition. *Atlas* files for bankruptcy in 1890 but quickly resurfaces as *Nya AB Atlas* (New Atlas Company). Under new management and with new strategies that included concentrating on steam driven machinery and machine tools, and abandoning steeple construction, the company does well. In fact they grow at a rapid pace, branching out into the area of pneumatic tools, compressors and drilling equipment. Their first rock drill is presented in 1905. The very first pneumatic tools are initially only intended for in-house use, but word of their quality soon spreads and before long other major workshops around the country are beating a path to *Atlas'* door.

In 1898 Marcus Wallenberg purchases the Swedish manufacturing rights for Rudolf Diesel's motor and founds a new company, *AB Diesels Motorer*, which goes on to merge with *Atlas* in 1917. Despite primarily being motor manufacturers it is the company's pneumatic tools division that proves most profitable. After the end of WWI *Atlas* launches *the Swedish method*, combining a light rock drill with pusher leg and drill steels with tungsten carbide drill bits that can be operated by one man.

It doesn't take much persuading to convince customers of the inherent superiority of the drill and before long the company's international breakthrough is assured. In order to support international sales, *Atlas* establishes sales companies around the world – a strategy that proves highly successful. But this is only the beginning of the success story. In the 1970s *Atlas* launches their revolutionary hydraulic rock drills which are far superior to pneumatic drills. The new drills are a runaway success for the company and a shot in the arm for Swedish exports.

However *Atlas* is still primarily focused on compressed air, a fact reflected when they take the name *Atlas Copco* in 1956. (*Copco* is an abbreviation of *Compagnie Pneumatique Commercial*). They deliver their first screw compressor in the 1950s and take another giant step when they develop the oil-free compressor at the end of the 60s. This innovation opens up a new world of possibilities in areas such as food production and pharmaceuticals, and helps the company conquer important new markets.

An oil-injected rotary screw compressor. Portable compressors are a reliable source of power for machines and tools in the construction industry.

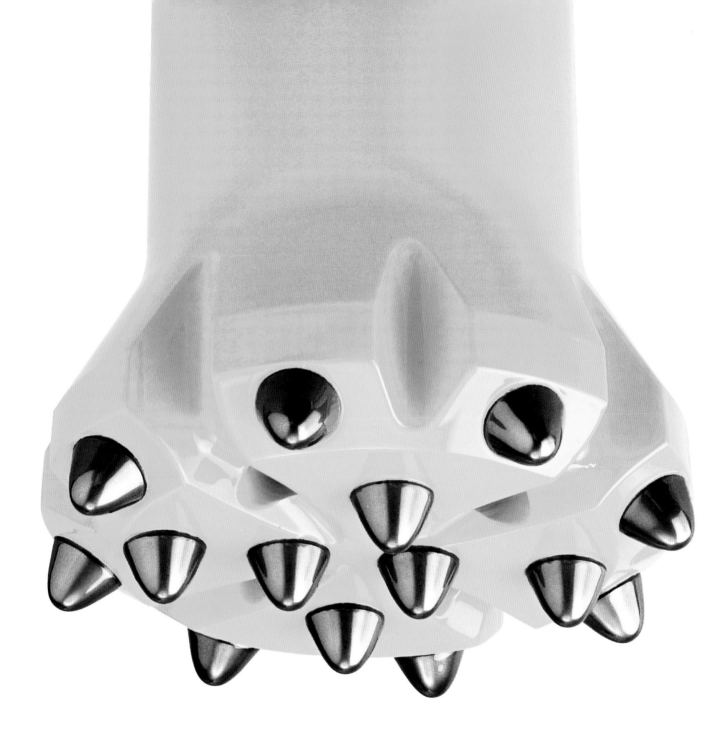

In the 1980s Atlas Copco strengthens their position on
major world markets when they embrace a conscious multi-
brand strategy. The company has demonstrated continu-
ous growth ever since. If the local market in one country
temporarily tapers off, they still have a broad base on which
to stand. Atlas Copco is represented in over 150 countries
around the world so diminished results in one market is
invariably compensated for by continued growth elsewhere.
In addition, Atlas Copco is spared the ravages of currency
fluctuations as most of their business sectors are currency
neutral.

Today Atlas Copco operates in three business areas; Compressor Technique, which accounts for half of the company's turnover; Construction and Mining Technique which accounts for 37 percent and Industrial Technique, which brings in around 13 percent. Three pillars that remain standing after 130 years of experience. Head Office is located in Stockholm.

COMPRESSOR TECHNIQUE

Compressors are used in anywhere air is used as a source of power or where it has a central role in a production process. Atlas Copco develops, manufactures and markets just about everything to do with compressed air, although they are primarily concerned with air and gas compressors. However, expansion turbines, generators and compressed air dryers are also to be found in their product range.

CONSTRUCTION AND MINING TECHNIQUE

In addition to mining, Atlas Copco are market leaders in major infrastructure projects such as power stations, roads and dams. Construction and Mining Technique manufactures and markets rock drills and rigs for tunnel construction and mining in addition to rigs for above ground work, loading and geotechnical drilling.

INDUSTRIAL TECHNIQUE

This division manufactures and markets high quality industrial tools and assembly systems, and provides products and services to distributors. Atlas Copco's power tools meet the rigorous demands sets by advanced industrial fabrication such as aircraft and vehicle assembly. Computerised assembly systems are primarily supplied to vehicle manufacturers.

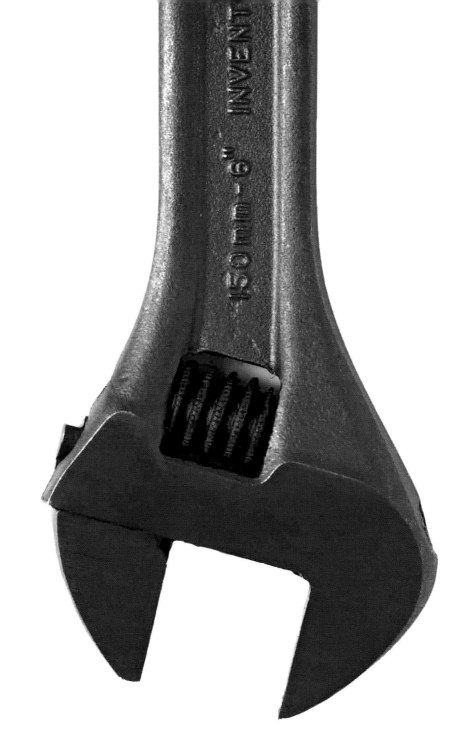

What we in Sweden
call a "skiftnyckel"

Every middle-aged Swede is familiar with the story where tennis coach Lennart Bergelin and his protégé Björn Borg become stranded in the French countryside. Lennart climbs out of their broken down car, promptly strides across a field and addresses a farmer in English. "Do you have what we in Sweden call a 'skiftnyckel'?"

The item he was hoping to borrow was an adjustable wrench, and even if his approach was unlikely to win any awards for cross-cultural communication, he could perhaps be forgiven for using the Swedish word. After all, the adjustable wrench *is* a Swedish device. By the 1840s hexagonal nuts have become standard, which means that every mechanical workshop needs an array of different sized spanners. Johan Petter Johansson can't understand why there isn't an adjustable spanner – so he makes one. His design is patented in 1891, and is still in use, practically unchanged, all over the world today. In the USA it is sometimes known as the Swedish wrench key and in Russian it is called *Sjedvik* which means *Little Swede*.

Johan Petter Johansson lives his life by the credo *necessity is the mother of invention*. He is also reputed to have said "When I see a need and am faced with the task of fulfilling it I follow the impulse 'Do it yourself'." This strategy takes this son of a poor tenant farmer a long way. Despite only 4 years of formal schooling, Johan Petter is awarded a total of 118 patents during his lifetime. Among these are the adjustable locking pliers, a revolution for plumbers who had previously required a battery of wrenches in various sizes.

He also founds international tools manufacturer Bahco, who will go on to sell several hundred million adjustable wrenches.

A Swedish genius

And his balls of steel

He may not have realised it at the time, but when process engineer Sven Wingquist invented the spherical ball bearing, he was doing far more than just solving irritating friction problems in his weaving mill. He was giving Swedish industrialism a major shot in the arm as well as laying the foundations of two major corporations: SKF (*Svenska Kullager-fabriken*) and eventually even Volvo.

SKF's story begins in a weaving mill in Göteborg where production is plagued by mechanical problems due to failing bearings. Power generated by a steam engine is transferred to the machines via long axles. The factory is built on muddy earth which continually subsides. This causes the axles to bend and the bearings to seize. No matter how often the bearings are lubricated they continuously overheat and the machines have to be shut down. They also pose an enormous fire risk. Not only does so much down-time cost Wingquist money, it is also a poke in the eye for Sweden's emerging industrial society and its catch cry of "cheaper, faster, more".

These mechanical problems drive Sven, a technically educated, laid back and persistent type, to the brink of despair. A man with a sense of social responsibility, he introduces paid vacations for SKF employees as early as 1913.

But back to his mechanical problems. He soon realises the wisdom in the old adage *if you want something done, do it yourself*. He does some research into ball bearings and discovers that they are actually nothing new. In particular, the increasing popularity of cycling as a sport at the end of the 19th century had led to the rapid development of the modern ball bearing. Contemporary ball bearings were perfectly adequate for bicycles but, as Sven was all too well aware, could not cope with the loads put on them by the machinery used in textile mills.

He continues his reading and discovers that ball bearings comprised of wooden balls were even used in the Middle Ages and Ancient Rome. Not that this helps him much. He is still stuck with seized bearings at the mill and the financial headaches they cause.

The biggest drawback with ball bearings is the limited contact area, which means they must be disproportionately large in order to bear significant loads. The ball bearing is perfectly adequate for bicycles but not for cars or railway carriages where roller bearings are required. The simplest form of roller bearing is cylindrical with cylindrical rollers and the axle attached on the inside. This type of bearing however cannot bear axial loads and is not self-aligning which makes it imperative that the axle is inserted perfectly straight. In order to overcome these limitations it is necessary to develop a roller bearing with the same self-aligning capabilities as the ball bearing. But calculating the dimensions of the rollers and axles for a roller bearing capable of withstanding the loads generated by belt-driven weaving machines is no easy task. However, in 1907, after spending countless hours at the drawing board, Sven Wingquist finally comes up with the *spherical self-aligning ball bearing* which can withstand heavy loads and is unaffected by axle misalignment. To demonstrate its properties, he builds a car which is placed in subsidiary a company – Volvo. Wingquist is also a skilled marketer and within a short time turns SKF into a world leader in their field. Millions of cars, planes and trains rely on this invisible component to give them the gift of movement.

The SKF group remains one of the world's leading bearing manufacturers. They celebrated their 100th jubilee by launching a new generation of energy efficient spherical roller bearings.

▶ Assembly of large size spherical roller bearings.

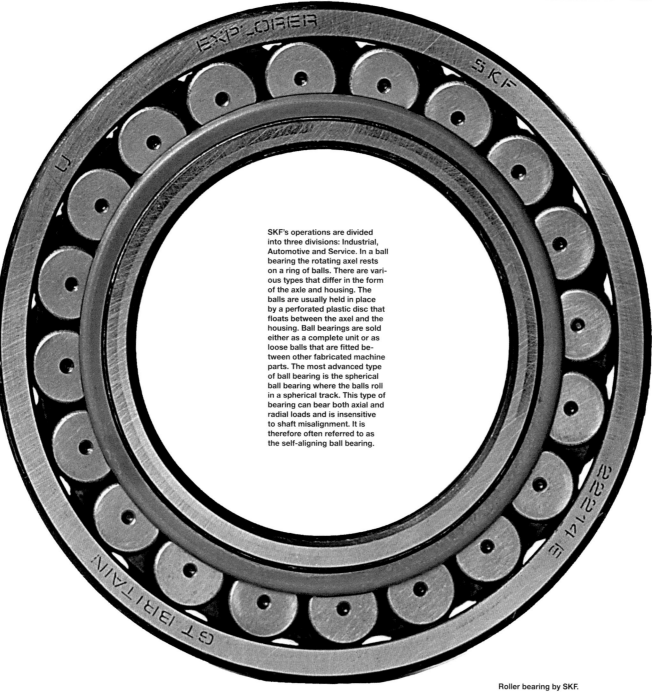

SKF's operations are divided into three divisions: Industrial, Automotive and Service. In a ball bearing the rotating axel rests on a ring of balls. There are various types that differ in the form of the axle and housing. The balls are usually held in place by a perforated plastic disc that floats between the axel and the housing. Ball bearings are sold either as a complete unit or as loose balls that are fitted between other fabricated machine parts. The most advanced type of ball bearing is the spherical ball bearing where the balls roll in a spherical track. This type of bearing can bear both axial and radial loads and is insensitive to shaft misalignment. It is therefore often referred to as the self-aligning ball bearing.

Roller bearing by SKF.

Few industrial products have been of such significance in Sweden as the Volvo Amazon. The PV model was the first to arouse foreign interest although the Amazon was the first great export success. For many years it was also the biggest selling car on the domestic market.

Re-Volvo-lution

Safety first

The Volvo story begins in 1924. A bakery, SKF ball bearings, a restaurant and a passion for Swedish crayfish all play their part in the saga. Two men – one an economist and the other an engineer – share a dream: to mass produce a Swedish car.

Assar Gabrielsson and Gustaf Larson know each other through SKF where Assar is Sales Manager and Gustaf an engineer. One day they run into each other at a bakery. "Lucky I bumped into you" says Assar. "You've worked in car manufacturing in England haven't you? We have to get together. I have a plan!" They don't have time to go into detail on this occasion as they are both on their way to celebrate Midsummer; however they meet later that summer at the *Sturehof Restaurant* in Stockholm where, surrounded by a pile of Swedish crayfish, they hatch their plans. They decide that the first car will be nicknamed *Jakob*, as it happens to be Jakob's name day. So it's not too much of an exaggeration to say that Volvo came into being as a side dish accompanying some delicious red crustaceans.

Volvo considers 14th April, 1927 to be their birthday. In fact, one could say that the delivery of the first vehicle is a breech birth; the differential is initially mounted back to front causing the car to go backwards. However, after some rapid "midwifery" beaming Sales Manager Hilmer Johansson finally drives it out through the factory doors – forwards this time – at 10 a.m. Assar Gabrielsson is convinced that the car will soon be embraced by the masses, however his timing is a bit off. Sales won't actually explode until after WWII.

Co-founder Gustaf Larson, on the other hand, has a different perspective and realises that there is a need for work vehicles such as trucks, busses and taxis. He believes that this market segment is concerned more with quality than price. Work on the first series of trucks commences at the end of 1926. The same motor and gearbox are used as in the cars, however all other parts are considerably more robust. The truck is well received and before long the first series is sold.

The first car, the OV4 or *Jakob*, is even called *The Swedish Car* when displayed for the first time. Volvo wants a symbol to illustrate this and decides to grace their radiators with the symbol for iron, the Mars symbol. In order to attach it to the car a diagonal metal strip is used.

Volvo loses money from day one and after a while majority owners SKF begin to tire. They contact the enormous American car manufacturers Nash and none other than Mr. Nash himself immediately boards a ship bound for Sweden. The evening before his arrival, an anxious Assar Gabrielsson contacts SKF boss Björn Prytz and manages to persuade him not to sell off the company. Assar even puts up his personal savings – said to be in the order of 220 000 Swedish crowns – and stops Volvo from becoming an American company. Part of the deal was that SKF would, in perpetuity, receive 25 crowns for every Volvo sold. This clause remained in effect until 1959 when the Swedish Taxation Courts finally decided the matter.

In 1929 Volvo finally makes a profit of 1579 crowns. Assar immediately sends a telegraph to SKF: "We are finally starting to see the light of day. This month we have shown a profit but alas, so small!" Given the size of the domestic market, establishing a car manufacturer in Sweden is quite an achievement. Volvo has often been compared to the bumble bee which, according to aeronautical theory, should not be able to fly. But fly it does!

In the 1960s Volvo's P1800 becomes an overnight sensation. Producers of the British television series *The Saint* are looking for a suitable car for the main character *Simon Templar*, played by the incomparably suave Roger Moore. Naturally they turn to exclusive British marque Jaguar. However they are unable to deliver a specially equipped car in time. The producers then approach Volvo about their P1800 model. Can they deliver a custom TV star on short notice? You bet your life they can! They deliver a fully equipped car plus a backup with a removable interior well before filming starts. *The Saint* becomes one of the most successful first-run syndicated shows in the history of television and the P1800, equipped with the new B18 mo-

241

▲ P1800. In 1961 Volvo's new sports model was unveiled, after which enthusiastic motoring journalists – in the interest, of thorough investigative journalism of course – thrashed it as much as possible around Swedish roads. At this time however Swedish roads were less than conducive to sporty driving. In spite of this the press corps was unanimous in their praise.

◄ Volvo Truck Series 1 1928. The very first Volvo truck model was often used for local delivery in communities, e g for transport of beer.

◄ The very first mass produced Volvo car (a.k.a Jakob) was built on a production line. There was only one slight hitch: legend has it that the differential was mounted back-to-front which meant that the car could only be driven backwards! True or not, who's to say? In any case the word Volvo means *I roll*, and backwards or forwards the first Volvo rolled off the production line in Hisingen, Göteborg just after 10 a.m. 14th April, 1927.

tor, rockets to international stardom immortalised as "The Saint Car". And just how much does this fortuitous product placement cost Volvo? As it happens the invaluable publicity doesn't cost them a penny! In fact, the film company pays list price for both cars.

In modern American films, Volvos are often driven by responsible, uninspiring, professionals in tweed jackets. Perhaps Volvo is a symbol for the international myth of the Swedish fixation with safety. Volvo's tradition of safety innovations began with the unveiling of the PV which included a laminated windscreen. The PV was also built on a so-called safety chassis, the actual safety of which is open to debate. It was however a huge selling point at the time. Journalists and photographers are invited to a safety conference in Germany and given an amazing demonstration of the PV544's safety features. A helmet-clad stuntman drives the car at 80 km/h up a ramp and drops the car on its nose after which it rolls over onto its roof. The driver – completely unscathed – climbs out through a hole in the windscreen before acknowledging the stunned crowd. The stunt creates headlines in the following day's newspapers, but one shudders to think of the headlines if it had all gone horribly wrong.

Nils Bohlin, an experienced engineer in Saab's aircraft division, exchanges planes for cars in 1958 when he is employed as Volvo's Safety Manager. His first assignment is to solve the seat belt problem. Up until this point, seat belts have gone diagonally across the body and the chances of flying out through the windscreen in the event of an accident were frighteningly high. Bohlin's experience from aircraft construction leads him to believe that the 3-point belt is also the best solution in cars. Comprehensive testing shows that he is right, and from 1959 onwards the 3-point belt is standard in all Volvos; a simple, ingenious construction that saves countless lives.

Perhaps the most significant event in the history of Volvo occurs in 1999 when Ford acquires the car division. Ford has practically always used SKF ball bearings, the invention that lead to the creation of Volvo, so in some ways the circle is closed. The acquisition evokes powerful emotions in Sweden as every Swede has some sort of relationship with Volvo. People fear that Ford will devour Volvo and one dramatic headline is followed by another. It is almost as if Sweden is at war. However, after the fact it can be said that the Volvo has undoubtedly remained a Swedish car. Ford purchased the brand which stands for Swedish quality and safety, and are no doubt keen on keeping one of the world's most famous brands intact – that of the safe Swedish car.

INNOVATIONS THAT CHANGED THE WORLD OF BOATING

Volvo Penta is the world's leading manufacturer of diesel engines for leisure boats. In 1956 the first ever mass-produced turbo diesel left Volvo Penta's factory. This was the first in a series of engines incorporating supercharging, which improves efficiency, reduces fuel consumption and increases longevity. Two years later an engine fitted with an intercooler was launched. This device reduces the temperature of the air coming from the turbocharger which results in improved fuel efficiency.

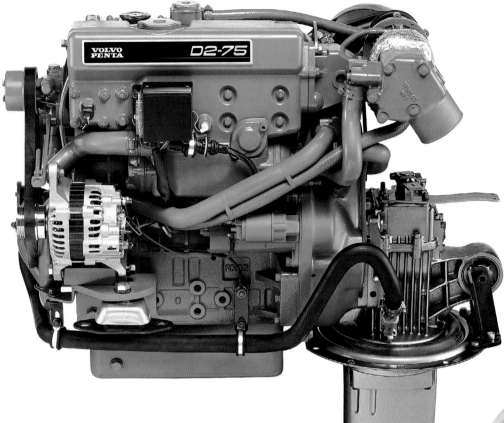

VOLVO TRUCKS

Volvo Trucks Global is Volvo's biggest business segment, manufacturing medium and heavy-duty trucks for long distance transportation and construction work.

Volvo's global expansion really took off in the 1950s. The subsequent acquisitions of Mack Trucks and Renault Trucks made them the second largest manufacturer of heavy-duty trucks in the world.

VOLVO AERO CORPORATION

Founded in 1930 under the name Nohab.

Flygmotorfabriker AB, the company initially manufactured aircraft motors under licence for the Swedish Air force. Collaboration with the defence forces in the development, manufacturing and maintenance of motors has been of vital significance throughout the post WWII period, however operations have since been complemented by the development and production of high-tech components for civil aviation and rocket motors.

The King of the forest

Moose on the loose

The moose is the largest terrestrial animal in Europe. The bull can reach heights of 2 m and weigh over 400 kg and has huge horns that stick out from the sides of its head. The moose likes to dine on water lilies and is a strong swimmer. It can even dive to a depth of 6 m and graze on aquatic plants. A Roman historian once wrote that the moose lacks joints and therefore often leans against a tree when sleeping. So to catch the moose, all you have to do is chop down the tree and he will fall over into your clutches. An amusing image but unfortunately completely untrue.

Road accidents involving moose are relatively common in Sweden which is why the *King of the Forest's* silhouette adorns traffic warning signs on country roads. This exotic triangular sign has become a popular trophy among tourists and is often stolen. The tourist industry has been quick to catch on and nowadays you can buy the sign in an endless variety of sizes in any souvenir shop.

If you come across a moose with its hackles raised and its ears pinned back – watch out. This is one angry moose! Get to safety as quickly as possible and don't dilly-dally on

the way because a moose can reach speeds of 60 km/h. And if it happens to be a cow with a calf, you'll need to turn it up a notch because your life may well be in danger.

In the 17th century King Karl XI introduced a cavalry unit that used moose instead of horses. This didn't work out too well however as moose are afraid of people and are sensitive to loud noises. During the 1700s the moose was extremely rare. Carl von Linné for example is said to have only seen a single moose in his whole life and this was a tame one belonging to the Mayor of Vänersborg. Nowadays moose numbers are good. In fact Sweden has the most moose in the world – as many as 350 000 moose steaks are wandering around in the forests.

A typically Swedish event is the annual moose hunt when men of all ages (yes, it is still a predominantly male past time) take time out to bag some big game. Some of them head out into the forests for quite a while as moose hunting season stretches from September to January in most parts of the country.

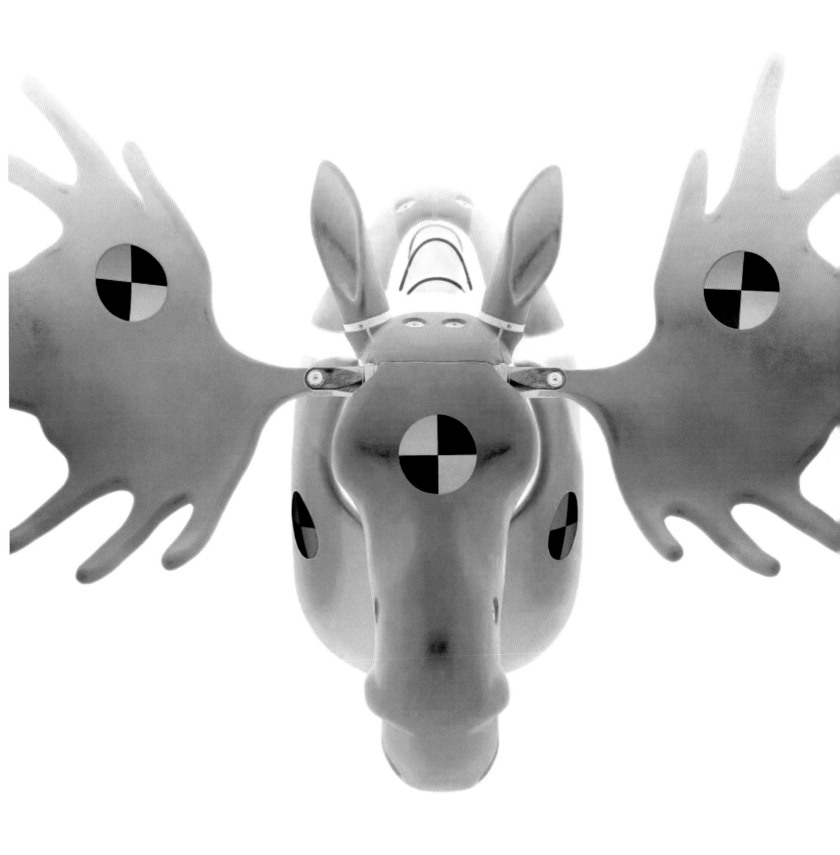

SAAB's crash test moose
helps to make Swedish cars
moose proof.

Look, we're flying, aren't we?

Saaaaab …

▲ Saab 92001: the first ever Saab. Just when the automobile industry was recovering after WWII, 15 of Saab's aircraft engineers were given the opportunity to test their skill and creativity; they were assigned the task of constructing a car. Free from the constraints of traditional automotive thinking, they produced a car unlike any other, with front-wheel drive and a transversely mounted two-stroke engine. However the most striking feature was perhaps the beautiful wing-shaped profile, a legacy of their aircraft heritage.

Tracing Saab's history is not easy. Planes have turned into cars that have grown into busses and trucks, names have been changed and ownership has changed hands numerous times. But fasten your seat belts and we'll give it our best shot …

Man has always dreamed of flying. Leonardo da Vinci sketches flying machines as early as 1493. Little did he know how his sketches would impact upon the future and even upon Swedish industry.

The Swedish Defence budget of 1936 was noteworthy in that large amounts of funds were suddenly allocated to the Air Force. This was naturally on account of the deteriorating political situation in Europe at the time. The clouds of war were gathering on the horizon and the Swedes were keen on having a powerful air force should hostilities break out. Domestic aircraft construction is started and the company *Svenska Aeroplan AB* (Saab) formed. At the factory

▲ The *Roadster* activity toy from Playsam, recommended for kids 1 year and older, is guaranteed to make any toddler's first car ride a joy. The design is archetypical with a steering wheel made of wood and steel just like the real sports cars of yesteryear. Playsam's sleek black Roadster is based on designer Sixten Sason's Saab prototype 92001, one of the most futuristic cars of its time.

▲ Saab's concept car, the Aero X. Clearly inspired by their aviation heritage, this car expresses an exciting, more progressive design vocabulary. An ingenious canopy negates the need for door or pillars. In the Aero X you simply lift the canopy and lower yourself into the cockpit, much as in a fighter plane, where you are treated to a full 180° field of vision through the panorama windscreen. The 400 bhp engine is designed to run "green" on 100% ethanol.

in Linköping plans for the first Swedish made metal aircraft, the B17, are drawn up with the help of American engineers. The plant even builds *Junkers* under licence. Over the years many different models of both military and civil aircraft are built including several classic fighter planes such as the *Saab 29 Tunnan* (Barrel), the *Saab 32 Lansen* (Lance) and the *Saab 35 Draken* (Dragon). The *Tunnan* sets two world speed records. During the 1980s Saab invested heavily in civil aircraft producing the *Saab 340* and the *Saab 2000*.

At the end of WWII, Saab come to the logical conclusion that the demand for aircraft will subside and they will have to find new ways to survive. So what should they do now? The civil aircraft market is simply too small for the company so they start to search for options. They consider manufacturing fishing equipment, prefabricated metal houses, aluminium-hulled boats, sinks … you name it. However after much hesitation, and perhaps with a little inspiration from Volvo, they finally decide that automobile manufacturing would suit them best.

The first model will be a small car with a two-stroke engine. Wing Engineer Gunnar Ljungström is assigned a small staff of around 15 people and given the task of creating a car. Designer Sixten Sason who helped design the *Hasselblad* camera, is brought in from the aircraft division to help. What results is an aircraft-inspired, technologically advanced car that differs markedly from other vehicles on the market. The preliminary drawings are ready by 1946 and a full-scale wooden model is built. A very Swedish thing to do. In order to reduce air resistance, the car resembles the cross section of an aircraft wing. In fact the whole car is reminiscent of an airplane without wings.

The first working test vehicle is hand built in 1946 and is mainly constructed from parts salvaged from a wrecking firm outside Linköping. *No1* is soon registered and

out on the roads, although rumour has it that none of the engineers involved actually had a driving licence. However, looking at the car, which resembles a wingless plane, one could fairly safely assume that all of them had their pilot's licence. The car is soon in production at the factory in Trollhättan, and the first car, a green Saab 92, rolls off the production line a few weeks later. Several million cars have since rolled out through the factory doors. For the first few years all the cars are painted the same bottle green colour. This was because the war had resulted in a surplus of paint in military colours which could be purchased for next to nothing. The first Saabs are powered by a transversely mounted 25 hp, 764 cm^3, two-cylinder, two-stroke engine. They are fitted with a 3 speed gear box and column shift. It even has a free wheel or overrunning clutch to prevent the engine from seizing when used as a brake. 13 cars are produced per day, although on Saturdays only seven are

rolled out. Why? Because at this time people in Sweden only worked half a day on Saturdays.

An advertising campaign from 1957 shows how the flagship 93 can be made up into a double bed. Someone happens to notice that the model in the photograph is not wearing a wedding ring. Not the done thing in the 50s! The photo is hurriedly touched up to give the model the obligatory wedding band. Of course no one would react in modern Sweden, which has one of the highest rates of de facto relationships in the world.

Saab first manufactures more than 10 000 cars in the year 1958. One can clearly see the airplane in each model and many of their technical innovations have had their origins in aircraft. To date, more than 4 million Saabs have seen the light of day.

The trials of the 1980s led to the automotive division being sold to General Motors and Investor.

Saab remains a leading company in the fields of defence, aeronautics and space, which may be a little confusing: aircraft that turn into cars and marry trucks that then drive in all directions with different names and owners.

Saab's operations are focused on the three strategic business segments; Defence and Security Solutions – Saab is a leader in advanced command and control and communication systems for military and civilian applications. The segment also comprises a wide range of integration services, integrated support and logistical solutions, and sophist-icated consulting services.

Systems and Products – Saab offers world-leading systems, products and components for defence, aviation, space and civil security. Also included in the segment are long-term maintenance and operational services for the systems it has delivered.

Aeronautics – Saab's extensive military and civilian aeronautics operations are dominated by the Gripen programme but also include the unmanned aerial vehicles of the future. In civilian operations, Saab is a supplier of structures and subsystems to the aircraft manufacturers Airbus and Boeing.*

▲ With the deliveries of its first aircraft, the light bomber and reconnaissance aircraft B17, Saab became the dominant supplier to the Swedish Air Force. Saab and the Swedish Air Force have progressed together through various generations of military jet aircraft, introducing world-leading technology every step of the way.

251

Swedish industrial heavyweight

From Skåne to Södertälje

Södertälje carriage manufacturer *Vabis* is founded in 1891 to produce railway carriages. Before long they start manufacturing cars and trucks. In 1911 they merge with Scania from Skåne in southern Sweden to form *Scania-Vabis*, which explains why most Swedes associate Scania with Södertälje despite the fact that this city is situated 500 km north of Skåne.

Scania started making international headway in the early 1950s and have since developed into a global heavyweight. In 1969 they joined forces with Saab and became *Saab-Scania*, however the 90s saw them go their separate ways. Scania's logo has always been the crowned griffin – Skåne's coats of arms. However during the Saab-Scania period this became the logo for the entire group, which explains why Saab's car and aviation divisions still have the griffin in their logo. Closer examination reveals that the logos do actually differ but it is only Scania that has any connection to Skåne, even if this was a long time ago.

Today Scania is a giant amongs heavy vehicle manufacturers, producing trucks, busses and even industrial and marine engines. They are currently active in over 100 markets.

Scania employs over 30 000 people worldwide of which 12 000 are in Sweden. An additional 20 000 work in Scania's independent sales and service organisation.

▲ Vabis A-car 1897. This is the first Swedish car. It was constructed by Vabis' engineer Gustaf Erikson who sits beside the driver. The driver is the MD at Vabis, Peter Peterson.

▼ Vabis 1902. The first truck designed by Vabis in Södertälje. The 1.5-tonner had a top speed of 12 km/h.

The Wallenbergare

A veal patty extra ordinaire

If there is one name that stands above all others in the world of Swedish business it is that of Wallenberg. They have often stressed that their immense assets constitute a family-oriented legacy where responsible management and long term viability are of the essence. In any case, the roll their group of companies has played in the advancement of Swedish industry cannot be overstated.

Outright ownership of one bank and majority holdings in another have provided the family with access to financial services and foreign contacts. More than any other financially influential family, the Wallenbergs have been willing to support companies wanting to invest in development and change.

Where does the Wallenberg story begin? The answer to that question lies in the middle of the 1800s, a time when Sweden is transforming from an impoverished agrarian nation into a modern industrial society. Exports of "Swedish gold" – timber – are on the rise. Burgeoning industrialism is accompanied by an increased need for investment capital which leads to the emergence of commercial banks backed by government guarantees. From the 1830s onwards smaller privately-owned banks begin to appear, some of which are granted the right to print their own bank notes. It was at this time that naval officer André Oscar Wallenberg arrives in Stockholm. Interested in political reforms, especially those concerning banking, he is elected into parliament where he uses his prodigious skills as a lobbyist to influence the banking system.

In 1856 André Oscar opens Stockholm's first privately-owned bank. The bank has the right to print its own notes but specialises in providing loans with reasonable repayment terms. By the turn of the century they have become the hub in a network of industrial enterprises. At this time the Wallenberg family owns 40 percent of the bank which serves to manage the family fortune.

At the beginning of the twentieth century the family shows great interest in the fledgling ASEA, lending them vast sums of money and acquiring a substantial stock holding. New legislation at the beginning of the 1900s limits the right of banks to own stock in industrial companies. As a result the investment management firm *Investor* is formed. *Investor* is not part of the bank but is nevertheless run by the same people.

In the 1920s the third generation of the Wallenberg family takes the helm with brothers Jacob and Marcus sharing responsibility. Marcus presides over the bank's industrial interests and becomes one of the most successful entrepreneurs in Swedish history. By the end of the 1920s *The Wallenberg Group* are majority owners of Separator (Alfa-Laval) and ASEA (ABB). Their journey continues with the acquisition of interests in LM-Ericsson, Atlas Copco, SKF and SAAB as well as leading steel and forestry companies. The post WWII world is bleeding heavily which creates a demand for industrial products and a boom for Swedish industry.

The legendary Raoul Wallenberg also belongs to this family. Mostly known for his daring exploits saving Jews in Hungary at the end of WWII, his bravery leads to him being made an honorary citizen in the USA, Canada and Israel.

The *Wallenbergare* is also a famous Swedish dish consisting of ground veal, eggs and cream served with green peas, mashed potatoes and lingonberries.

Legend has it that the *Wallenbergare* originated one night when Marcus Wallenberg and a friend were dining at a restaurant in Stockholm. They were keen on having a ground veal dish they had eaten abroad, so Marcus persuaded the chef to prepare the first ever *Wallenbergare*, a dish that is still served in countless bank cafeterias, restaurants and homes. The dish can be prepared in various ways although many insist that a true *Wallenbergare* should consist of leg meat which is ground twice and then flavoured with the spice mix *épice riche*; a mixture of marjoram, thyme, oregano, tarragon, sage, allspice, black pepper, fennel, cumin and cloves. Eating a *Wallenbergare* is an experience you are bound to want to repeat.

WALLENBERGARE FOR 2

250 g ground veal
2 egg yolks
200 ml cream
salt
white pepper
épice riche
Mie de pain (white breadcrumbs)

Condiments:
lingonberry preserve
green peas
mashed potatoes

Make sure that all the ingredients for the patties are well chilled. Place the veal, eggs and spices in a mixer. Mix for a while with the lid on, and then slowly add the cream in a fine stream while mixing. Make sure the cream mixes in well but do not over mix. This may raise the temperature and cause the mixture to separate.

Place half of the breadcrumbs on a plate. Dip your hands in cold water and then form the patties. Place them on the plate of breadcrumbs. Pour the remaining breadcrumbs over the patties. Fry the patties in butter at a low temperature. If need be cook them in the oven for a while to make sure they are thoroughly cooked, moist and tender.

Lars Magnus Ericsson

Swedish telephone king

Lars Magnus Ericsson was born in 1846 and grew up on a farm in Värmland in western Sweden. As a child he displayed an unusual technical ability on one occasion constructing a telephone that ran from the play house, to the house, and on to the boy next door's place. Lars Magnus's first phone consisted of a string attached at each end to a cow's bladder. The bladders acted as a membrane that vibrated when someone spoke and hey presto, all of a sudden Mum could talk to her son out in the play house! No one knows how he came up with the idea but it was just one of many. For example he also built a music box for his sister and an organ.

Lars Magnus loses his father at the age of 12. For a family that was already struggling to make ends meet this is a dire turn of events. Now the sole breadwinner in the family, Lars Magnus moves to Norway where he serves as a blacksmith's assistant in the mines, a physically demanding but well-paid job that allows to him send much-needed money home. After a few years he returns to Sweden to work on the railways but yearns for a real trade. He becomes a metalworkers apprentice and in the evenings he studies. One day he realises that he has learnt all he can, so he packs his bags and heads off towards Stockholm. After a week's travelling he arrives only to find himself in a bit of a bind; he doesn't have any references! A poor farmer's son with no money and no references alone in a big city has few prospects. However, he promptly sets about knocking on doors and is finally given a position at *Öller & Co's* telegraphic workshop. He works for them for six years, becoming an expert in low voltage electricity. He is also awarded a government scholarship to travel abroad and study.

By the age of 30 he has managed to borrow enough money to open a small workshop in a kitchen on Drottninggatan in downtown Stockholm. What happens next is the stuff of legend. Whether or not it actually happened this way is unclear, but here's how the story goes:

Errand boy Gabriel is sent off to jeweller Cedergren's to buy silver to make electrical contacts. Once in the shop he spies a telephone and bursts out "My boss makes those, only much better!" Mr Cedergren is naturally curious and dons his coat to go and see for himself. He and Lars Magnus meet for the first time, and thus the seed of the renowned Swedish telecommunication business is sown.

When he starts his workshop, Lars Magnus is well aware of the potential of the telephone. But there is one major problem. Who will buy his phones? The international *Bell Telephone Company* who holds the patent to Alexander Graham Bell's telephone has been granted monopolies in several countries effectively blocking Ericsson from entering these markets. Bell is able to charge high fees for their services which prevent the telephone from reaching beyond the upper classes. However, for some inexplicable reason, Bell did not file for patents in Sweden or Germany. Whether this was due to complacency or merely an oversight no one knows, but one thing is for sure: it helped pave the way for Lars Magnus.

Jeweller and engineer Henrik Tore Cedergren is one of the very first to acquire a telephone in Bell's network. He calculates what it would cost to construct a competing network and concludes that it need not cost the subscriber more than 100 crowns per year. However, in order to start a telephone company he needs phones and switchboards. And this is exactly what Lars Magnus has in his workshop! It's interesting to toy with the idea of what might have happened if the errand boy had chosen another jeweller or had failed to mention his boss' telephones.

Cedergren founds a telephone company called SAT that uses Swedish components to provide telecommunication services to the general public at considerably lower prices than Bell. The goal is to install telephone lines to every building and every apartment and by the middle of the 1880s Sweden has one of the largest telephone networks in the world consisting of over 4 800 subscribers, a feat made possible by the lower charges. Another factor is the way the

When the Museum of Modern Art in New York chose the 300 best examples of industrial design in the early 1970s , the inclusion of Ericsson's Cobra was a given. The first model was launched in 1956.

▲▲ Lars Magnus Ericsson.

▲ Telephone, 1878 model. The first Ericsson telephone.

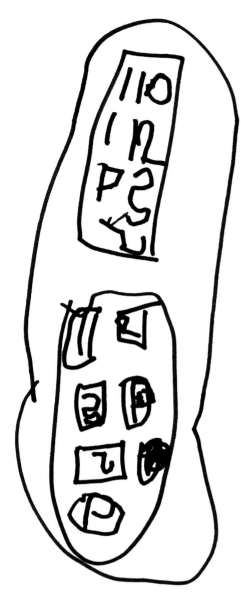

The foundations for modern cell phone networks were established in the 1950s but the equipment was clumsy and the range hopeless. The size of a suitcase and weighing around 40 kg, getting one installed in your car costs as much as the car itself. At this time the network had around 100 subscribers so it could hardly be called a success. However, in time the equipment shrank and fierce competition broke out to see who could develop a first generation cell phone network. One could almost be so bold as to claim that Ericsson won that race. They managed to look deeply into their crystal ball and see cell phones for the man on the street.

Since 2001, development and sales of cell phones has been handled by subsidiary company *Sony Ericsson* in which Ericsson holds a 50 percent share.

◀ Mobile cell phone by John, 4 years.

Lars Magnus is a progressive employer. His workforce during the 1880s is better paid than workers elsewhere and their working week has been reduced to 57 hours. In 1891 he introduces free medical care and burial assistance for all LME employees. He has an eye for talent and is willing to invest in the young and untried. His preference for practical training goes hand in hand with his sceptical attitude towards highly educated "paper engineers".

In 1878 he marries Hilda. She contributes to LME's development as Lars Magnus' colleague, business partner and confidante. On top of this she runs the household and raises four children. However some claim that her greatest contribution was the way she can keep her melancholy husband emotionally balanced. It is said that Lars Magnus is burdened by a dark disposition and that it is only his creativity and work that keep him going. If he has nothing to do he quickly plunges into the depths of despair where not even Hilda can reach him. His contemporaries describe him as someone who is very withdrawn and dislikes attention. He declines an honorary doctorate from Stockholm University and avoids any type of praise or congratulatory event. On his 50th birthday a group of singers from the company are let into his house to sing for him. Unfortunately when Lars Magnus gets wind of this he runs off and hides. The next day however each one of the singers receives a thank you card expressing his appreciation.

Ericsson is of great importance in Sweden. In the 1880 Stockholm has the highest number of telephones per capita of any city in the world, and over a century later Sweden is one of the countries in the world with the highest rate of cell phone usage.

In the 1920s Ericsson delivered their first electronic switchboard. Another major breakthrough occurred in the 1970s with the launch of the computerised AXE system. This system laid the foundations for both the development of land-based telecommunications for the remainder of the century and the emergence of services such as ISDN and cell phone networks. And even if one is aware that AXE is a digital switchboard it is perhaps difficult to appreciate the role it has played in the daily life of the average telephone subscriber. Let's put it this way: no matter where you are, if you pick up a phone, AXE is involved. It is the biggest selling telephone system in the world and one of Sweden's greatest ever export successes.

The period 1970-1999 is one of the most eventful in company history, and sees the traditional telephone company transformed into a cutting edge telecommunications Group.

local state-run telegraphic company *Telegrafverket* actively competes with SAT for customers in the Stockholm area. Fierce competition encourages rapid technological innovation and increased efficiency. By the beginning of the 1890s the number of telephone calls made in Sweden exceeds the number of letters posted.

While the telephone is taking Sweden by storm, Lars Magnus continues to refine and develop its construction. One development that he becomes famous for is the *hand micro-telephone*, what we call the handset. Up until this point users couldn't listen with and speak into the same unit. This ingenious idea is said to have come from two co-workers who, when testing lines, attach a speaker and microphone to a broom stick.

By 1896 Lars Magnus' company has grown into quite a large concern employing over 500 people and exporting the majority of their phones. At this point there are over 100 000 phones around the world bearing the Ericsson logo. Just like his compatriots Gustaf Dalén and Sven Wingqvist,

Is it possible to make better looking base stations? Ericsson launches a new type of concrete cell phone tower. *The Ericsson Tower Tube* is approximately 5 m in diameter and 40 m tall. Thanks to its ingenious construction, it uses 40 percent less power and carbon dioxide emissions during manufacturing are considerably lower. The tower is designed by Thomas Sandell. Aesthetically pleasing? Well, beauty is in the eye of the beholder ...

Refrigerators from Sweden?

The ingenious use of heat to cool

As a teenager, Baltzar von Platen dreamed of a perpetual motion machine that would extract heat from the cold environment and provide heat for people's houses. A desire that is easy to understand given that cold is in plentiful supply in Sweden, at least in the winter. The pursuit of a *perpetuum mobile* drives Baltzar throughout his long life, although he never fully succeeds in developing one. He does however succeed in exactly the opposite – producing cold from heat in the form of one of the world's first refrigerators for domestic use. Indeed, the fridge that Baltzar von Platen and Carl Munters construct in 1922 formed the basis of what has become the global company Electrolux.

Baltzar von Platen was a strange child whose profile seems to match the stereotype of the mad inventor; a one-of-a-kind who always has to do everything his own peculiar way and who doesn't fit well into the contemporary school system. But then again, which school has ever succeeded in encouraging the originality of geniuses? Baltzar is failed every year from the age of 12 until he graduates. A subject he fails is biology and one story on the subject goes like this. The pupils are on a biology field trip when the Principal asks: "Baltzar. What is the Latin name of that flower?" Baltzar doesn't answer. "Why don't you answer me?" asks the Principal. "I couldn't hear you because I was wondering how on earth the tree gets water up to the highest leaves. They can't possibly suck water that high."

Unfortunately this candid answer earns him an *F*. What the 12-year old Baltzar is wondering about is capillary action, the ability of water to climb up a tube or in this case the trunk of a tree.

When he commences studies at Lund University he is failed in physics, this time because he insists on solving an equation his own way. He is probably right, but locking horns with his professor gets him nowhere except expelled. He moves to Stockholm and enrolls at the Technical University where he runs into Carl Munters. After just a few

days they are well on their way to constructing a cooling machine with no moving parts, where one end turns cold when the other one is heated. Carl Munters comes from an innovative family and has excellent business sense. While WWI was raging, he realised that there was a shortage of soldering flux so he started manufacturing his own. Sales went well, so well in fact that he was forced to employ other people. After all there was a limit as to how much school he could get away with skipping.

While a student at the Technical University he creates his first inventions such as the kickback-proof start crank for cars, his first patent. Earlier models could suddenly spin backwards breaking the hand or arm of the person starting the car. Carl sells this invention to *Scania-Vabis*. When Carl and Baltzar put their heads together they decide to work on an idea they got from Carl's Dad – a refrigerator. Refrigerators had been in existence since the early 1900s but were unwieldy and run by noisy compressors. They set their sights on producing a compact, low-maintenance version without a compressor or moving parts. The idea has been around for a long time but no one has actually succeeded in producing one. After a year of working after school the prototype refrigerator is finally ready. Or perhaps *freezer* is a better term seeing as it produced temperatures of around minus 40 degrees Celsius! But in 1922 the two proud "parents" could present their refrigerator to the world and apply for a patent. The apparatus takes the world by storm. Even Albert Einstein expresses his amazement over the ingenious device. Their invention incorporated so many innovations that one would need a whole book to describe them and degrees in chemistry and physics to understand them. Let's just say that it was revolutionary.

In 1923 they display the refrigerator at an exhibition in Stockholm, and in 1925 Electrolux buys the rights and employs the two inventors to continue its development. They each receive 560 000 Swedish crowns, an incredible amount

in those days, and royalties to
the tune of 50 Swedish öre per
machine sold. All of a sudden
they are men of considerable
means.

Electrolux was founded
in 1919. Appliances such as refrigerators and vacuum cleaners have been the cornerstone of
their success, and today they are
one of Sweden's leading companies
employing over 50000 people in over
56 countries. They were quick to realise
the importance of design and began using
leading designers such as Robert Loewy, *The
Father of Industrial design,* as early as the 1930s.
Loewy is famous for his bold, beautiful work with
things such as Greyhound buses, locomotives, cars,
household appliances and those famous rounded
car fridges.

ELECTROLUX

Electrolux was founded in 1919 when kerosene lamp manufacturer *AB Lux* and vacuum cleaner producer *Elektromekaniska AB* merged. Refrigerators and vacuum cleaners formed the basis for Electrolux' success and they went on to become one of Sweden's leading global companies selling over 40 million products annually in 150 countries. White goods account for close to half of their sales whereas their vacuum cleaners have around a 5th of the world market.

DUST MATE

With time at a premium, why not combine two necessary activities: cleaning and exercise? Normally, shoes track dirt throughout homes. But with Dustmate, shoes are used as a cleaning apparatus, sucking dirt into special shoes as you walk, run or dance through your home. Comfortable to wear, easy to store.

262

THE FULLY AUTOMATIC VACUUM CLEANER – THE ABILITIES OF A BAT

The Electrolux *Trilobite* is one of the world's first commercially available automatic vacuum cleaners. The prototype was presented to the public in 1997 on the BBC TV programme *Tomorrow's World*. Considerable research has gone into the project where the goal has been to cram a lot of cutting-edge technology into a compact format at an affordable price. The device navigates using harmless ultrasonic signals and returns to its charger if the battery runs out before it is done vacuuming. When it is finished, it puts itself to bed. If you're allergic to dogs and cats you might consider having one as a pet …

About the size of a curling stone, its rounded shape lets it manoeuvre between table and chair legs without getting stuck. It is a high-end product intended to blend in to the home environment while exuding a sense of exclusivity. Inese Ljunggren has been responsible for its design and has worked with engineers, researchers, sonar and software experts and the military to make the vision a reality. The fact that the *Trilobite* has been given a place at the Nationalmuseum in Stockholm is a testament to its success. Praise and awards from within the design world have also been heaped upon it.

Carl and Baltzars' goal was to produce a compact, low-maintenance refrigerator without a compressor or moving parts. The fridge took the world by storm and was a huge sales success for Electrolux. The inventors each received 560 thousand kronor, an incredible amount in those days, and royalties of 50 Swedish öre per machine sold. All of a sudden they were financially independent.

263

The AGA lighthouse –
a brilliant Swedish idea

Gustaf Dalén – an optimistic genius

Gustaf Dalén, a farmer's son from Stenstorp in Västergöt-land, first saw the light of day in 1869. An uncommonly heavy sleeper, as a child he is forced to resort to extreme methods to get himself out of bed in the morning. He repairs an old alarm clock and fits it with a strip of sandpaper. Against the sandpaper he places a stick of phosphorous and a rocker arm. When the alarm clock rings, the phosphorous ignites and is fed through an array of spindles and string to the wick of an oil lamp. A coffee pot is placed above the lamp. After about 15 minutes, when the coffee is hot, a small hammer attached to the clock movement makes sure that Gustaf and his brother are woken to the wonderful aroma of freshly-brewed coffee.

After a while he decides he needs to further develop his invention because the hammer often fails to wake him up. He proposes suspending the bed on two poles that will tip the sleeping boys out onto the floor when the alarm rings. Yes, at the age of 13 Gustaf Dalén is already a fully-fledged inventor! However, his brother Hjalmar refuses to be subjected to the indignity of being thrown onto the floor every morning. When speaking of his three sons, Gustaf's father, a farmer and teacher, says, "I can make men out of Gottfrid and Albin, but Gustaf is good for nothing."

But Gustaf is an inventor and has absolutely no intention of working on the land. For one thing farm life involves getting up at the crack of dawn, something that definitely doesn't suit young Gustaf. Instead of studying agriculture he chooses engineering in Göteborg and then at Polytechnikum in Zürich. He finds employment working on Laval's steam turbine, but continues to develop his inventions on his own time together with his eccentric companion Henrik von Celsing, an interesting young man who is often seen walking around the streets of Stockholm in the company of a tame moose. In the summer of 1901 Gustaf marries his childhood sweetheart Elma. By now he is Head Engineer at *Karbid & Acetylen* AB and is simultaneously running his own engineering firm together with Henrik.

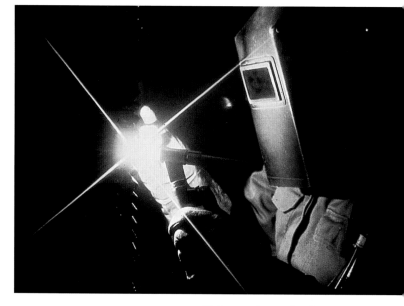

Modern operations are based upon industrial gas applications such as welding, freezing, heating, metallurgy, environmental protection, the manufacture of glass and electronic products and pharmaceuticals.

German industrial *The Linde Group* acquired AGA in 1999 incorporating it into their gas division. British *BOC* was acquired in 2006 making AGA and its family the largest industrial company in the world.

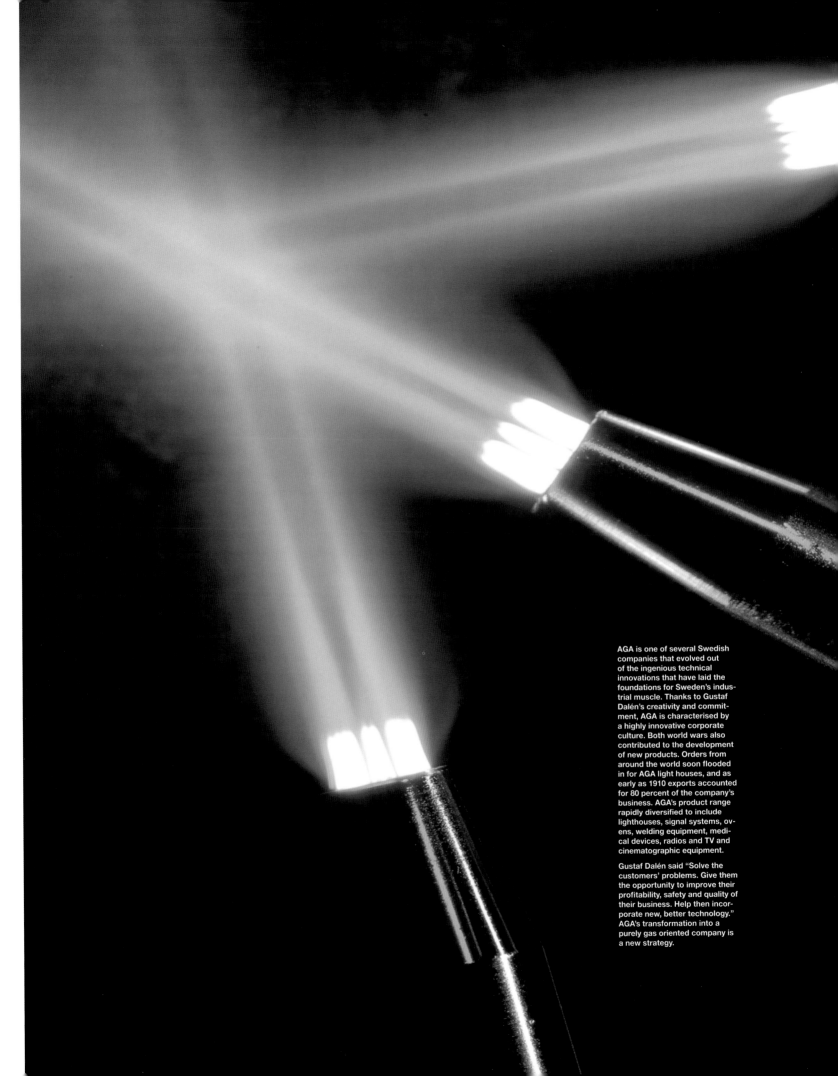

AGA is one of several Swedish companies that evolved out of the ingenious technical innovations that have laid the foundations for Sweden's industrial muscle. Thanks to Gustaf Dalén's creativity and commitment, AGA is characterised by a highly innovative corporate culture. Both world wars also contributed to the development of new products. Orders from around the world soon flooded in for AGA light houses, and as early as 1910 exports accounted for 80 percent of the company's business. AGA's product range rapidly diversified to include lighthouses, signal systems, ovens, welding equipment, medical devices, radios and TV and cinematographic equipment.

Gustaf Dalén said "Solve the customers' problems. Give them the opportunity to improve their profitability, safety and quality of their business. Help then incorporate new, better technology." AGA's transformation into a purely gas oriented company is a new strategy.

Acetylene, with its bright, light is an excellent fuel for use in lighthouses but is prohibitively expensive when burnt all day. In 1905 Gustaf invents the intermittent light regulator – widely known as the *Dalén Flasher* – a device that ignites and extinguishes the light at regular intervals thereby dramatically reducing gas consumption. A membrane is fitted within a cylindrical housing. A spring connects the membrane to a reciprocating valve which regulates the gas inlet and outlet ports. When gas is fed into the system the membrane rises and in so doing simultaneously closes the inlet valve and opens the outlet which leads to the burner. When the gas has flowed out, the membrane returns to its original position, once again opening the inlet valve and closing the outlet. Gas is ignited in the burner by a small pilot light. *The Flasher* reduced gas consumption by around 90% because gas was only burned during the flash and the pilot light required very little gas. One year later he launched the ingenious sun valve, a device that automatically lights the beacon at dusk and extinguishes it at dawn. News of Dalén's sorcery is met with scepticism by the rest of the world and none other than Thomas Alva Edison is reported to say, "It will never work." The German Patent Office greets the news with a single word; "Impossible".

Dalén then sets about solving the problem of safely transporting the inflammable acetylene gas by improving the porous AGA compound. His first attempt fails but after endless experimentation he finally works out how to reduce the risk of explosion by embedding the gas while simultaneously increasing the intensity of the beacon. The *automatic mantel exchanger* now also makes its entrance which suddenly means that a beacon need only be serviced annually. Dalén's lighthouses face their greatest challenges out at sea where they must produce a characteristic, reliable and safe light to guide shipping through treacherous waters. Dalén's lighthouse system is used all over the world throughout the 20th century.

The AGA cooker can be run on wood, gas, oil or electricity. The rounded form is a result of the now blind Dalén wanting to avoid sharp corners. It burns around the clock, requires a minimum of supervision and is incredibly economical to run. The unit is manufactured out of cast iron and weighs at least 400 kg, which is why the load bearing capacity of the floor should always be checked before installation. There are two-oven, three-oven and four-oven models.

Selma Lagerlöf, one of Sweden's foremost authors, receives one as a personal gift from Gustaf Dalén. She is particularly proud of her AGA. In fact, the only time she sets foot in the kitchen is when she shows it to her guests.

At the time of the great Stock Market collapse in 1929 Gustaf Dalén is blind and financially hard pressed. He orders small badges bearing the words "BE OPTIMISTIC" and every time he meets a prophet of doom he promptly pins one on the whiner's lapel. He personally wears a badge at all times.

In 1912 he receives an extremely prestigious order, the illumination of the Panama Canal. Later that year Gustaf is involved in a serious gas explosion when testing the new AGA compound. His clothes are engulfed in flame, one of his eyes is blown out and his hands are horrendously burned. The first doctor to arrive on the scene wants to give him morphine but he refuses. He wants to know how many hours he has to live and insists on meeting his wife and four children before he dies. However, against all odds he actually survives. His brother Albin who is Sweden's leading ophthalmologist desperately tries to save Gustaf's sight, but to no avail. It is said that disappointment at his failure turned his hair grey overnight. Gustaf Dalén, the man who had used light to serve humanity will spend the rest of his life in darkness.

Upon coming home from hospital he is greeted with the joyful news that he has been awarded the Nobel Prize for Physics 1912. He donates some of the money to the workers at AGA, who each receive an extra week's pay, and uses the rest to create scholarship funds at Chalmers Technical University. Despite his disability, Gustaf continues to run *Aktiebolaget Gas Ackumulator* (AGA) and conduct research with the assistance of a colleague and his son Gunnar.

Eight years later Gustaf starts to look into why ordinary wood-burning stoves are so uneconomical. Eureka! The highly-efficient AGA cooker is born and goes on to be an international success: The AGA is still enormously popular – a prized cultural object for anyone fortunate enough to own one. Labour is in short supply when the AGA comes on the market, and it suddenly becomes an ace up the sleeve of those seeking to entice and secure the services of the best domestic staff. Some families are so proud of their AGA that they place it in the living room for all to see and admire. Gustaf Dalén is a creative genius and is awarded a total of 99 patents. He retains the position of Managing Director of AGA until his death in 1937.

Medical innovations

Power puffers and pills for your ills

Astra got off to a flying start in 1913, the year that the state monopoly on pharmaceutical production was abolished, and have gone from strength to strength ever since. Their success can largely be attributed to a series of revolutionary medical innovations.

Pharmacist Adolf Rising, the founder of Astra, is a man with a vision. He envisages a Swedish pharmaceutical company based on contemporary German and Swiss models. Pharmaceuticals had been produced on an industrial scale in Europe since the 1800s but Swedes have always had to rely on imported medicines, a situation that often leads to indignant headlines in the local press. The first tentative steps towards domestic production are taken by a few pharmacists with well-equipped laboratories, among them Adolf Rising. His first product catalogue included 60 preparations including heart medicine *Digotal* which would prove to be a great success. In fact it would remain on the market well into the 1950s. Spurred on by his success he dreams of large-scale production and global marketing. And he is well on his way, even if the road is strewn with various obstacles such as government monopolies.

One of the keys to Astra's success is an early commitment to research. New medicines are rarely discovered by accident. They are invariably the product of a complex and costly experimental process. Astra's first international success is the sulfur preparation *Sulfatiazol*, the profits from which are ploughed back into further research which in turn results in *Xylocain*. This local anaesthetic turns Astra into a global pharmaceutical company almost over night. This is at the end 1940s.

After a shaky start Astra shifts into high gear becoming a major player and one of the most successful Swedish companies of the 1900s. When antacid *Losec*, the product of 20 years' research, is launched in 1988 it becomes the world's biggest selling pharmaceutical, treating over 200 million patients around the world.

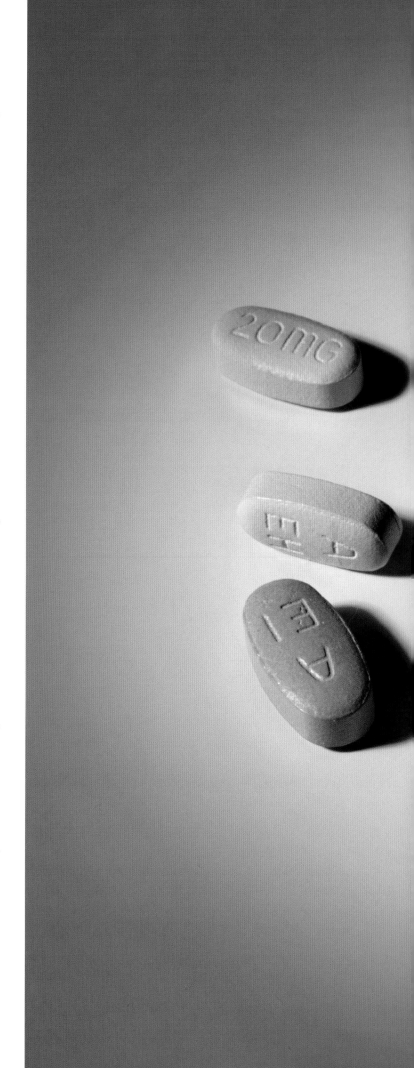

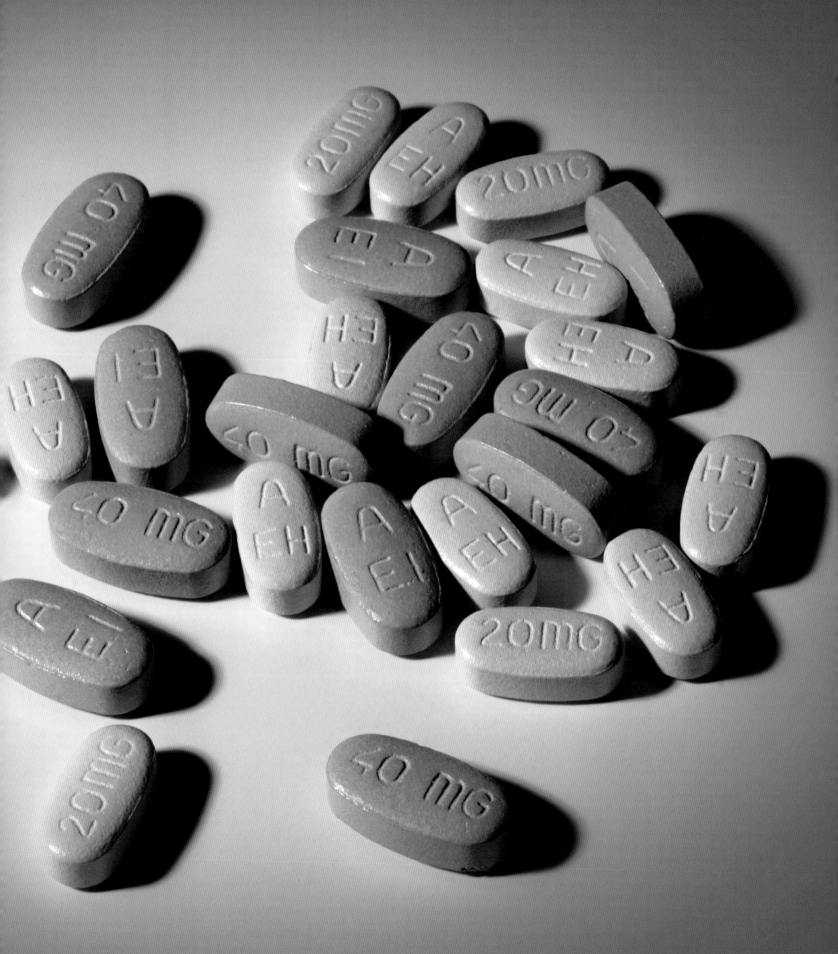

Two Australian researchers investigate another avenue and discover the link between the bacteria *Helicobacter pylori* and stomach ulcers. This causes a sensation in the world of medical research but naturally is a potential disaster for Astra. What happens when a well-established medical "truth" turns out not to be true? Losec was unchallenged in its field and Astra's cash cow. So what do they do now? They immediately change the direction of their research in gastro-intestinal and infection diseases. This pays dividends and AstraZeneca, as they are now known after merging with British Zeneca in 1998, are first onto the market with a combined proton pump inhibitor and antibiotic to treat the nasty little *Helicobacter pylori* bacteria. Eventually they can register two combination treatments of this type. They also create a research unit dedicated to developing an antibacterial substance that specifically targets *Helicobacter*. A condition that would have meant a lifetime of discomfort and treatment or even surgery can now be treated with a seven-day course of drugs. Such quantum leaps are rare in medical circles. Imagine if Alfred Nobel had lived to see this – a man who suffered from continual stomach pain and probably lived his whole life with *Helicobacter*. In 2005 the two Australians Robin Warren and Barry Marshall are awarded the Nobel Prize in Medicine.

AstraZeneca's operations are concentrated in six health-care areas, namely respiratory/inflammation, oncology, neuroscience, cardiovascular, infection and gastrointestinal. Astra's commitment to research has resulted in a wide portfolio of advanced products. Their goal is to develop pharmaceuticals to reduce the suffering of mankind. Astra's efforts have changed the lives of many people who suffer from asthma and allergies. An asthma attack is sometimes described as like trying to breath through a straw. This chronic condition is extremely common and the numbers of those afflicted are, at least in Sweden, continually increasing. Mortality has been halved since the 1970's largely due to increased awareness and better drugs. It is no exaggeration to say that medical treatment of asthma has undergone a revolution in the past few years. In 1966 Swedish researchers Leif Svensson and Kjell Wetterlin developed the bronchodilator *Bricanyl* thereby making life easier for countless sufferers at a time when the medical establishment still believed that asthma was caused by abnormalities in the smooth muscles of the airways.

Ten years later, researchers discovered that asthma is an inflammatory condition that is better treated by bronchodilators and local cortisone. As a result of this research the preparation *Pulmicort* is developed. In addition the *Turbuhaler*

is launched. This is an ingenious little inhaler that dispenses exactly the right amount and eliminates the risk of overdosing, something that is critical when administering cortisone. What happened next on the asthma fighting front? The latest development has been the miraculous *Symbicort* which contains both *Pulmicort* and *Oxis*, a long acting bronchodilator of the type beta-2 stimulator. This is Astra's very own *Kinder Surprise* with several gifts in the same inhaler. Research has enabled asthma sufferers to live a life that years ago they could only have dreamed of.

The evolution of Astra from an insignificant little laboratory at the beginning of 1900s to one of the world's leading pharmaceutical companies is unique and yet another example of just what Swedish entrepreneurship and innovation can achieve. Their success story is inextricably linked to the pharmaceuticals *Sulfatiazol*, *Xylocain*, *Bricanyl*, *Aptin*, *Pulmicort*, *Penglobe*, *Seloken* and *Symbicort*.

THE MORE (pharmaceutical companies) THE MERRIER

In the 1960s three Swedish pharmaceutical companies began collaborative research in the area of receptor mechanisms. They succeeded in producing substances that target receptors and as a result were able to develop drugs that improved the functioning of certain organs such as the heart. These drugs are known as Beta blockers and are used to manage a number of medical conditions. Beta blockers reduce the effects of our body's' stress hormones.

Several of the pharmaceuticals produced by this Swedish project have gone on to be market leaders. Produced in 1965, *Aptin* is used to prevent over-stimulation of the heart in patients suffering from cardiovascular disease. *Aptin* was produced by Astra Hässle in Göteborg. Arguably the most famous drug to come out of the project is *Bricanyl* which dilates the bronchia of asthmatic patients without affecting cardiovascular function. Launched in 1969 by Astra Draco, this drug has been of great importance to asthmatics around the world. *Seloken* is a selective Beta blocker that simultaneously lowers blood pressure and blocks the sensation of pain in the heart. *Seloken* limits the damage caused by heart attacks and prevents the occurrence of new cardiac events by increasing the oxygen supply to the heart. Developed by Astra Hässle, *Seloken* is a leading blood pressure medication and can be used for years at a time.

Approximately eight percent of the Swedish population suffers from asthma and many more from some other form of allergy or hypersensitivity. In other worlds asthma and allergies are extremely common ailments. Fortunately in recent times asthma treatment has come on in leaps and bounds. Modern medicines work better and are easier to administer than ever before.

Symbicort combination inhaler is the latest in asthma treatment containing both anti-inflammatory and bronchodilating agents. This means asthma patients only need one inhaler. Other pharmaceutical companies have similar products in their portfolio. *Symbicort* is Astra Zeneca's very own *Kinder Surprise*.

The artificial kidney

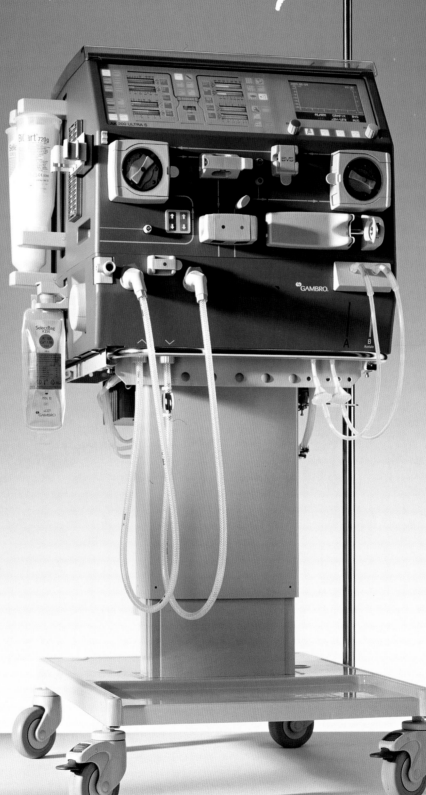

The year is 1946. Time – 3 a.m., but at the medical clinic in Lund nobody is asleep. A man, 47 years of age, has been brought in. He is suffering from uremia and silicosis complicated by pneumonia. His kidneys have ceased functioning.

The surgeon on-call has made two incisions in the man's wrist under local anaesthetic and has inserted cannulae into a vein and an artery. On the floor is a strange machine that has been assembled in the hospital workshop. It consists of a large glass jar and a cylinder of stainless steel mesh. A flat tube, that is actually 11m of sausage casing, is wound around the jar. When the machine is connected to the patient blood flows from the artery through the sausage casing and is returned, clean, to the patient. The exchange of substances that occurs via the sausage casing is the first ever dialysis. The peculiar machine has been manufactured by Nils Alwall, physiologist, pharmacologist and doctor of internal medicine. He has always found the plight of kidney patients to be particularly moving as there is no cure for their condition. At the time, kidney failure is treated with strict bed rest and a diet devoid of egg whites, salt or spices. After several weeks in bed the boredom becomes un-bearable. But let's get back to the 47-year-old dialysis patient. Overnight the patient regains consciousness and can now speak and open his eyes. The experiment was a success but unfortunately the patient dies a few days later – not from kidney failure but from pneumonia. Dialysis rapidly becomes an important method for dealing with temporary kidney malfunction.

The artificial kidney was the result of animal experiments and Alwall's extensive physiological knowledge. This ground-breaking medical innovation eventually evolved into Gambro, a market-leading, multi-national health care company specialising in blood component technology and the treatment of kidney disorders.

The kidneys are vital organs. However, thanks to dialysis these days many people live a full and active life even when their kidneys aren't fully functional. The first artificial kidneys were constructed in the late 1960s and since then have helped hundreds of thousands of people around the world. Development commenced in Lund and soon developed into the company *Gambro*. Industrialist Holger Craaford was one of the people who realised the importance of the development of this life-giving device. Gambro backs the Craaford Foundation in Lund, one of the country's most important sources of research funding.

These days Gambro is a global health care company that develops and markets dialysis products and services for hospital and domestic environments as well as blood purification equipment for Intensive Care Units. Gambro has been a market leader in its field for decades and has been responsible for the introduction of many ground-breaking innovations.

The idea of regulating heart rate using electrical impulses has been around since the beginning of the 19th century, but it wasn't until inventor Rune Elmqvist developed a small battery powered pacemaker in the 1950s that surgeons could finally put the theory into practice. The pacemaker's task is to stimulate the heart muscle into contracting when it doesn't have the strength itself. Åke Senning performed the world's first pacemaker implant at the Karolinska Hospital in Stockholm in 1958. There is no record of the outcome but it is fairly safe to assume that the operation was a success as the invention itself went on to be highly successful.

The first pacemaker was pieced together in a coffee cup and turned out to be quite a clumsy gadget. A modern pacemaker however weighs between 14 and 40 grams and can be implanted under local anaesthetic. It can even be adjusted to suit the patient's needs via a remote connection to the doctor's control panel. To date this Swedish invention has helped over a million heart patients live a normal life.

Rune Elmqvist also invented the *Mingograph*, an extremely sensitive printer with the ability to immediately register and record series of minute changes. The *Mingograph* is used as a chart recorder in conjunction with sensitive medical equipment such as electrocardiographs (ECG).

The beat goes on ...

1958

1969

1976

1988

1995

1996

2007

St. Jude Medical is one of the world's leading medical device companies.

The Hasselblad camera

First on the moon

The inspiration for Victor Hasselblad's ingenious camera came to him when travelling the world photographing birdlife. He was a bit of a rare bird himself – an unlikely combination of skilful captain of industry and highly educated ornithologist. His passion for birds accompanied him deep into the inner reaches of the business world where his ability to combine a fascination with nature with technical innovation would eventually give rise to a camera that would revolutionise photography.

Victor's grandfather had been given a camera by Kodak founder George Eastman while on his honeymoon in London, and had fallen in love with photography. He began selling photographic equipment through the family company and soon became Kodak's sole Swedish distributor. This proved to be an astute move. As a young man, Victor Hasselblad was a lost, upper-class lad growing up in a palatial house with a disapproving father. Fortunately however, he inherited Grandad's interest in photography which, together with a fascination for birds that bordered on the fanatical, would eventually forge one of the world's most recognisable brand names.

In 1937 Victor opened a photographic shop in Göteborg and espoused his views on the ideal camera construction for wildlife photography in several well received articles. When WWII broke out he was approached by the Swedish Air Force and asked to develop a camera for aerial surveillance – something he achieved in record time. He continued to develop highly innovative cameras for the defence forces throughout the war and his company prospered. Meanwhile, he made it clear to his staff that he fully intended to produce a camera for the civilian market – one that would be hand-held, multi-purpose and consist of interchangeable components. Orders from the armed forces waned when the war ended, so prototypes for a civilian camera were developed.

The Hasselblad camera, launched at a press conference in New York in 1948, was an instant success, praised both for its bold design and innovative technical features. The first Hasselblad for consumer use was a single lens reflex camera with the same basic structure we see today – a housing containing a mirror and view finder, an interchangeable lens and film magazine.

The Hasselblad modular concept lends itself well to development. As a result, the look of the cameras has been retained even though their internal components have changed radically. Modern digital cameras are still instantly recognisable as Hasselblads, and even though they may use Japanese optics and are owned by the Chinese, they are still manufactured in Göteborg. Victor had the pleasure of seeing many renowned photographers create classic photographs with his cameras. For example several of Phillipe Halsman's portraits, Neil Leifer's award-winning sports photographs, the spectacular landscape photography of Ansel Adams and Lennart Nilsson's ground-breaking documentation of the inner world of the human body have all been captured on Hasselblads.

Creating contacts came easily to Victor Hasselblad and years of travelling led to a solid international network. He was a personal friend of many of the great photographers and was himself a pioneer of wildlife photography, spurred on by an almost obsessive passion for ornithology.

Victor was said to be conservative man, but was nevertheless curious about modern things. At home he combined classical furniture with works of art by Picasso and Giacometti. Victor and his life partner Erna remained childless – a source of great personal sorrow to them – but left a substantial legacy of 78 million Swedish crowns to a research foundation. Each year the foundation awards the prestigious Hasselblad Prize, the photographic world's equivalent of the Nobel Prize.

In 2002 Hasselblad was acquired by Hong Kong-based former general distributor House Shriro. Hasselblad was subsequently amalgamated with Danish manufacturer of digital components and scanners, Imacon, to form Hasselblad AB, which now consists of two subsidiaries; Victor Hasselblad AB in Göteborg and Hasselblad AS in Copenhagen.

Hasselblad first rocketed into world focus when the American astronauts used Hasselblads to photograph earth from space. The defining moment came in 1969 as Neil Armstrong and Buzz Aldrin finally stepped onto the surface of the moon. When pictures of the event were wired out to an eagerly-waiting globe, Hasselblad instantly became one of the most famous brands on the planet.

The Swedish Spark

Burning safely

Lighting a fire at the beginning of the 19th century required a fair bit of equipment: flint, steel and tinder for the most part. In 1827 Englishman John Walker invented the match, which he called the *friction light*. These are difficult to light so it is dubious if they could be called an invention. In any case he was on the right track.

Shortly thereafter manufacturers in Germany and France started producing phosphorus matches. The problem is that they are too volatile and start many fires as they tend to self-combust. Instead of a cosy open fire you could end up burning down the house. Another problem is that they are highly poisonous. Significant doses of yellow phosphorus can actually be lethal. The substance is used to induce abortions at great risk to the mother. Workers in match factories suffer the most, many of them becoming seriously ill. Their teeth fall out; their jaw bones decay which in severe cases lead to death. The ones who dip the sticks into the combustible coating are at greatest risk.

Two Swedes change all this. Jöns Jacob Berzelius, who is best known as the man behind the modern system of chemical notation, discovers that it is possible to use red phosphorous which is practically harmless instead of yellow. However he never quite works out how to put it into practice. This problem is solved by his protégé Gustaf Erik Pasch – a gifted guy who also develops waterproof cement for the construction of the Göta Canal – produces a new type of paper for printing notes, manufactures vinegar, raises silk worms and plays the bassoon. When the versatile Gustaf Pasch solves the problems of self-combustion and toxicity the modern safety match sees the light of day. He replaces yellow phosphorus with red which instead of being on the match head is placed on a strip on the box. Now the match cannot spontaneously combust as it must first be struck against a substance with which it reacts. Pasch is awarded a patent in 1844 and starts manufacturing matches in a factory in Stockholm. Unfortunately producing red phosphorus is expensive and the strips on the box soon ware out. Pasch's patent expires in 1852 without large-scale production ever becoming a reality. He dies, destitute ten years later.

Safety matches based on Pasch's patent eventually become a commercial success due to the efforts of the Lundström Brothers at the Jönköping match factory, *Tändsticksfabriken*. The product is soon a runaway international success and Sweden becomes synonymous with matches. Money rolls in to the business but instead of raising wages the company builds houses for its employees. This dramatically improves their standard of living and creates a loyal and dedicated workforce. By the end of the 1800s there are over 30 match factories in Sweden and in 1903 the two biggest factories amalgamate. This merger results in the formation of AB *Förenade Svenska Tändsticksfabriker* under the leadership of Ivar Kreuger, the man who comes to be known as *The Matchstick King* and who would control three-quarters of the global production of matches.

Ivar Kreuger begins his career as a civil engineer in the USA where he learns to work with reinforced concrete. Back in Sweden he starts the construction firm Kreuger & Toll who build Stockholm Stadium and City Hall designed by Ragnar Östberg. Kreuger stumbles across matches when he is asked to reorganise a match factory in Kalmar. This leads to a series of mergers and acquisitions which culminate in the formation of *Svenska Tändsticks Aktiebolaget* (STAB), a holding company for Kreuger & Toll. A remarkable journey now begins. By emitting new stock and bonds Kreuger is able to raise enough money to buy other match manufacturers as well as real estate, industrial factories and mining operations. An unmanageable frenzy of acquisitions both in Sweden and abroad is now underway. All of a sudden Kreuger is one of the richest men in the world who, on paper at least, is good for several billion crowns. He becomes an international celebrity but his success depends on his ability to continually raise new capital. He even lends money to federal governments in return for a match stick monopoly in their country. The great stock market crash

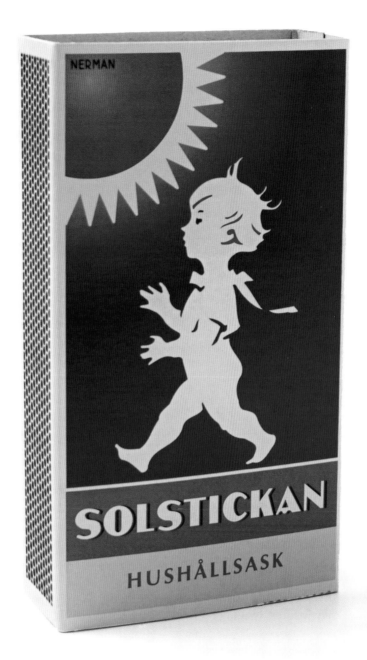

of 1929 bursts Kreuger's bubble and he finds himself in the throws of a serious cash flow crisis. Throughout the winter of 1931-32 he attempts to keep afloat by purchasing his own stock. When the Swedish Central Bank audits the company they discover that around 125 million crowns are missing – around 3.3 billion in modern terms. Hardly peanuts!

In March 1932 Kreuger is found dead in an apartment in Paris, shot through the chest in an apparent suicide. Others claim that he has been murdered. The case is a huge story in Sweden and the subject of constant discussion. His death is the final nail in the coffin of the matchstick empire and as a result thousands of Swedes are ruined. It even comes to light that Prime Minister Ekman had accepted

a financial "contribution" from Kreuger, a revelation that leads to his political downfall. The depression that follows hard on the heels of the so-called *Kreuger Crash* fosters a deep mistrust of capitalism amongst the Swedish people. The Social Democrats come to power and retain it for the next 44 years. Kreuger's death also allows the powerful Wallenberg family to tighten their grip on several of Sweden's leading companies.

The fate of The Matchstick King has titillated the Swedish imagination since 1932 and rumours and stories abound. However one thing is for sure. The crash led to a commercial and political paradigm shift in the Swedish corridors of power.

Ingenious simplicity

Packaging should save more than it costs

One of the most successful inventions ever to come out of Sweden is the Tetra Pak. However, this revolutionary product was hardly the result of a single inspired idea. In fact it took decades to develop.

Ruben Rausing, the founder of Tetra Pak, is an ingenious entrepreneur who inspires his colleagues to develop a unique product that opens the world of food production to previously unimaginable possibilities. The son of a master painter, Ruben proves to be a determined visionary who dares challenge conventional wisdom and do what others claim is impossible. The motto behind Tetra Pak's phenomenal success is quite simply *Think differently*.

The Tetra Pak story begins in the beginning of the 1920s when the young economist Rausing wins a scholarship to the USA. Here he comes in contact with the *supermarket* and realises that this concept will undoubtedly find its way to Europe. He also sees a need for new types of packaging, particularly for groceries. Packaging dry groceries is not particularly difficult but how could one make a practical, cheap and sterile container for perishables like milk? By the 30s he is on the case but during WWII people have more pressing issues to consider. However in 1944 Rausing puts his foot down and demands results. His Lab Chief has been conscripted so newly-employed assistant Erik Wallenberg takes his place. A breath of fresh air unburdened by previous failures, Erik is given carte blanche. His proposal, which is given a lukewarm reception at first, is to take a cylinder and press it into a tetrahedron. However, this ingeniously simple paper packaging goes on to become one of Sweden's greatest export successes, further cementing its reputation as a world leader in industrial design.

In 1946 engineer Harry Järund presents the prototype for all future Tetra Pak packaging machines. All that remains is to develop a suitable packaging material. Coating heavy paper with a thin layer of polythene proves to be the ticket. This makes the paper waterproof which means the container can be heat-sealed in the filling machine. In 1951 the newly-formed Tetra Pak Company presents its packaging system to the press and causes an absolute sensation; at this time people were either buying their milk directly from the farmer or in glass bottles .One year later the first Tetra Pak machine is delivered to the *Dairy Association* in Lund and the rest, as they say, is history. The classic tetrahedron may have over 50 years under its belt, but it is still one of the most popular packages in the world.

It isn't long before dairy producers around the world are clamouring for the miraculous machine. Work on a sterile packaging system is commenced and the first machines for packaging milk in one litre containers are installed. Then things really start to happen. The rectangular Tetra Brik is launched and the T/1 machine that can package fluid volumes between 200 ml and one litre. What follows is an indescribable journey that conquers the packaging world. Of course many people contribute to Tetra Pak's enormous success, however Ruben Rausing and Lab Chief Erik Wallenberg are perhaps those who deserve most of the credit.

As Tetra Pak celebrated its 50th birthday another milestone is passed. For the first time ever annual production of Tetra Pak packages exceeds 90 billion. Development of new packages and machines continues. Thanks to the extraordinary vision and persistence of Ruben Rausing, Tetra Pak goes on to become the largest manufacturer of cardboard packaging in the world. However, in spite of being a global company, Tetra Pak remains true to its southern Swedish roots. All R&D is overseen from Lund, a stone's throw from the old dairy where customers were the first in the world to take their cream home in an ingenious paper package.

The cream of the crop

And 92 different patents

Describing Gustaf de Laval is difficult, not only because his genius was so all-encompassing, but also because he was often so far ahead of his time that in some cases we are still yet to catch up to him. As a child in the mid-1800s he was unusually gifted and innovative and went on to graduate with a degree in engineering before completing a PhD.

In an era when kerosene lanterns were considered luxury items Gustaf was already dreaming of airplanes, rockets and being able to cross the Atlantic in a boat in ten hours. He even dreamed of a more just society and how industrialism can raise the standard of living for everyone. He is reported to have said "Sweden could be the world's leading industrial nation." He envisages blast furnaces and iron works along the banks of the Lule River and goes so far as to imagine northern Sweden as a new California. Environmental care also figures in his thinking even though Sweden at this time was still a predominantly agricultural society. He predicts that Great Britain's coal will run out and that the Swedes will turn to peat. In short he predicts a modern industrialised Sweden before industrialism had even taken root. Talk about being ahead of his time!

Most people associate Gustaf de Laval with the invention of the milk separator. Butter has always been used as cooking fat and up until the middle of the 19th century it was made by hand. In 1878 Gustaf patents the separator, a machine that automatically separates milk from cream. This invention results in the emergence of several large dairy operations in Sweden. But what has Gustaf seen that other inventors have missed? He realises the importance of speed in the separation process. His separator uses centrifugal force in conjunction with a series of metal cones that distributes the milk in a thin film and increase the speed of the separation process. The separator is successfully exported and in so doing revolutionises dairy farming operations around the world. Gustaf was a prolific inventor who was awarded a total of 92 patents and founded 37 companies. Reviewing his body of work is difficult as he was active in so many different fields and was often way ahead of his time. A fearless character with a brilliant mind, his ideas included everything from helicopters to high speed ships. His inventions still create employment for millions of people. For example the innovations used in his steam turbine from 1883 are still used in power stations around the world, not to mention the *de Laval nozzle* which is an essential component in rocket motors. The list of his innovations is lengthy indeed.

The private Gustaf is described as a difficult loner. It is said that he only has two interests in life; himself and his inventions. He marries for the first time at the age of 50 to Isabel who is 20 years his junior. She is reputed to be a very considerate woman who patiently listens to Gustaf while he incessantly talks of his projects. One of his few surviving personal notes reads, *Got a boy, October 18, quarter to nine.* He is buried in the Northern Cemetery in Stockholm where his tombstone bears the epitaph: *The man of high speeds.*

▲ The centrifugal milk separator was launched in 1879. Gustaf's invention quickly became a world sensation laying the foundations for a new global industry.

After more than 120 years in the dairy business DeLaval can, without fear of contradiction, claim to be market leaders in their field.

During his lifetime Gustaf de Laval collects hundreds of projects under the title *Something to think about for the future*. He spends his last few years researching into energy and peat exploitation projects at a time when environmental concerns are not an issue. He even sketches an automatic milking machine.

When Gustaf de Laval dies in 1913 his estate files for bankruptcy on account of its enormous debts. Never able to manage his finances he dies a destitute genius. His innovations however, survive.

283

THE BRIDGE

The slipway for the Öresund Bridge is in Malmö. From here it's a stone's throw from Copenhagen and the European continent is just a short press on the accelerator away.

A consortium led by *Skanska* is charged with the task of building the bridge that will connect Sweden and Denmark. Minimizing the environmental impact of the project was top priority.

After discussing the matter for over 100 years a permanent connection between Sweden and Denmark was finally opened in 2000. The connection is 15.4 km long and includes the longest cable-stayed bridge for both motor and rail traffic in the world. The bridge is supported by four pylons that at 204 m tall are the tallest constructions in Sweden. The best view of the bridge is from the *Luftkastellet* restaurant in Lernacken.

When cement works

Southern cement plant spawns global success

Skånska Cementgjuteriet (Cement plant) was founded in 1887 by Rudolf Fredrik Berg, the man known as the *King of Limhamn* – Malmö's harbour – on account of the influence he exerted over practically everything that went on in the area at the time. An astute and charismatic chemist, Berg may have been quick to realise the role concrete and cement could play in the construction industry, but he was not responsible for their invention. These materials had been used extensively in ancient building works only to disappear until their rediscovery in the 18th century. Concrete consists of cement, water and aggregate, usually sand or gravel, which means that it can withstand much greater loads than its cousin cement.

Increased pressure from burgeoning fishing and mining industries necessitated a modern harbour in Malmö and work commenced at Limhamn in 1880. The introduction of dynamite had quickly seen the local limestone quarry expand to a depth of over 100 meters. Ore could no longer be transported by barrows and a steam-driven paternoster with containers on wires was built.

The railway between the limestone quarry and the harbour started operating in 1884 after long and heated discussions as to whether horses or steam engines were to be used. The fear of a locomotive pulling 35 fully loaded carriages through a densely populated residential area was great, so in the interests of public safety a person waving a green flag always ran ahead of the train. The 4 km long stretch of track was a runaway success. In addition to freight and the daily trips of the fish hawkers and their barrows, the number of recreational trips to summer houses and sea baths also increased. Berg even had his finger in this pie, offering trips combining train and horse drawn carriages for "tourists" from central Malmö. The railway also meant that people could now commute between Limhamn and Malmö and the run became highly lucrative. Rudolf certainly had an eye for a good deal.

However, *Skånska* were not content only with producing cement and soon branched out into the construction business where they played a significant role in creating Sweden's infrastructure, including power stations, bridges and even prestigious buildings such as the Royal Opera House and government offices and residences.

Rudolf F Berg founded countless companies and organisations. As a local politician in Malmö he initiated the establishment of the free port and steam boat connections between Malmö and Copenhagen. In many ways he was way ahead of his time. He was not afraid to try new ideas and possessed exceptional organisational skills and business acumen. Personable and approachable, he strove to create a harmonious and contented workforce founding savings banks, life and accident insurance and free medical care. His vision was of a more trusting, humanitarian society founded on the principles of cooperation, justice and freedom.

A mere ten years after starting operations, the company received an order from the British telephone company for one 100 km of hollow concrete blocks to house telephone cables. It would be interesting to know how the Brits came into contact with the *Skånska* cement plant in southern Sweden.

The company became a serious player on the international market in the 1950s. This was largely due to their technical know-how and ability to adapt to local markets, something that has continued to serve them wherever they establish operations, be it the Middle East or Africa. *Skanska* is often thought of as a local company which may partly explain their international success.

In 1984 the company dropped the Swedish letter *å* and became *Skanska*. The Swedish alphabet includes three extra vowels with hovering dots and rings, and when a company drops them it is clear indication that they have substantial international ambitions.

Not for the rich, but for the smart

DIY Swedish style

IKEA is unique. A group of companies worth four times as much as the combined fortune of Sweden's pre-eminent financial dynasty, the Wallenbergs, and created in the space of just one generation. The work of a determined boy – one who set the bar high. One who said "I want to be as rich as Ivar Kreuger" – the Swedish magnate who was one of the most powerful businessmen in Europe in the interwar period. IKEA's founder, Ingvar Kamprad, is said to be a frugal workaholic with a big heart and a firm belief in walking the talk. His concept is that IKEA's prices will not be beaten anywhere.

Just about every Swede knows at least one Kamprad story, most of which revolve around his spartan lifestyle or engagement as a business leader and environmentalist. Tales of the richest man in the world flying economy class and riding the underground with a battle scarred brief case and in well-worn clothes abound. One such story has Kamprad declaring IKEA to be the realm of a more intelligent breed of shopper – something that led to the advertising slogan "Not for the rich – but for the smart". These tales also describe a man who rises at the crack of dawn and starts working long before ordinary mortals have wiped the sleep from their eyes. One woman tells of a dawn business meeting at IKEA. As she approaches the building she spies a lone figure in the dark crouching down in the flower beds near the entrance. It turns out to be none other than Kamprad himself doing a bit of weeding!

The secret behind IKEA's phenomenal success may well be Ingvar's ability to unite people in a common purpose. The year is 1943 when 17-year-old Ingvar starts a mail order business. The company is christened IKEA, an acronym formed from his name, the farm *Elmtaryd* where he grew up and the district of *Agunnaryd* in which it is situated. The first product catalogue is distributed to Swedish homes in 1951. The characteristic idea of naming each product comes into being because Ingvar has difficulty remembering product codes. Two years later he buys a furniture workshop in Älmhult and converts it into a furniture showroom. IKEA's pricing policy enrages the Swedish furniture industry, which is hardly surprising given that they take a resounding beating from the upstart. Their suppliers boycott them, but IKEA simply segue into a new strategy based on imports, large production series and short warehousing periods. Large pieces of furniture require a lot of storage space so Ingvar decides to sell them in kit form introducing the now famous *flat pack* in 1955. Three years later IKEA open their first retail store in Älmhult in Ingvar's home county of Småland.

The concept of letting customers transport their own goods turns out to be a stroke of genius. And if they don't happen to own a set of roof racks IKEA is naturally more than happy to sell them a pair at a very reasonable price. As they put it, "We're not out to make money by selling roof racks, but from all the packages that will be loaded onto them." In addition the do-it-yourself assembly concept makes the ubiquitous Allen wrench synony-

The concept of customers assembling their own furniture is so strongly associated with IKEA that the humble Allen wrench has practically become a part of the IKEA identity. IKEA furniture is so popular that you will find it in approximately every second Swedish home, where countless people have scratched their heads and cursed while putting together their new household item. Despite the headaches it cannot be denied that success brings a well-deserved feeling of achievement.

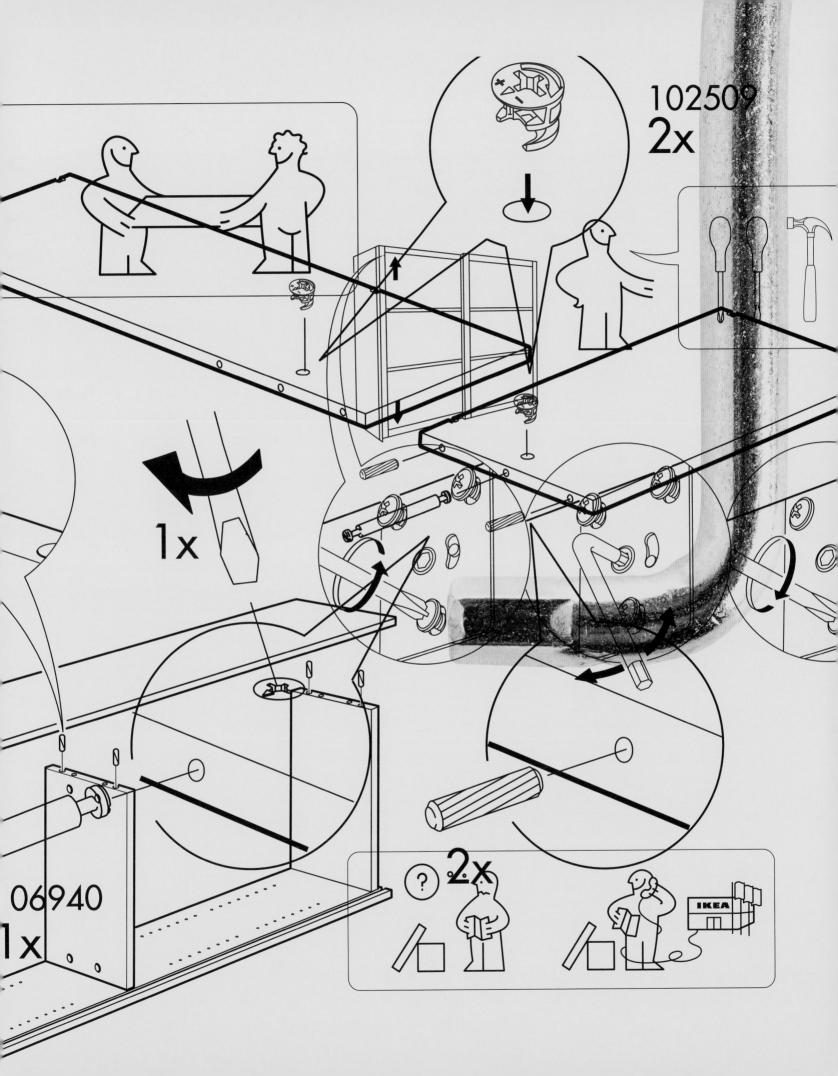

102509
2x

1x

06940
1x

2x

IKEA

mous with IKEA, in effect incorporating it into the brand identity.

At 191 million published copies in 27 languages, IKEA's annual product catalogue is the most widely distributed free of charge publication in the world and is third on the *Most Read Books* list after the Bible and the Koran. Regardless of your opinion of IKEA one cannot help but be impressed by the way little Älmhult turned the world of home products on its ear. Naturally the catalogue has played an important role in the success of the company – after all, mail order was where it all started. Many Swedish households plaster the message *No unsolicited mail* on their letter boxes, often with an accompanying sub-text: IKEA *catalogue welcome*. Such is its status.

Ingvar Kamprad is probably the most lauded Swedish entrepreneur of the 20th century. An icon for many Swedes, he personifies the American Dream although this time in Swedish garb. His story is one that shows that with nothing more than two empty hands, hand work and a nose for business anything can be achieved. As it happens money and power have never been the driving forces for Ingvar Kamprad. Rather he has been quoted as saying "Happiness is not reaching your goal. Happiness is being on your way." He still regards himself as a small business owner even if he happens to be one of the richest men on the planet.

The birth of Christ is the event commonly used to signify the start of the current epoch, however in Norrbotten County in north-east Sweden it's the arrival of IKEA that counts. This is the remarkable story of how local councilman Sven Erik Bucht buttonholes Ingvar Kamprad and charms him into believing that the sparsely-populated county is practically the centre of the civilised world and that IKEA would be crazy not to open a store here. This fateful meeting leads to Ingvar defying his own Board of Directors to initiate a project christened *Ingvar's own*. Ingvar steamrolls sceptical bean counters with his own figures and sales projections, claiming that the proposed site in Haparanda on the Swedish/Finnish border is within an hour and a half's journey for 500 thousand people. Expand the customer catchment area slightly and suddenly the purchasing power of a million consumers in northern Sweden, Finland, Norway and Russia is within reach. And in these parts a drive of a 90 minute journey is peanuts.

Naturally Ingvar is on site for the grand opening of the Haparanda store in 2006. All of a sudden the counties of Norrbotten and Västerbotten which had been in decline become high growth areas. Forestry, mining and smelting operations change up a gear and the population drain of the last few decades is stemmed. In fact, for the first time in longer than anyone cares to remember the population of the region actually increases. A turnaround of this nature is remarkable. But then again, so is IKEA.

Rocking-chair *Gullholmen*,
Maroa Vinka

Desk *Jonas*

Sofa *Klippan*

Watering can *Vållö*
Monica Mulder

Stool *Benjamin*, Lisa Norinder

Drawer unit *Erik*

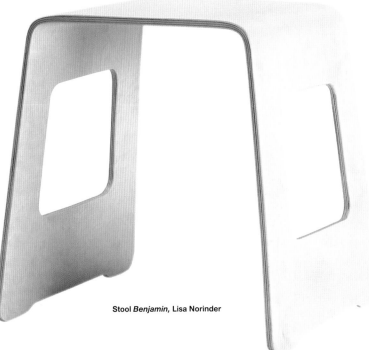

The Hennes & Mauritz story

From meat, cheese and pens to clothes

H&M, one of Europe's leading clothing retailers, has a simple business concept: youthful clothes at reasonable prices.

Founder *Erling Persson* grows up in a family that owns a modest butcher's shop run by Mum, Dad and three employees. Erling is no fan of school and has no intention of following in his parents' footsteps even though they expect him to. At the age of 21 he packs his suitcase and moves to Stockholm where he founds a company that sells cheese. He makes cash purchases from wholesalers and then cycles around to restaurants where he sells the cheese for cash with which he buys more cheese. Cycling around Stockholm on a bike laden with cheese is a heavy job which teaches the future founder of H&M the importance of financing and transport. After a while he starts selling knives to restaurants. Soon the advent star *Glimmering crystal*, pens and penholders also find their way into his product range.

In 1943 Erling becomes Swedish distributor for Mont Blanc pens and founds *Pennspecialisten* (The Pen Specialist) with partner Björn Wennberg. Björn loves books and opens a bookshop but Erling thinks that the turnover rate for books is way too low and wants to move on to bigger things. He travels to the USA where, somewhere between New York and the Rockies, he comes up with the idea of selling women's clothing in high volumes at low prices. He has long pondered the value of timing and location. In 1947 he returns to his hometown of Västerås and opens a boutique downtown. He christens the store *Hennes* – Swedish for *Hers*. Shops in Uppsala, Jönköping and Stockholm soon follow – all situated in the best downtown locations.

But when does *Mauritz* come into the picture? When the company acquires new premises in Stockholm they also happen to acquire a collection of leftover sports clothes owned by *Mauritz*. All of a sudden the chain of women's boutiques is transformed into his and hers clothing stores with the name *Hennes & Mauritz*.

The secret behind H&M's success is really no secret. One factor is a clear business concept. According to Erling Persson a good idea is worth more than money. The notion that good design need not cost a fortune has been a fundamental company value since its inception in 1947.

A lot has happened since butcher's son Erling Persson founded H&M. The retailing giant is so well-established in Sweden that as far back as 20 years ago it was worked out that every Swede owned at least four H&M items. You could say that Erling Persson dressed the *People's home* as much as Per Albin Hansson built it or Ingvar Kamprad furnished it. *Hennes & Mauritz* is one of the most successful Swedish companies of the post-war era. Their policy today is much the same as it always has been; high-quality, fashionable clothes at affordable prices. There is nothing revolutionary behind their success, but rather the admirable qualities of common sense and a sprit of enterprise.

◄ **H&M shop in Shanghai**
The original boutique in Västerås has since spawned over 1 400 other stores around the world. H&M is currently eyeing up a particularly interesting market in Asia. Other established high-end brands have planted their flags in China and they are soon to be joined by a Swedish fashion giant. Look out! And no one in their right mind believes that H&M's development is about to wane. Their goal has always been continued expansion which usually results in about 80 new shops per year – equivalent to a growth rate of 10–15 percent.

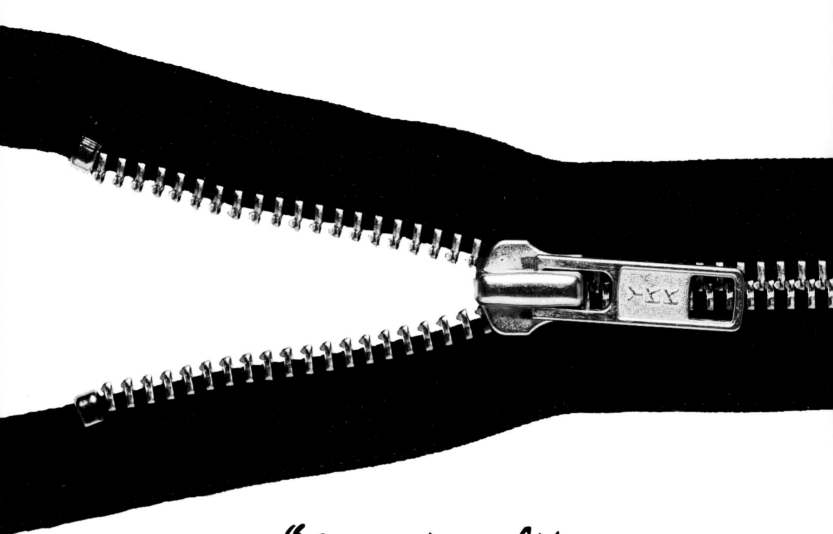

"Opening like
a smile,
closing like a line
drawn on water"

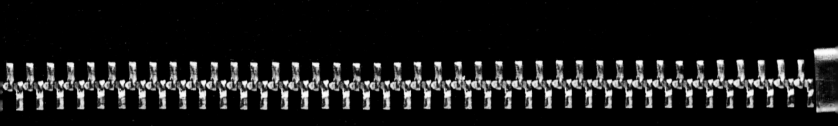

The zipper has been around for a long time; however the earliest types were clumsy and unreliable. Gideon Sundbäck constructed a device in 1900 that consisted of punched teeth attached to a strip of cloth that was sown into clothing. In 1913 he was granted a patent in the USA where he started a factory and marketed his product with the remarkable slogan: "Opening like a smile, closing like a line drawn on water".

However, despite its ingenious construction and memorable slogan, initial sales of his *separable opener* were poor. It first began to catch on during WWI when it reached the rest of the world as part of the American soldiers' uniforms. The appearance of what became known as the *zipper* has remained unchanged for over a 100 years, even if these days plastic teeth are often used instead of metal.

A Swedish propeller that changed the world

And a tragic love story

John Ericsson was born in Värmland in western Sweden in 1803. A fiery, bold lad, he is quick of mind and deed. Fiercely independent, at times he has trouble bending to the will of others, but his heart is definitely in the right place. John is an active little tyke, perhaps even hyperactive, although it's difficult to say for sure 200 years later. His family moves to Västergötland where his father works on the Göta Canal project. John and his brother Nils receive a technical education at home and both display a particular aptitude for things mechanical. With their father's assistance they too start working on the canal. Suddenly John, at the ripe old age of 13, is in charge of over 600 people and answers directly to project leader Baltzar von Platen.

It doesn't take long for John to outgrow Sweden. After all, he is a technical genius intent on conquering the world. Brother Nils remains in Sweden and builds railways while John, now 23, moves to England. Once in London, he enters an engineering competition where contestants are required to build a steam engine weighing at least six tonnes that can haul three times its own weight and travel at a speed of at least 16 km/h. It takes John six weeks to construct *Novelty*, which, with a top speed of 50 km/h, is three times faster than any of his competitor's machines. On the third day of the competition one of *Novelty*'s boilers bursts and he loses the competition. Construction of the engine has cost a small fortune and he now has debts that he cannot pay. He spends a year in Debtor's prison where he continues to sketch his innovations; a wheel-driven fire pump, a surface condenser, a depth sounder and, above all, a unique propeller. It appears that the prison environment fosters technical innovation.

Once he is released he sets about constructing various devices including propellers and steam engines. He receives financial support from USA's Consul General Francis B. Ogden, and thanks to the American, is able to build a propeller-driven boat that he displays on the Thames in 1837. Ericsson's ship is the first of its kind to be driven by a steam engine and propeller – a unique propeller that imitates the swimming action of water fowl, and which propels the boat up the river at an amazing ten knots. However, despite this auspicious maiden voyage the English are not interested in Ericsson's innovation. This time it is England that John has outgrown and he turns his attention westwards to America – the land of opportunity.

Francis B Ogden puts John in contact with American Naval Officer Robert F. Stockton who is in the market for a new propeller-driven steam ship. John's ship proves its seaworthiness in 1839 when it crosses the Atlantic, and later that same year the USA decides to commission three propeller-driven frigates based on his design. The first, christened *Princeton*, is launched in 1843 with a highly delighted Robert F. Stockton at the helm. Stockton takes the credit for John's innovation and, rumour has it, blocked the Navy from paying John's 15 000 dollar fee. It doesn't take long however for John to receive new orders and in the following few years he builds over 50 propeller-driven ships. The English may not have understood his invention but Ericsson certainly had the last laugh.

Around this time John launches his *hot air engine*. He began working on this idea in Sweden and now it begins paying dividends providing him for the first time in his life with a guaranteed income. The device, a so-called *caloric engine*, remains a lifelong project which he hopes will eventually replace the steam engine.

The outbreak of the American Civil War sees the Confederate Navy's ironclad *Merrimack* lay waste to all resistance. The Union forces desperately seek a vessel that can stand up to the strange ship from the south, and a series of coincidences leads to John Ericsson presenting models of his ship the *Monitor*. He is given the task of building a ship but has only 100 days to deliver. He succeeds and the *Monitor* finally meets the southern ironclad on 9th March 1862 at Hampton Roads. The *Monitor*'s task is to prevent its opponent from entering the river that leads to Washington, and

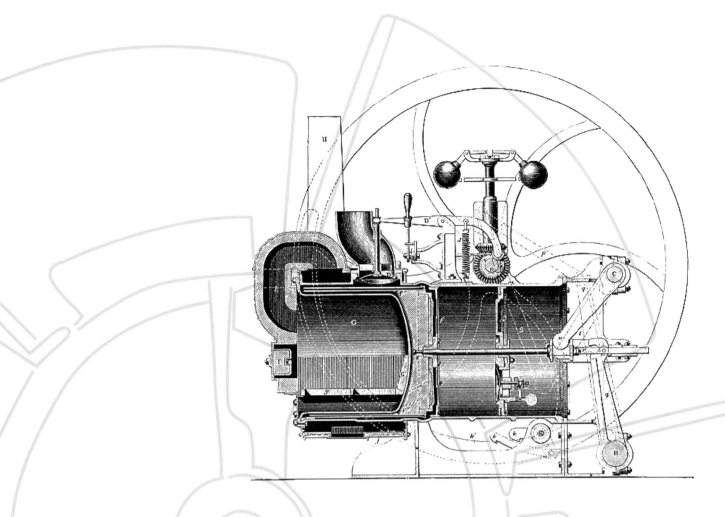

John Ericsson's lifelong quest was to construct a hot air engine, often called a caloric engine, that he envisaged would replace the steam engine.

manages to inflict major damage to the Confederate ship despite being a quarter of the size. The *Monitor* is a revolutionary naval vessel – the area above the water line is low, it is heavily armoured, it has rotating gun turrets and the machinery and crew are safely housed below the waterline. John is hailed as a war hero and quickly receives new orders for new monitors. Swedish John Ericsson and his ingenious ship play a decisive roll in the American Civil War. His fame spreads throughout the US and even reaches Europe.

John Ericsson is usually way ahead of his time and as a result he often has to fight to win support for his ideas. Few appreciate his genius, and developing his innovations proves difficult as people simply regard them as too fantastic. But he is persistent and usually succeeds, even if it means

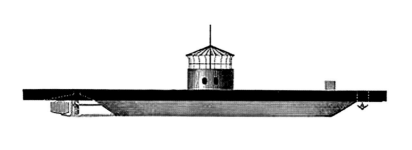

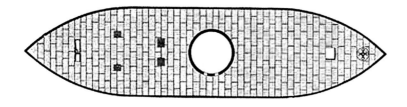

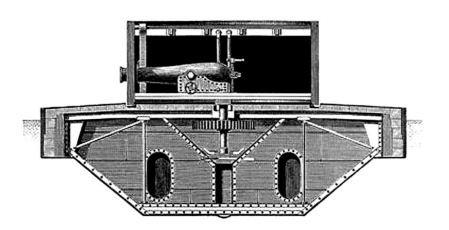

spending time behind bars. One vision he doesn't live to see realised is the harnessing of solar energy – something that he truly believes is possible. However, he does succeed in constructing a solar powered water pump that sells well in the US. John Ericsson is a genius and his innovations in the fields of solar energy and thermodynamics are still relevant 100 years after his death. Despite his success John lives frugally. He lives most of his life in a small, dark apartment in one of New York's roughest neighbourhoods, and any money he receives is immediately ploughed into new inventions. A man with manic tendencies, he spends all his waking hours working, he never socialises unless it is absolutely necessary to market an innovation or secure financing for a new project, and he never returns to Sweden – which is strange given that his ships regularly cross the Atlantic. Nor does he ever build a family, although oddly enough,

it turns out that he has a son in Sweden! Hjalmar is all of 52 when he first meets his father in America.

But how is it possible that he has a son? Before leaving Sweden John has a relationship with a girl by the name of Carolina Liljesköld who gives birth to a son in 1824. Unfortunately Carolina's father believes that a common Ericsson is beneath his daughter and does everything in his power to end the affair. All letters between John and Carolina are intercepted by her father and as a result John never gets to know that he has fathered a son. Both of them wonder why their letters aren't being answered but never hear a word from each other. (Feel free to reach for a tissue now). When John leaves for England he is unaware that Carolina is pregnant. But the misery doesn't end there. In a final tragic twist, Carolina is sent away to give birth and is forced to give up her child.

John Ericsson dies at the age of 85 in 1889 while working on another invention. His final wish is to be buried in
Swedish soil. The USS Baltimore ships his body to Stockholm from whence it is transported by train to Värmland.
All along the route people gather by the railway tracks to
honour the local boy who is finally returning home. John is
buried in Filipstad and statues are erected in his honour in
Stockholm, Göteborg and New York. He may have become
an American citizen, but to the people of Sweden John
Ericsson remains a Swede – a true patriot working tirelessly
on behalf of his homeland. "America is just where I work"
he is reputed to have said, for all the while his heart was in
Sweden. Swedish people always speak of him with pride
– and who wouldn't be proud of such a genius! The whole
world knows who John Ericsson was and the whole world
knows that he was Swedish!

One of John's greatest achievements was his warship the
Monitor. More of a submarine
than a battleship, most of the
vessel was hidden below the
waterline. The *Monitor* included
40 innovations that Ericsson
could have patented. However
he generously gave them to the
USA. The boat had its detractors
and was variously described as
a tin can on a shingle, a cheese
cover on a raft and an iron
coffin. The *Monitor* was 52.4 m
long, 12.5 m wide, weighed
776 tonnes and was fitted with
two guns in the rotating turret.
The crew was made up of 59
volunteers.
During the American Civil War
the small monitors defeated the
much larger confederate ship
the *CSS Virginia* – an ironclad
that ironically had been built
from the salvaged remains of
the scuttled Union ship *USS
Merrimack*.

Swedish icons

INGMAR BERGMAN

Ingmar Bergman is unquestionably one of the greatest film and theatre directors of the 20th century. His strength lay in his ability to wrest powerful emotional performances from his actors. On the whole Swedes haven't realised how highly the old recluse is regarded by the rest of the world.

Bergman's father was a Lutheran minister. Bergman's relationship with his country was complex and not unlike all the hopeless marriages portrayed in his films. He married five times and fathered eight children.

Ingmar's debut as director was *Crisis* from1946. His first films went largely unnoticed but his breakthrough came in 1953 with the film *Sommaren med Monika*, the story of two young lovers that run away to the Stockholm Archipelago. The film's nudity certainly contributed to its success although it was actually heavily censured in Sweden. In the USA however the film's promotion centred mainly on the nudity which is reflected in the local title *Monika, The story of a bad girl*. When the film premiered in LA, the cinema manager was arrested and the film confiscated by the Vice Squad as alleged pornography. Better publicity would be hard to come by ... Ingmar was unable to make films in the year preceding *Monika* due to a producers' lock out in protest over a proposed entertainment tax. To support himself he made commercials and filmed a total of nine for an anti-bacterial miracle soap. One of the world's leading directors was producing "soaps"!

The late 1950s and early 60s are generally considered his greatest period with films such as *The Seventh Seal*, *Wild Strawberries* and *Persona*. The quality of his films fluctuated during the 70s although *Cries and Whispers* is highly regarded. In 1983 he directed *Fanny and Alexander* which was a huge success.

The films *Through a glass darkly*, the *Silence* and *Persona* are often known as the *Faith Trilogy* – a reference to the silence of God. Many pundits consider these films to be Bergman's best. Whether or not the public at large agrees with them is another matter, although one thing is for sure: everyone has an opinion about Bergman. His career as a theatre director is unsurpassed with over 170 plays under his belt.

Ingmar Bergman lived on the island of Fårö in northern Gotland – a landscape that has been immortalised in a number of films. Apparently he was partial to chamomile tea, biscuits and watching TV. Like the other "great one", Greta Garbo, he was seldom seen in public, although he always spoke openly about his health problems and personal demons. The question "Who was Bergman?" is impossible to answer. Perhaps he said it best himself. "He is many people." Bergman died in summer 2007.

INGRID BERGMAN

Ingrid Bergman is one of the most famous of all Swedish actresses being one of the few, alongside Greta Garbo, that has succeeded in becoming a major Hollywood star.

Sometime at the beginning of the 20th century a young German woman visits Sweden where she meets Justus Bergman, a charming but impoverished landscape artist. They have a daughter whom they name Ingrid. Justus opens a photographic studio and celebrates his daughter's first two birthdays with photographs of mother and daughter together. There is however only one photo from Ingrid's third birthday – that of her placing flowers on her mother's grave.

Ingrid's acting career starts with lessons at the Royal Dramatic Theatre of Sweden where she is given a bit part in the film *Munkbrogreven* (English title: *The Count of the Old Monk's Bridge*). After a dozen or so films in Sweden, she establishes contact with Hollywood producer David O. Selznick. Her first film on the other side of the Atlantic is *Intermezzo*. Her natural beauty and freshness is quickly embraced by movie-goers, particularly after her heart wrenching performance as Maria in *For whom the bell Tolls*.

One of her most famous performances is given in *Casablanca* opposite the legendary Humphrey Bogart. Her line "Play it again, Sam. For old time's sake" goes down in history as one the most famous and misquoted lines of all time. The fact is, she never actually says what everyone quotes her as saying.

In 1950 Ingrid meets Italian director Roberto Rossellini. Sparks fly and they become lovers. At the same time she is given a roll in his film *Stromboli*. Their relationship creates a media circus and she is punished for the scandal with fewer rolls. She does however receive rave reviews for her roll in *Anastasia* in 1956, and 20 years later she is given a roll in Ingmar Bergman's *Höstsonata* (English title: *Autumn Sonata*) reclaiming her place in the constellation of Hollywood supernova with a performance that many film critics regard as her best. Ingrid Bergman left a unique legacy of cinematic work spanning over 50 years of acting. Her star will always shine over the world of film.

GRETA GARBO

Dustbin man's daughter Greta Garbo grew up in a little apartment on the island of Söder in southern Stockholm. Her father dies when she is 14 and to support herself she starts working as a shop assistant in the PUB department store where she also works as a model. Director Erik A. Petschler spies her in an advertisement for hats and offers her a roll in the film *Peter the Tramp*.

In the beginning of the 1920s, Greta studies at the Royal Dramatic Theatre's drama school where she meets film director and teacher Mauritz Stiller. He gives her a part in the film *The Atonement of Gösta Berling* and christens her Greta Garbo. When he heads off to Hollywood with a Metro-Goldwyn-Mayer contract in his hand, he takes his beautiful student with him. However, the more famous Greta becomes the worse their friendship fares.

Greta's voice is heard for the first time in the film *Anna Christie* which is promoted with the tagline "Garbo speaks!" The film is a runaway success. Every inch the movie star, Garbo is famous for threatening to return to Sweden when things do not go her way – an effective tactic that invariably results in her being appeased. She insists on closed sets where even the other actors and studio executives are barred from seeing her work. Greta is a dyed in the wool diva.

In 1932 she plays the seductive WWI spy *Mata Hari*. Her revealing clothing raises the ire of film critics and leads to a contract dispute with MGM. After two years of negotiations they finally agree on a new contract that gives Greta almost total control over her films. She replaces leading man Laurence Olivier with John Gilbert in *Queen Christina* and insists on being cast both as *Anna Karenina* in the Tolstoy classic and as Camille in the film of the same name where she gives arguably the greatest performance of her career.

The comedy *Ninotchka* is promoted with the tagline "Garbo laughs".

Greta Garbo is infamously reclusive and is known as "The Divine Mystery". She never gives interviews, sign autographs or attends premieres.

When the film *Two-Faced Woman* is panned by critics she walks away from it all, at the ripe old age of 37. She never appears in another film. She withdraws into a cocoon and lives a reclusive life in New York. Today when Swedes say that they are "doing a Garbo" they mean they are withdrawing.

Greta Garbo's ashes are interred in Skogskyrkogården (the Woodland Cemetery) in southern Stockholm.

SELMA
LAGERLÖF

PHILOSOPHIAE
DOCTOR

GOODWIN
1917-20

SELMA LAGERLÖF

In 1909 Selma Lagerlöf becomes the first woman ever to receive the Nobel Prize in Literature. Born in Mårbacka in Värmland County in western Sweden, she is born with a deformed hip joint. Described as more serious and quieter than other children, this is probably due to the fact that she is in constant pain. Like most children at this time, Selma is educated at home as the national school system has yet to be fully developed. A bright child, she reads her first novel at the age of seven and decides to become an author. She reads the Bible at the age of ten and writes a lengthy poem two years later.

Literature studies lead her to the conclusion that the characters she has heard about in her native Värmland are just as interesting as the people her literary predecessors Bellman and Runeberg wrote about. She feels compelled to write a story about Värmland and its people but it takes many years to complete. *Gösta Berlings Saga* is finally published in 1890. A tale of life in Värmland in the late 1800s it becomes a Swedish classic. It defies contemporary literary trends by eschewing Realism and receives mixed reviews from critics.

Her most famous work is *The Wonderful Journey of Nils Holgersson* which is originally intended as a geography book using the device of a boy flying around Sweden on the back of a goose.

Selma Lagerlöf is the first woman ever to be inducted into the Swedish Academy: When Hjalmar Gullberg succeeds her he says, "She is the queen of our literature. The most famous Swedish woman since Saint Bridget".

In 1992 Selma Lagerlöf became the first woman to be depicted on a Swedish bank note. Not only does the twenty crown note bear her likeness it also includes an excerpt from *The Story of Gosta Berling*. The back of the note shows *Nils Holgersson* flying on the back of his goose.

AUGUST STRINDBERG

Not only is August Strindberg one of Sweden's most prolific writers who totally dominates the Swedish literary scene for four decades, he also becomes a giant on the world literary scene. As a young man he meets Siri von Essen who happens to be married. But this is no hinder to August. He simply tells her he is sterile, impregnates and marries her. What a guy!

Strindberg's professional breakthrough occurs in 1879 when his novel *The Red Room* is published and his play *Master Olof* is set up. The following year he produces the historical work *The Swedish People at Work and Play* and the novel *The New Country*, both criticizing practically all the institutions of contemporary society. As a result he becomes a controversial figure – so controversial in fact that he leaves Sweden and settles in Paris. Here he writes and publishes autobiographical novels such as *Married*, *Son of a Servant* and *A Madman's Defense*; plays such as *The Father* and *Miss Julie* and socially critical novels such as *Utopia in Reality*. Strindberg doesn't hesitate to attack the political and literary establishment, who on the other hand, never take long to counterattack. In 1884 Strindberg is formally charged with "blasphemy against the holy sacrament" on account of his work *Married*. Strindberg receives widespread support in his fight for freedom of speech and is eventually acquitted.

Some of his other works earn him a reputation as a misogynist. His marriage to Siri becomes increasingly strained – something that is reflected in the way he portrays women in his novels.

Strindberg often spends his summers on the island of Kymmendö in the Stockholm archipelago and it is here that he writes *The Natives of Hemsö*, *The Life of an Island Lad* and *By the Open Sea*. This magnificent landscape inspires him to paint powerful impressionist canvases that clearly reflect the tortured state of his soul. Whenever these painting come on the market they are guaranteed to fetch seven figure sums. Less well known is Strindberg's interest in alchemy, an art that remained popular in Swedish occult circles well into the 19th century. On one occasion Strindberg succeeds in making iron pyrite – "fool's gold" – and believes it to be the real thing.

August and Siri divorce and Strindberg moves to Berlin. Strindberg enters a paranoid psychotic phase which is depicted in *Inferno*, *Legends* and *The Road to Damascus*. By now he is a renowned author but this doesn't stop him from revolting against all and sundry. Once back in Sweden he writes *Black Banners* in which he picks a fight with the Swedish cultural community and manages to alienate his few remaining supporters.

He has however become an icon for the working class struggle. In his last works *A Blue Book* and *The Great Highway* he attacks the scientific establishment and sides with religion. He dies at the age of 63. His final words are "Everything personal has now been obliterated" upon which he places a bible on his chest and expires.

"Travel is a laxative that purges me of Sweden and Swedish stupidity" is just one of the 33 provocative Strindberg quotations paved into the street of Drottinggatan in downtown Stockholm.

ASTRID LINDGREN

In 1944 Astrid Lindgren wins second prize in a Girls' story competition with *Britt Marie lättar sitt hjärta* (Britt Marie gets something off her chest). The following year she wins with *Pippi Longstocking*. She had previously sent a copy of *Pippi* to major publishing house *Bonniers* who turned her down – a monumental blunder that is still talked about in Swedish publishing circles 60 years after the fact. Astrid Lindgren's books have been translated into 76 languages and sales outside of Sweden have exceeded 80 million copies.

Astrid is famous for her children's books – primarily *Pippi Longstocking*, *Karlsson on-the-Roof* and *Emil of Maple Hills*. Her primary source of inspiration is her own childhood in Vimmerby, Småland. Her great strengths as an author are her ability to write from a child's perspective and her sense of mischief. She remained a little girl until her final breath at the age of 94. She wrote over 30 children's books that formed the basis for 50 films.

It is only natural that such a prominent author is both praised and attacked – the more so in Astrid's case as her works have always been interpreted politically as much as emotionally and morally. As she said herself: *Death and love are the greatest things man experiences – these interest all age groups. One shouldn't scare children to the point of anxiety, but just like adults they need to be shaken up by art.*

In 1976 the tabloid *Expressen* publishes Astrid's satirical allegory *Pomperipossa in the World of Money* – a story that unleashes a heated political debate on the subject of taxation. Swedes are the most highly taxed people on the planet and usually suffer in silence. Astrid however has discovered that she is actually being taxed at the rate of 102 percent and decides to strike a blow for common sense. Treasurer Gunnar Sträng – a name which interestingly means *strict* in English – ridicules her in parliament saying *She may be good at writing stories but she can't count.* He is later forced to eat humble pie when it comes to light that Astrid has received her figures from none other than the Swedish Tax Agency. The Social Democrat government is ousted at the next election – their first loss in 40 years.

Astrid is a champion of the underdog and fights her whole life for the rights of children and animals. She writes a book called *My cow wants to have fun* and pursues a determined animal rights campaign in the media. In the end the Prime Minister passes animal rights legislation although Astrid is not impressed by its scope. Famous for her turn of phrase she describes it as "farty".

A German publishing house presents her with a peace prize after which she writes a speech entitled *Never Violence* comparing violence at home with violence in the world. This causes an outcry in Germany. She claims that those presenting the prize should have known that she would always champion children. The speech has a great impact and thousands of copies are printed.

In 1996 the Russian Academy of Science names an asteroid after her, which causes her to exclaim "From now on you may call me Asteroid Lindgren."

BIRGIT NILSSON

Blessed with rare tone and power *La Nilsson* was one of, if not *the* greatest sopranos of the 20th century and a frequent guest on the leading opera stages of the world.

A farmer's daughter from Skåne County in southern Sweden, she realises early on that music flows in her veins. She has perfect pitch and a big voice and longs to be a singer. Her father, however, will hear nothing of it. He had always wanted a son to take over the farm and had even promised the midwife 50 Swedish crowns if his wish came true. Unfortunately for him his only child is a girl, albeit one with an angel's voice. Luckily there is someone in her life who encourages her singing: a sympathetic farmhand named Otto. Eventually she is admitted to the Conservatory of Music in Stockholm, but even here she is actively discouraged. "My dear Birgit. Singing is not for peasants" as one teacher kindly put it.

But Fate has other things in mind. She makes her debut in the Stockholm Opera Company in 1946 and breaks through the following year as Verdi's Lady MacBeth. Birgit Nilsson becomes Sweden's most famous opera singer, adored around the world, above all for her performances in Wagner's *Tristan and Isolde*, *Lohengrin* and *The Ring* suite.

Her Electra is generally regarded as the finest of the 20th century. Her breakthrough at the Metropolitan Opera in New York comes in the roll of Isolde – a part she would go on to play 209 times. She holds the world record in encores.

Birgit Nilsson conquers the great opera stages of the world. Her career spans a remarkable 35 years, which is highly unusual for an opera singer. Famous for her rapier wit she is loved in Sweden for her humility and down to earth nature – the country bumpkin that outshone most other stars. She is the only other singer ever to achieve the status of Maria Callas, however unlike *La Divina*, *La Nilsson* is mainly remembered for being an exceptional dramatic soprano and vocal force of nature.

Birgit Nilsson dies at home in Skåne in 2005. Her family succeeds in keeping her death out of the media for a full two weeks. When the news finally leaks out the headlines practically write themselves. "A great voice is silenced."

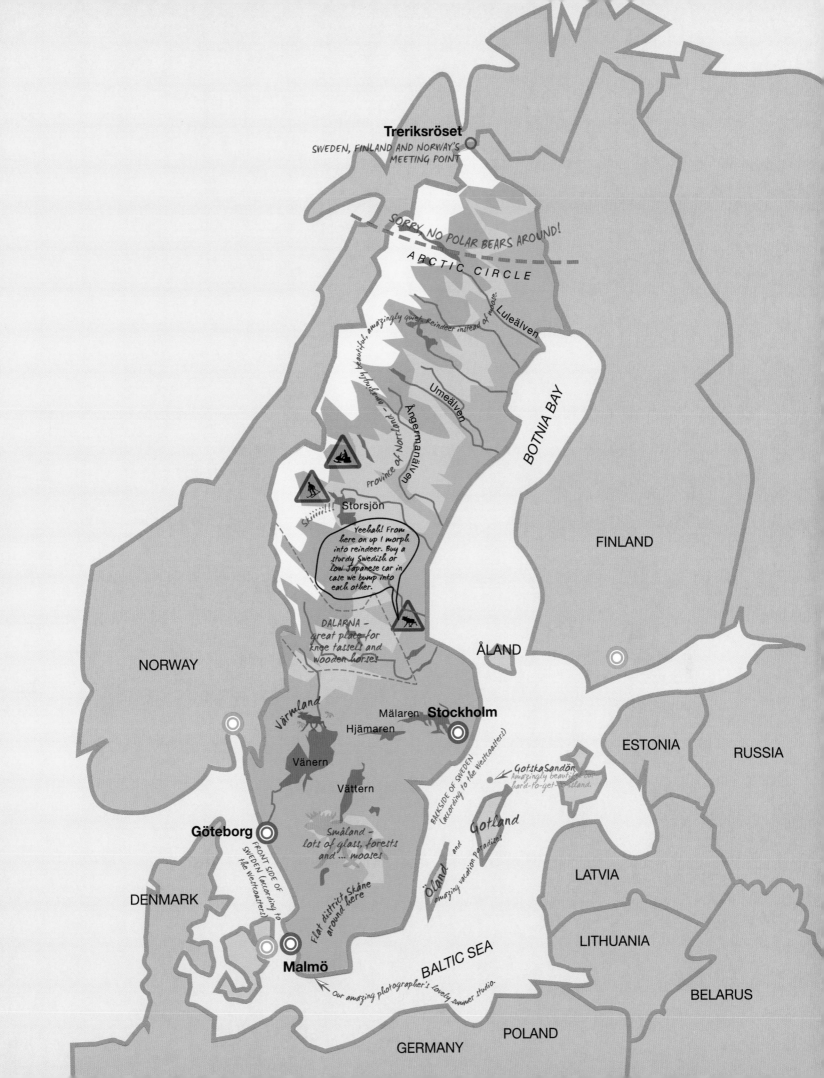

Photo Credits

What ever happened to the Swedish Viking?
p 7 Hjälm från Vendel **©Christer Åhlin** Statens historiska museum, Historiska museet
p 9 Svärd **©Christer Åhlin** Statens historiska museum, Historiska museet

Stockholm & The Stockholm Archipelago
p 10 Slussen **Lena Koller**
p 12 Kulturhuset **Bruno Ehrs** Scanpix
p 13 Suddiga profiler **Lena Koller**
p 15 Skärgårdsbåt **Lena Koller**
p 16 Sandhamn **Lena Koller**
p 17 Björnö, Ingarö **Lena Koller**
p 19 Segelbåt **Oskar Kihlborg**

The Monarchy
p 20 Kungafamiljen **Charles Hammarsten** IBL Bildbyrå
p 21 Svenska flaggan **Lena Koller**
p 22 Drottningholms slott **Lena Koller**
p 22 Riksregalierna **Alexis Daflos** ©Kungliga Husgerådskammaren
p 23 Högvakten **Lena Koller**

The balance of power
p 25 Rosenbad Lena Koller

Göteborg
p 26 Götaplatsen **Kjell Holmner** Image Bank Sweden
p 27 Göteborgsoperan **Richard Ryan** Image Bank Sweden
p 28 Skadjursplatå **Lena Koller**
p 29 Götheborg **©Dick Gillberg**
p 30 Kallbadhuset i Lysekil **Lena Koller**
p 31 Badhuvud **Lena Koller**

Malmö
p 32 Turning Torso **Pierre Mens** HSB Turning Torso
Västra hamnen och Turning Torso **Pierre Mens** HSB Turning Torso
Ribergsborgs kallbadhus **Lena Koller**

Holidays and festivals
p 34 Fyrverkeri **Mårten Johnér** Johnér Bildbyrå
p 35 Markus i hatten **Lena Koller**
p 36 Semla **Lena Koller**
p 37 Påskkäringar **Jan Tham** Image Bank Sweden
Valborgsmässoeld **Maria Ravegård**
p 38 Midsommarsill och flagga **Lena Koller**
Jordgubbstårta **Lena Koller**
p 39 Nils i krans **Lena Koller**
p 40 Midsommarstång **Lena Koller**
Livstycke på folkdräkt **Lena Koller**
Resning av midsommarstång **Lena Koller**
p 41 Midsommarkyss **Lena Koller**
p 42 Kräftkalas **Lena Koller**
p 43 Kräftor **Lena Koller**
p 44 Burk med surströmming **Lena Koller**
Ål **Mats Svensson** Åhus
Gäss **Lena Koller**
Adventsljus **Lena Koller**
p 45 Adventsljus **Lena Koller**
p 46 Glöggflaskor **Lena Koller**
p 47 Lussebullar **Lena Koller**
p 48 Pepparkakor i julgran **Lena Koller**
p 49 Lucia **Vykort från Leopolds antikvariat**
p 50 Julflicka **Lena Koller**
p 51 Julkrans på dörr **Lena Koller**
p 52 Julskinka **Lena Koller**
p 53 Sillsallad **Lena Koller**
Köttbullar **Lena Koller**
Jansons frestelse **Lena Koller**
p 54 Knäckebröd **Lena Koller**
p 55 Laxrullar **Lena Koller**
p 56 Kock och mattallrik **Lena Koller**
p 57 En kopp fika **Lena Koller**

The Swedish passion for snaps
p 59 Två snapsare **Lena Koller**
p 60 Häller upp snaps **Lena Koller**
p 62 Dill **Lena Koller**
p 63 Potatis **Lena Koller**
p 65 Sillar **Lena Koller**

Sweden's national drink
p 66 Ärtsoppa **Lena Koller**
p 67 Punsch **Lena Koller**

The best glass in the world
p 68 Karaff Barbara **Nina Jobs**
p 69 Glas Difference **Roland Persson** Orrefors
p 70 Parispokalen **Orrefors**
Vaser i kraka-teknik **Orrefors**
Äpplet **Per Larsson** Orrefors
p 71 Glasblåsning **Lena Koller**
p 72 Vas Starline **Roland Persson** Orrefors
p 73 Ingegerd Råman **Lena Koller**
p 74 Dreams Bertil Vallien **Hans Bonnevier** Kosta Boda
Atle II **Mats Jonasson Målerås**
Peacock fat **Lindshammar glasbruk**
Skulptur Scandinavian **Nybro Glasbruk**
p 75 Ljuskrona **Pukeberg**
Skulptur House Gods **Rolf Hörlin** Kosta Boda
Skål Seaside **Rolf Hörlin** Kosta Boda
Vas Soft spot **Rolf Lind** Orrefors

Elegant simplicity – Design
p 76-77 Cloud **Monica Förster**
p 79 Lampa Do Swing **Patric Johansson**
Ljusstakar Fire **Anna Kraitz**
Lampor Lampel **Bengt O. Pettersson** Bsweden/Belysningsbolaget
Lampa Grace **Bsweden/Belysningsbolaget**
Lampa Original **Pukeberg**
p 80 Brudstol **Ölands museum**
Stol Concrete **Källemo**
p 81 Fåtölj Norrsken **Robert Eldrim**
Fåtölj People **Patric Johansson**
Fåtölj Lamino **Swedese**
Fåtölj BD Relax **Björn Dahlström**
Fåtölj Model 36 **Bruno Mathsson International**
Fåtölj Pebbles **Bitetto Chimenti**, **Walter Gumiero** Image Bank Sweden
Stol Lilla Åland **STOLAB**
Stol Hug **Gärsnäs**
Stol Odenslunda **www.1700-collection.com**
Stol Vitemölla **Design House Sthlm**
Stol Glide **Monica Förster**
Soffa E-seat **Offecct**
Fåtölj IKEA PS **Sandell & Sandberg**
p 82 Kudde Lustgården **Design House Stockholm**
Matta Röd flossa **Märta Måås-Fjetterström**
p 83 Texil Tulpan **Svenskt Tenn**
Textil Tistlar **Jobs Handtryck**
Textil Jungle **Nina Jobs**
Matta Trädgård vid havet **Kasthall**
p 84 Silverarmband **Mats Håkanson**
p 85 Silverarmband Fortune Bangle **Pia Wallén**
Armbandsur Vivianna **Georg Jensen**
Kaffepanna **Svensk Form**
Lövdosa **Fredrik Wahlberg**
Bestick Focus **Gense**
Tennvas **Svenskt Tenn**

Knee Tassels, painted wooden horses and Swedish handicrafts
p 86 Dalahäst **Lena Koller**
p 87 Knätofs och sko **Lena Koller**
p 88-89 Folkdräkter **Lena Koller**
p 90 Sameknív **Fredrik Ludvigsson** Naturbild
Keramikfat **AB Nittsjö Keramik**
Träskor **Grannas A. Olssons Hemslöjd AB**
Ljuslykta Snowball, Ann Wärff **Kosta Boda**
Osthyvel **Lena Koller**
Högklackade träskor **Åsa Westlund**
p 91 Lovikabikini **Lena Koller**

Gustav Vasa
p 92 Gustav Vasas intåg i Stockholm **Nationalmuseum**
p 93 Ornässtugan **Lena Koller**

Swedish art
p 94 Suzanne Roslin **Nationalmuseum**
p 95 Gustav III:s kröning **Nationalmuseum**
Vädersolstavlan **Nationalmuseum**
p 96 Näcken **Nationalmuseum**
p 97 Une premiére **Nationalmuseum**
p 98 Vinterstugan **Nationalmuseum**
Frukostdags **Nationalmuseum**
p 99 Den döende dandyn **Moderna Museet**
Ateljeinteriör **Moderna museet**
p 100 A Mediterraneo **Moderna museet**
p 101 Aiyam 1955 **Gerhard Kassner, Berlin. Courtesy to Galerie Nordenhake**
"Första mötet" **Galleri Magnus Karlsson**
p 102 Guds Hand **Pelle Höglund**, Millesgården
p 103 Krucifix **Galleri Andersson Sandström**

Dalhalla
p 104-105 Dalhalla **Martin Litens** Dalhalla

The Abba story
p 106 ABBA **Anders Hanser** www.rockshot.com
p 107 The Polar Music Prize **The Royal Swedish Academy of Music**

Alfred Nobel and The Nobel Prize
p 109 Alfred Nobel **Scanpix**
p 111 Nobel Diploma **Susan Duvnäs**
p 113 Nobelservis **Rörstrand**
Nobelbankett **Jonas Ekströmer** Image Bank Sweden

Cold faces, warm hearts
p 114 Carolina Klüft **Gero Breloer, Scanpix**
Annika Sörenstam **Don Ryan, Scanpix**
Björn Borg **Jacob Forsell, Scanpix**
J-O Waldner **Joerg Sarbach, Scanpix**
Zlatan Ibrahimovic **Mikael Sjöberg**

The swedish sin
p 117 Sommaren med Monika **Louis Huch** ©1953 AB Svensk Filmindustri

Snuff
p 118 Emma med snus **Lena Koller**
p 119 Snus i bakficka **Lena Koller**

Swedish nature
p 120 Lappländsk sjö **Lars Thulin** Johnér Bildbyrå
p 122-125 Lapporten **Claes Grundsten** Scanpix
p 127-128 Store mosse, Småland **Bengt Hedberg** Naturbild
p 130-131 Vindelälven **Roine Magnusson** Naturbild
p 132-133 Trappstegsforsen, Saxnäs, Västerbotten **Lars Thulin** Johnér Bildbyrå
p 135 Faldreven, Västergötland **Bengt Hedberg** Naturbild
p 136 Jämtland **Kjell Ljungström** Naturbild
p 138-141 Bergslagen **Lena Koller**
p 143 Ramsjön, Bergslagen **Lena Koller**
p 144 Vargkitteln, Kilsbergen, Bergslagen **Lena Koller**
p 146-149 Skåne **Lena Koller**
p 151 Sandhammaren, Skåne **Lena Koller**
p 152 Böda, Öland **Lena Koller**
p 153-154 Raukar, Fårö, Gotland **Lena Koller**
p 155-156 Gotska Sandön **Lena Koller**
p 157-158 Yttre Huö, Bohuslän **Bengt Hedberg** Naturbild
p 159-160 The Stockholm archipelago **Jeppe Wikström** Johnér Bildbyrå
p 161 Katterjåkk, Lappland **Lars Thulin** Johnér Bildbyrå
p 162 Låktatjåka midnightsun, Lappland **Lars Thulin** Johnér Bildbyrå
p 163-165 Lapporten, Abisko, Lappland **Lars Thulin** Johnér Bildbyrå
p 166 Slädhundar **Lena Koller**

Celsius
p 167 Snölandskap **Lena Koller**
p 168 Termometer **Lena Koller**

Off Track
p 169 Vasaloppet **Nisse Schmidt** Scanpix
Ingmar Stenmark **Örjan Björkdahl** Scanpix
Anja Pärson **Jonas Lindkvist** Scanpix
p 170 Skidåkare **Lars Thulin** Johnér Bildbyrå

Ice – friend or foe?
p 171 Fyra skridskoåkare **Ingemar Aouell**
p 173 Isspricka **Ingemar Aouell**
p 174 Skiktad is **Bengt Stridh**

The Icehotel
p 175-176 Entrance 2006-07 **Big Ben**
p 177 Main Hall **Big Ben** Artists: Jessica (chairs) by Jörgen Westin
p 178 Ice Church **Big Ben** Artists: Marjolein Vonk, Cindy Berg, Jan Willem van de Schoot and Marinus Vroom

Absolut Vodka
p 179 Icebar **Big Ben**
p 180 Absolut Vodka annons-reproduktioner och Absolut Vodka flaska ABSOLUT®VODKA. ABSOLUT COUNTRY OF SWEDEN VODKA AND LOGO, ABSOLUT, ABSOLUT BOTTLE DESIGN AND ABSOLUT CALLIGRAPHY ARE TRADEMARKS OWNED BY V&S VIN & SPRIT AB (publ). ©2007 V&S VIN & SPRIT AB (publ)

The Swedish indigenous people
p 182 Same **Staffan Widstrand** Naturbild
p 184 Renskiljning **John M. Pavval** Sameportalen.se

Land of contraste
p 186 Norrsken **Imagebank Sweden**

Carl von Linné
p 188 Tulpan **Lena Koller**
p 190 Vilda blommor **Lena Koller**

Trespassers welcome
p 192 Svampkorg **Lena Koller**
p 193 Höstlöv **Lena Koller**
p 194 Bilder från Ännaboda, Bergslagen **Lena Koller**

Architecture
p 195-196 Hötorgsskrapor **Lena Koller**
p 197 Allmogeentré **Scanpix**
p 198 Kina slott, Drottningholm **Lena Koller**
p 200 Detalj från Ornässtugan, Dalarna **Lena Koller**
p 201 Grindstuga, Pershyttan **Lena Koller**
Domaregården, Pershyttan **Lena Koller**
p 202 Villa Karlsson **Åke E:son Lindman** Tham, Videgård, Hansson Arkitekter AB
p 203 Stockholms stadshus **Lena Koller**
p 204 Stockholm stadion **Lena Koller**
Staty **Lena Koller**
p 205 Skogskyrkogården **Lena Koller**
Skogskapellet **Lena Koller**
p 206 Stockholms stadsbibliotek **Lena Koller**
p 207 Flygledartornet, Arlanda **Lena Koller**
p 208 The Mill House **James Silverman**
Citadellbadet **Gert Wingårdh**
p 209 Parvilla Danderyd **Åke E:son Lindman** Tham, Videgård, Hansson Arkitekter AB
Weekendhouse Arkö **©Marge Arkitekter**
p 210 Gåshaga **Åke E:son Lindman**
p 211 Gustavianska stolar **www.1700-collection.com**
p 212 Bord med kaffekopp **Lena Koller**

Fruit of the Swedish forest
p 213 Papper **Stora Enso**
p 214 Timmer **Lena Koller**
p 215 Pappersbruk i Norrland **Lena Koller**
Trädkronor **Lena Koller**

Hidden riches
p 217 Stånggång, Pershyttan **Lena Koller**
p 218 Hyttan i Pershyttan **Lena Koller**
p 219-220 Kirunavy **LKAB**
p 220 Tackjärn **Stig-Göran Nilsson** Jernkontorets bildbank
Gruvarbete vid skärm **LKAB**

A true man of steel
p 221 Tappning av råstål **Stig-Göran Nilsson** Jernkontorets bildbank
p 222 Stålrör **Sandvik Media Base**
p 223 Trådläggare i trådvalsverk **Stig-Göran Nilsson** Jernkontorets bildbank
p 224 Produktbilder, 3 st **Sandvik Media Base**

ABB
p 226 High-voltage direct current **ABB**
p 227 Kontrollrum **ABB**
p 228 Robot **ABB**

Atlas Copco
p 229 Kompressor **Atlas Copcos bildbank**
p 230 Secoroc drill bit **Jonas Frid** Atlas Copcos bildbank
p 231 Compressors **Atlas Copcos bildbank**
Rocket Boomer E2 **Atlas Copcos bildbank**
p 232 Hydraulic impulse nutrunner **Niklas Hagelbeck** Atlas Copcos bildbank
p 233 Skiftnyckel **Lena Koller**

SKF
p 236 Rullager **SKFs bildbank**

Re-Volvo-lution
p 237 Amazon **Lena Koller**
p 239 P1800 **©Volvo Car Corporation**
Volvo Truck Series 1 **©Volvo Car Corporation**
The very first mass produced Volvo car **©Volvo Car Corporation**
p 240 Båtmotor **Volvo Penta image gallery**
Buss **Volvo Bus image gallery**
Operator **Volvo construction equipment image gallery**
Flygplan **Volvo Aero image gallery**

The king of forest
p 241-242 Mooses **Bengt Olof Olsson** Scanpix
p 243 Älgskylt **Vägverket**
p 244 Krockälg **Saab Picture & Art Service**

SAAB
p 245 Saab 92001 **Rony Lutz** Saab
The Roadster **Playsam**
p 246 Saab Aero X **Adrian Bert** Saab
p 247-248 Fågelstreck **Lena Koller**
p 248 Saab B17 **©Saab AB**

Scania
p 249 Vabis A-car **Scania Image Bank**
Vabis 1902 **Scania Image Bank**
p 250 Lastbil front **Scania Image Bank**

The Wallenberger
p 252 Wallenbergare **Lena Koller**

Lars Magnus Ericsson
p 254 Porträtt LM Ericsson **Ericssons arkiv hos Centrum för Näringslivshistoria**
Telephone 1878 **Ericssons arkiv hos Centrum för Näringslivshistoria**
Kobra-telefon **Lena Koller**
p 255 Mobile phone **John Ravegård**
p 256 The Ericsson Tower Tube **Steve Bush**

Electrolux
p 258 Hydrosphere **Electrolux Group Image Bank**
p 259 Trilobite **Image Bank Sweden**
Dust Mate **Electrolux Group Image Bank**
p 260 Porträtt Carl och Baltzar **Electrolux Group Image Bank**

AGA
p 261 Svetsare **Linde Media Base**
p 262 Tre svetslågor **Linde Media Base**
p 263 Solventil **AGA:s arkiv hos Centrum för Näringslivshistoria**
p 264 AGA-spis **AGA Consumer Products Ltd**

Medical innovations
p 266 Piller **Astra Zeneca**
p 268 Raketer **John Ravegård**

The Hasselblad camera
p 270 Victor Hasselblad **Hasselblad A/S**
Astronaut **Hasselblad A/S**

Gambro
p 273 Dialysmaskin **Gambro**

Pacemakern
p 274 Pacemakrar **Lena Koller**

The Swedish Spark
p 276 Tändsticksask **Swedish Match Image Bank**

Tetra Pak
p 278 Pojke och mjölk **Tetra Pak Image Bank**

Gustaf de Laval
p 279 Mjölkningsorgan **De Laval Image Bank**
Separator 1910 **Alfa Lavals arkiv hos Centrum för Näringslivshistoria**
p 280 Ko **Stefan Berg** Johnér Bildbyrå

When cement works Skanska
p 281 Öresundsbron **Lena Koller**

IKEA
p 284 Collage **Maria Ravegård**
p 285 Ingvar Kamprad **IKEA**
p 286 6 st produktbilder **IKEA**

Hennes & Mauritz
p 287 Butiksbild **H & M Hennes & Mauritz AB**
p 288 Modebild **H & M Hennes & Mauritz AB**
p 289-290 Blixtlås **Lena Koller**

John Ericsson
p 292 Varmluftsmaskinen **Tekniska museet**
p 293 Ritning på Monitorn **Tekniska museet**
p 294 Tavla Monitor och Merrimac **Tekniska museet**

Swedish icons
p 296 Ingmar Bergman **Gunnar Seijbold**, Scanpix
p 297 Ingrid Bergman **Topham Picturepoint**, Scanpix
p 298 Greta Garbo **Scanpix**
p 299 Selma Lagerlöf **Henry B. Goodwin** Image Bank Sweden
p 300 August Strindberg **J.M Marcus** Image Bank Sweden
p 301 Astrid Lindgren **Ulla Montan** Image Bank Sweden
p 302 Birgit Nilsson **Scanpix**

References

SFS nr: 1974:152

Skandinavisk design Charlotte & Peter Fiell. Taschen 2002

Stockholm genom sju sekler Per Erik Lindorm, Läsförlaget, Centraltryckeriet Borås, 1998

Sundborn ou les jours de lumière Philippe Delerm, Éditions du Rocher, 1996

Svensk slöjdkonst Uuve Snidare, Forum 2005

Svenska Hus Thomas Hall/ Katarina Dunér, Carlsson Bokförlag, Omnigraf, 2002

Svenska innovationer Kjell Sedig, Svenska Institutet, Kristianstad Boktryckeri, 2002.

Svenska Snilleblixtar 1 Börje Isakson, George Johansson, Natur och Kultur, Gummessons Tryckeri AB, Falköping 1993

Svenska Snilleblixtar 2 Börje Isakson, George Johansson, Natur och Kultur, Gummessons Tryckeri AB, Falköping 1994

Svenskt glas 1900-1960 Dag Widman,Cordia

Svenskt Glas W&W, Ove Halls Offset AB, Växjö, 1995

Svenskt konstglas André Laszlo, Sellin & Blomquist,

Sveriges historia under 1800 och 1900-talen Lars I Andersson, Stockholm, Liber, 2003

System och passion Linné och drömmen om naturens ordning, Nils Uddenberg, Natur och Kultur, 2007

The Atlas Copco way Page One Publishing Stockholm 1998

Turning Torso Björn Raneild, HSB

Underbara uppfinnarbragder Jansson, John, Stockholm 1948

Ur Svenska Hjärtans Djup bilder från Oscar II:s Stockholm, Gotthard Johansson, Mats Rehnberg, Gösta Selling, W&W 1987

Vägen gick via Operan Carl-Gunnar Åhlén, Svenska Dagbladet, 31 juli 2007

Per aspera ad astra Astra 1913-1999, Sven Sundling, Ekerlids förlag, Trosa tryckeri, 2003

Svenskt Glas K. Wickman, G. Holmér, E. Anisimova. T.Rappe, SI, Vida Museum Öland, Statliga Eremitaget, Sankt Petersburg, KalmarSundTryckeri AB 2003

Då och Nu Svenskt Konstliv under 150 år, Bo Lindwall, **Sveriges Allmänna Konstförening** Bohuslänningen AB, Uddevalla 1982

Sweden style Angelika Taschen. Taschen 2005

web.telia.com Robert Karlsson
www.ki.se
www.nobelprize.org/alfred_nobel/
www.nobelprize.org/alfred_nobel/will/testamente
www.susning.nu/Nobelpriset
www.slu.se
www.ab.lst.se
www.abb.se
www.abbamuseum.com
www.absolut.com
www.aga.se
www.ahusstrand.com
www.alagille.com
www.algar.se
www.amazonklubben.se
www.antikviteter.net/design
www.archipelago.nu
www.arkitekturmuseet.se
www.arlanda.se
www.assa.se/inside/profilen/0602
www.astrazeneca.com
www.astrazeneca.se
www.astridlindgren.se
www.astridlindgrensallskapet.se
www.astro.uu.se/history/celsius
www.atlascopco.com
www.bahco.com
www.bgf.nu
www.bgf.nu/historia/7/snillen.
www.biblioteket.stockholm.se
www.bohusgillet.se
www.bohuslan.com
www.bokhyllan.se/Nobel/nobelpriset
www.borlange.se
www.burkar.nu
www.carllarsson.se
www.chalmers.se
www.chemicalnet.se
www.chemicalnet.se/iuware.aspx?pageid=792
www.dalarna.se
www.dalhalla.se
www.designmuseum/bernadotte.
www.dn.se/DNet/road/Classic/article
www.dn.se/Ingmar Bergman,Magikern som trollband hela världen, Maaret Koskinen, 2007
www.dranghuset.se
www.edu.linkoping.se
www.ekeroturism.se/birka
www.electrolux.com/designlab
www.electrolux.se
www.ericsson.com
www.ericssonhistory.com
www.falurodfarg.com
www.file.se/artiklar/
www.filipstad.se
www.fjallen.nu
www.folkdrakt.se
www.fyr.org
www.fyrar.se
www.gaaltije.se
www.gambro.se
www.glafo.se
www.glasakademin.net
www.goteborg.com
www.goteborg.se
www.greatbuildings.com

www.handlasvenskt.se
www.hasselblad.se
www.hasselbladfoundation.org
www.historia.su.se
www.historiska.se
www.hm.com
www.holmen.com
www.holmenskog.com
www.hummerfiske.com
www.hummersafari.se
www.icehotel.com
www.illvet.se
www.ingmarbergman.se
www.investorab.com
www.irf.se/norrsken
www.isa.se
www.iswebb.se
www.iva.se
www.jagareforbundet.se
www.jagrullar.se
www.jernkontoret.se
www.jarnriket.com
www.johnericsson.net
www.jordbruk.nu
www.jul-i-sverige.se
www.karlshamnsmuseum.se
www.karlskoga.se/kulturhistoria/personligheter/nobel
www.katolik.nu
www.kemi.uu.se/Nobelpristagare
www.klassbols.se
www.kostaboda.se
www.kungahuset.se.
www.kva.se
www.lankskafferiet.skolutveckling.se
www.largestcompanies.com
www.linnaeus.uu.se
www.linnaeus.uu.se/online, Linnés liv, Hans Odöö, Idéerna och historien, Carl Frängsmyr, Magdalena Hydman och Ragnar Insulander, Växterna och djuren, Mariette Manktelow, Linné och läkemedlen, Håkan Tunón, Fysikens kosmos, Johan Rathsman och Mats Thunman, Linné och ekologin, Ragnar Insulander
www.linnaeus.uu.se/online/fysik/makrokosmos/norrsken
www.linne2007.se
www.lkab.com
www.lrf.se
www.malmo.se
www.millesgarden.se
www.mimersbrunn.se
www.modernamuseet.se
www.moosefarm.se
www.moviebox.se/profiler/ingridbergman
www.msi.vxu.se/fysik/teknik/
www.naringslivshistoria.se
www.nationalencyklopedin.se
www.nationalmuseum.se
www.naturensbasta.se
www.naturinorr.nu
www.naturskyddsforeningen.se
www.naturvardsverket.se
www.ninet.se Mats Bergman
www.nobelmuseetikarlskoga.se
www.nordiskamuseet.se
www.nykarlebyvyer.nu
www.nyteknik.se/nyheter/innovation/forskning
www.olm.se/bjc/pershyttan
www.orebrolansmuseum.se
www.orrefors.com
www.ostindiefararen.com
www.passagen.se/kent.andersson
www.passagen.se/rente/uppf/sulfit
www.passagen.se/skiftnyckelnsvanner/jp_johansson
www.playsam.com
www.polarmusicprize.com
www.politiskamord.com
www.popularhistoria.se
www.prv.se
www.raa.se
www.raa.se/varldsarv
www.regeringen.se
www.riksdagen.se
www.rollspel.nu/juneborg/Historia/Hela_Sveriges_historia.
www.rorstrand.se Nobelservisen
www.rottneros.se
www.royalcourt.se
www.runeberg.org
www.rymdforum.nu
www.rymdportalen.com
www.saabgroup.com
www.saabklubben.com
www.saabsverige.com
www.sandellsandberg.se
www.sandhamn.com
www.sandhamn.org
www.sandhamn.se
www.sandvik.com
www.sandviken.se/kommun/omsandviken/historia
www.sapmi.se
www.sca.com
www.scandinavia.nu/klassbol
www.scandinaviandesign.com
www.scania.com
www.selmalagerlof.org
www.sfv.se/fastigheter
www.sgu.se
www.shenet.se
www.si.se
www.sjm.se
www.skane.com
www.skansen.se
www.skanska.se
www.skargardsstiftelsen.se
www.skf.com
www.skiftnyckel.com
www.skonahem.com Karin Björquist mfl
www.smalandsmuseum.se
www.smhi.se
www.sna.se/Klimat, sjöar och vattendrag
www.snilleriket.se

www.snusbutiken.se
www.snusexpress.com
www.snusfabriken.com
www.soderhamn.se
www.sodra.com
www.soic.se
www.sonyericsson.com
www.sr.se
www.ssc.se
www.stadsmuseum.stockholm.se
www.stockholm.se
www.stockholm.se/stadion
www.stockholmtown.com
www.stopminpost.com
www.storaenso.com
www.strindbergsmuseet.se
www.student.educ.umu.se
www.sub.su.se
www.sub.su.se
www.sub.su.se/national
www.sund.com
www.surstromming.se
www.svd.se/Fragmentets och ögonblickets mästare, Carl-Johan Malmberg, Under strecket, 2007
www.sveaskog.se
www.svenskaakademien.se
www.svenskakyrkan.se
www.svenskdamtidning.se Nobelservisen
www.svenskform.se
www.svenskkulturarv.com
www.svenskt-porslin.nl
www.sverigeresor.se/resor/sverige/kulturmiljoer-och-byggnader/borlange
www.sverigeturism.se
www.svid.se
www.svt.se Nobels fredspris
www.sweden.se
www.swedensite.com
www.swedishmatch.com
www.swedishtrade.se
www.t.lst.se/t/amnen/Kulturmiljo/riksintressen/Nora/Pershyttan
www.tacitus.nu/svenskhistoria/kungar/bernadotte.
www.tacitus.nu/svenskhistoria/kungar/vasa/gustav
www.tarnaby.se
www.tasteline.com
www.teknikenshus.se
www.tekniskamuseet.se
www.tekniskamuseet/elkraft/snilleblixtar/se
www.tetrapak.se
www.tidningenkulturen.se
www.turningtorso.se
www.ungafakta.se/vikingar
www.uppfinnare.se
www.upplevmittsverige.nu
www.varldsarvetfalun.se
www.vartgoteborg.se
www.vasaloppet.se
www.vasamuseet.se
www.vasteras.se
www.vikinguppsala.se
www.vinterviken-nobel.se/nobel.
www.visitsweden.com
www.volvo.com
www.volvop1800club.se
www.wasa.com
www.wingardhs.se
www.zorn.se

* www.saabgroup.com
** www.wingardhs.se

1000 år En svensk historia, Olle Häger, Jan Hugo Norman, Hans Villius, Brombergs, Almqvist&Wiksell, Uppsala 1980

19002000 Den moderna formen. Cilla Robach, Nationalmuseum 2004

17 uppsatser i svensk idé och lärdomshistoria, Bokförlaget Carmina, Uppsala, 1980

Absolut story Kenth Olsson, Accent, 2002

Älskade Älgar Torsten Blomquist, Media Express Förlag, 2004

Astma hos vuxna Kjell Larsson, redaktör, Astra Zeneca AB, Elanders Berglings, 2005

Birger och Fredrik Ljungström-uppfinnare Sven A Hansson, Nordiskt Rotogravyr, Stockholm 1955.

Blodstämmare och handpåläggare, folklig läkekonst och magi i Tornedalen, Jörgen I Eriksson, 1992

Den skandinaviska stilen Ingrid Sommar. Stockholm Valentin 2003

Designed in Sweden Bradley Quinn. Arvinius Förlag 2004

Ericssonkrönikan John Meurling, Richard Jeans Informationsförlaget, 2001

Folkkonst – en värld av prakt och grannlåt. Johan Knutsson, Mats Landin. Nordiska museets förlag 2005

Företagsminnen tidskrift från centrum för näringslivshistoria, nr 2 1998, nr1 1999, nr1 2001, nr1 2002, nr2 2003, nr1&2 2004, nr2 2005

Från Galtströms järnbruk till SCA Bertil Hasleum, SCA, Köping, 1993

Från Vårgårda till Bacho, Kempe, L-Å, skiftnyckelns uppfinnare J.P Johansson I, Västgötabygden, 1992

Gamla Stan-historia som lever Beatrice Glase, Boförlaget Bra Böcker, Trevi 1988

Gammalt glas Jan Erik Anderbjörk, Ica bokförlag

Guide till Sveriges arkitektur Byggnadskonst under 1000 år, Arkitektur Förlag AB, Värnamo 2001

Gustav Vasa upprorsmakaren som befriade Sverige, Dag Sebastian Ahlander, Natur&Kultur, 2004

Handelsmännen Bo Pettersson, Månpocket, 2003

Havsbad Marie Dahlberg, Lena Koller, Maria Ravegård, W&W, Fälth &Hässler, Värnamo, 2004.

Historien om IKEA Bertil Torekull,W&W, STC Avesta 2005

Husen på Malmarna En bok om Stockholm, Marianne Råberg mfl, Bokförlaget Prisma, Bröderna Ljungberg Tryckeri AB, Södertälje 1985

Icehotel food and experiences in Jukkasjärvi, Lars Magnus Jansson, Lars Petterson, Goda Sidor, Fälth&Hässler

Jean-Baptiste Bernadotte Från revolutionssoldat till svensk kronprins, Margareta Beckman, Stockholm, Prisma, 2003

La Nilsson Birgit Nilsson, Fischer&Co, 1998

Mångkulturalism – etniska grupper i skilda skolor eller överlappade identiteter inom den allmänna skolan? Gerle, Elisabeth, Utbildning & Demokrati. Tidskrift för didaktik och utbildningspolitik,8(2) 20 s (s 23-42),1999.

Möbelstilarna Erik Andrén, Nordiska Museet, Bohuslänningen, Uddevalla, 1981

New Design in Sweden Susanne Helgeson, Swedish Institute 2002

Nobel – en biografi. Staffan Tjerneld, Bonniers 1972

Ostindiefararen Götheborg seglar igen, Ingrid Arensberg, Warne Förlag

Phaidon Design Classics Phaidon 2006

Propellerns pionjär och Monitors mästare: glimtar av John Ericssons liv och verk/Björn Hallerdt. Stockholm: Ideella fören. John Ericssons-jubileet 2003, Tekniska museet, 2003.

Reimersholms Snapsakademi Jonas Odland, Steffo Törnquist, V&S

Så länge vi har marker Lennart Lundmark, AiT Scandbook, Falun 1999

Samer – ett ursprungsfolk i Sverige Jordbruksdepartementet, Edita Västra Aros, 2004

Sandhamnsledens öar Skärgårdsstiftelsen och författarna, Skärgårdsstiftelsens årsbok, Gummessons Tryckeri 1995

Acknowledgements

Edward Blom
Fredrik Cederbor
May Britt Dahlberg
Uno Dahlberg
Susan Duvnäs
Patrik Fallberg
Anders Gidlöf
Christina Gustavsson
John Hasselberg
Svante Hultquist
Karl Wilhelm Olsson
John Ravegård
Magnus Ravegård
Markus Ravegård
Kerstin Strid-Gustavsson
Bengt Stridh, Västerås
Mats Svensson, Åhus
Helena Thornes
Mats Åkerman
Maria Wessberger
Martin Wickström
Annie Widman
Carl Widman
Marit Widman
Johan Åkerman
Per Åkerman

Special thanks to Craig Andrew Pratt, our magician, for surviving working with us with a smile on his lips.

... and many others who have graciously withstood having their brains picked and their patience tried by the authors.